JOURNAL FOR THE STUDY OF THE OLD TESTAMENT
SUPPLEMENT SERIES
156

JSOT Press
Sheffield

The LORD's Song

The Basis, Function and Significance of Choral Music in Chronicles

John W. Kleinig

Journal for the Study of the Old Testament
Supplement Series 156

Copyright © 1993 Sheffield Academic Press

Published by JSOT Press
JSOT Press is an imprint of
Sheffield Academic Press Ltd
343 Fulwood Road
Sheffield S10 3BP
England

Typeset by Sheffield Academic Press
and
Printed on acid-free paper in Great Britain
by Biddles Ltd
Guildford

British Library Cataloguing in Publication Data

A catalogue record for this book is available
from the British Library

ISBN 1-85075-394-6

CONTENTS

PREFACE

This book began more by accident than design. In preparing a course on worship in the Old Testament for the students at Luther Seminary, I made two discoveries. First, Chronicles is the only set of books in the Old Testament which explains in some detail how liturgical music was arranged in the temple at Jerusalem and why it was arranged as it was. Secondly, even though much work had been done on the identification and nature of the musical instruments used in Israel's worship, no scholar had considered the ritual function and theological significance of sacred song within the sacrificial ritual as described in Chronicles. These two discoveries led in due course to a dissertation on this topic for the University of Cambridge which was successfully defended in January, 1991. That dissertation has been abbreviated and lightly revised for publication in this book.

Many people have given me personal, material and financial support for my year of research at Cambridge in 1989. First, there are my colleagues at Luther Seminary in Adelaide. They not only supported my application for study leave and encouraged me to work towards a doctorate, but they also filled in for me in 1989 and gave me time to complete the work for it in 1990. Secondly, the President of the Lutheran Church of Australia, Dr L.G. Steicke, its First Vice-President, Dr J.G. Strelan, and its Secretary, Revd K.J. Schmidt, together with the members of the General Church Council and the Standing Committee for Scholarships, approved of my leave from teaching, provided generous financial support in difficult times, and encouraged me in my project. Thirdly, my parents-in-law, Mr and Mrs W.J. Bentley, my mother, Mrs E.E. Kleinig, and an anonymous donor provided the financial support needed for my family to spend 1989 with me in Cambridge. Fourthly, I am most grateful for the hospitality extended to me at Westfield House in Cambridge by its Preceptor, Revd R. Quirk, and its Tutor, Revd G.E. Zweck, as well as for the generosity of the Evangelical Lutheran Church of England in providing housing for me and my family at a rather nominal rate. Besides these, there are many other friends and acquaintances who have supported us with their prayers and encouraged us in this undertaking.

When I first investigated the possibility of enrolling for a doctorate at the University of Cambridge I got in touch with Dr G.I. Davies to discover whether it would be feasible. He not only encouraged me to apply but offered to act as a referee for my application. Subsequently, he was appointed my supervisor. I owe much more than I can say to him for his gracious friendship and unstinting encouragement, his clear guidance and incisive criticism, his wide knowledge of Old Testament theology and his tactful counsel. He proved to be an ideal supervisor for me in my circumstances. After I returned to Adelaide at the end of 1989, Dr N.C. Habel generously took over the role of supervisor for the completion of the dissertation. From his wide understanding of ritual symbolism, he gave me good advice on strengthening my case and on presenting my findings in tabular form, for which I am most grateful. Besides these, I should also like to thank my colleague Dr J.T.E. Renner for reading through this work and making some helpful suggestions for improvement.

I dedicate this monograph to the members of my immediate family. My wife Claire has sustained me during its preparation and inspired me by her passion for church music. She has been my partner in its production, helping me sort out my ideas by discussing them with me. My children, Louise, Timothy, Hilary and Paul, have all had their lives disrupted by this project. My hope is that they, who are so fond of music, will be enriched in their appreciation of church music by the discussions which resulted from this work.

John W. Kleinig, Luther Seminary
Adelaide, South Australia

ABBREVIATIONS

AASH	Acta antiqua academiae scientiarum hungaricae
AARSR	American Academy of Religion Studies in Religion
AB	Anchor Bible
AJBA	*Australian Journal of Biblical Archaeology*
AOAT	Alter Orient und Altes Testament
ATD	Das Alte Testament Deutsch
ATANT	Abhandlungen zur Theologie des Alten und Neuen Testaments
AUR	*Aberdeen University Review*
BA	*Biblical Archaeologist*
BARev	*Biblical Archaeology Review*
BASOR	*Bulletin of the American Schools of Oriental Research*
BBB	Bonner biblische Beiträge
BBLA	Beiträge zur biblischen Landes- und Altertumskunde
BDB	F. Brown, S.R. Driver and C.A. Briggs, *A Hebrew and English Lexicon of the Old Testament*
BEATAJ	Beiträge zur Erforschung des Alten Testaments und des antiken Judentums
BET	Beiträge zur biblischen Exegese und Theologie
BHS	*Biblia hebraica stuttgartensia*
Bib	*Biblica*
BeO	*Bibbia e oriente*
BJRL	*Bulletin of the John Rylands University Library of Manchester*
BKAT	Biblischer Kommentar: Altes Testament
BN	*Biblische Notizen*
BSac	*Bibliotheca Sacra*
BT	*The Bible Translator*
BTB	*Biblical Theology Bulletin*
BZ	*Biblische Zeitschrift*
BZAW	Beihefte zur *ZAW*
BZNW	Beihefte zur *ZNW*
CBC	Cambridge Bible Commentary
CBQ	*Catholic Biblical Quarterly*
CJT	*Canadian Journal of Theology*
ConBOT	Coniectanea biblica, Old Testament
CTM	*Concordia Theological Monthly*
EH	Europäische Hochschulschriften

EncJud	*Encyclopedia Judaica*
ERE	*Encyclopedia of Religion and Ethics*
ETL	*Ephemerides theologicae lovanienses*
Ev	*Evangelium*
EvQ	*Evangelical Quarterly*
EvT	*Evangelische Theologie*
ExpTim	*Expository Times*
FOTL	The Forms of the Old Testament Literature
FT	*Faith and Thought*
FTS	Freiburger theologische Studien
FRLANT	Forschungen zur Religion und Literatur des Alten und Neuen Testaments
FZ	*Freiburger Zeitschrift für Philosophie und Theologie*
GHAT	Göttinger Handkommentar zum Alten Testament
GKC	*Gesenius' Hebrew Grammar*, ed. E. Kautsch, trans. A.E. Cowley
HALAT	L. Koehler and W. Baumgartner (eds.), *Hebräisches und Aramäisches Lexikon zum Alten Testament*
HAR	*Hebrew Annual Review*
HAT	Handbuch zum Alten Testament
HBT	*Horizons in Biblical Theology*
HDB	J. Hastings (ed.), *A Dictionary of the Bible*
HKAT	Handkommentar zum Alten Testament
Holl	W.L. Holladay, *A Concise Hebrew and Aramaic Lexicon of the Old Testament*
HR	*History of Religions*
HSM	Harvard Semitic Monographs
HSS	Harvard Semitic Studies
HTR	*Harvard Theological Review*
HUCA	*Hebrew Union College Annual*
IB	*Interpreter's Bible*
IBD	N. Hillyer *et al.* (eds.), *The Illustrated Bible Dictionary*
ICC	International Critical Commentary
IDB	G.A. Buttrick (ed.), *Interpreter's Dictionary of the Bible*
IDBSup	*IDB*, Supplementary Volume
IEJ	*Israel Exploration Journal*
IJPR	*International Journal for the Philosophy of Religion*
Imm	*Immanuel*
Int	*Interpretation*
ISBE	G.W. Bromiley (ed.), *International Standard Bible Encyclopedia*, rev. edn
JAAR	*Journal of the American Academy of Religion*
JAOS	*Journal of the American Oriental Society*
JBL	*Journal of Biblical Literature*
JBR	*Journal of Bible and Religion*

JETS	*Journal of the Evangelical Theological Society*
JJS	*Journal of Jewish Studies*
JLH	*Jahrbuch für Liturgik und Hymnologie*
JNES	*Journal of Near Eastern Studies*
JQR	*Jewish Quarterly Review*
JR	*Journal of Religion*
JRAS	*Journal of the Royal Asiatic Society*
JSOT	*Journal for the Study of the Old Testament*
JSOTSup	*Journal for the Study of the Old Testament*, Supplement Series
JSS	*Journal of Semitic Studies*
JTS	*Journal of Theological Studies*
Jud	*Judaica*
KAT	Kommentar zum Alten Testament
KHAT	Kurzer Handcommentar zum Alten Testament
LCL	Loeb Classical Library
LTJ	*Lutheran Theological Journal*
LTQ	*Lexington Theological Quarterly*
MGWJ	*Monatsschrift für Geschichte und Wissenschaft des Judentums*
MQ	*Musical Quarterly*
MVAG	Mitteilungen der Vorderasiatischen-ägyptischen Gesellschaft
NCB	New Century Bible
NES	Near Eastern Studies
NICOT	New International Commentary on the Old Testament
NTT	*Nederlands theologisch Tijdschrift*
OBT	Overtures to Biblical Theology
OLP	Orientalia lovaniensia periodica
Or	*Orientalia*
OrAnt	*Oriens antiquus*
OTL	Old Testament Library
OTS	*Oudtestamentische Studiën*
RB	*Revue biblique*
Rel	*Religion*
RGG	*Religion in Geschichte und Gegenwart*
RTP	*Revue de théologie et de philosophie*
SBLDS	SBL Dissertation Series
SBLMS	SBL Monograph Series
SBLSP	SBL Seminar Papers
SBM	Stuttgarter biblische Monographien
ScrHier	Scripta Hierosolymitana
SEÅ	*Svensk exegetisk årsbok*
SJLA	Studies in Judaism and Late Antiquity
SJOT	*Scandinavian Journal of the Old Testament*
SOTSMS	Society for Old Testament Study Monograph Series
SR	Symbolik der Religionen
StBT	*Studia Biblica et Theologica*

TA	*Tel Aviv*
TDOT	G.J. Botterweck and H.H. Ringgren (eds.), *Theological Dictionary of the Old Testament*
THAT	E. Jenni and C. Westermann (eds.), *Theologisches Handwörterbuch zum Alten Testament*
ThS	*Theologische Studien*
ThWAT	G.J. Botterweck and H.H. Ringgren (eds.), *Theologisches Wörterbuch zum Alten Testament*
TJ	*Trinity Journal*
TLZ	*Theologische Literaturzeitung*
TOTC	Tyndale Old Testament Commentaries
TQ	*Theologische Quartalschrift*
TRE	G. Krause and G. Müller (eds.), *Theologische Realenzyklopädie*
TRu	*Theologische Rundschau*
TS	*Theological Studies*
TSK	*Theologische Studien und Kritiken*
TTQ	*Tübinger theologische Quartalschrift*
TTS	Trierer theologische Studien
TWNT	G. Kittel and G. Freidrich (ed.), *Theologisches Wörterbuch zum Neuen Testament*
TynBul	*Tyndale Bulletin*
TZ	*Theologische Zeitschrift*
UF	*Ugarit-Forschungen*
UUÅ	Uppsala universitetsårsskrift
VD	*Verbum domini*
VT	*Vetus Testamentum*
VTSup	*Vetus Testamentum*, Supplements
Yuv	*Yuval*
WBC	Word Bible Commentary
WMANT	Wissenschaftliche Monographien zum Alten und Neuen Testament
WO	*Die Welt des Orients*
WTJ	*Westminster Theological Journal*
YNER	Yale Near Eastern Researches
ZAW	*Zeitschrift für die alttestamentliche Wissenschaft*
ZDPV	*Zeitschrift des deutschen Palästina-Vereins*
ZPEB	M.C. Tenney (ed.), *The Zondervan Pictorial Encyclopedia of the Bible*
ZTK	*Zeitschrift für Theologie und Kirche*

Chapter 1

THE LORD'S SONG IN CHRONICLES

The Nature and Purpose of this Study

At 2 Chron. 5.13 in his copy of the Calov Bible Commentary,[1] J.S. Bach adds the marginal gloss: 'In devotional music God is always present with his grace'.[2] This is not an isolated comment but is connected thematically with two other comments. In response to Calov's remarks on 1 Chron. 25.1 that the temple musicians were to proclaim God's word in the composition of their psalms and sing them to the accompaniment of musical instruments, Bach declares, quite emphatically, that this chapter was the true foundation for all God-pleasing church music.[3] The reason for this is given at 1 Chron. 28.21, where Calov had remarked that David had not arranged the temple and its services on his own initiative but rather at the LORD's instruction.[4] Bach notes there that, through David, God's Spirit had instituted church music together with all the other aspects of the divine service at the temple. It seems then that Bach was influenced by Chronicles in his understanding of liturgical music. It had been instituted by God himself to proclaim his word and grant his gracious presence to his people in their worship of him.

This is not a monograph on Bach's theology of music but rather a treatment of the ritual function and theological significance of liturgical music in Chronicles. It has, however, been inspired by these remarks

1. This three-volumed commentary of the Bible by A. Calov, which was printed in Wittenberg in 1681–82, is now found in the Concordia Seminary Library, St Louis. Facsimiles of all the marginal comments in Bach's hand with an English translation and commentary have been produced by Leaver (1985). For accounts of its discovery and significance, see Trautmann 1969, 1972 and Leaver 1976.

2. Leaver 1985: 97.

3. Leaver 1985: 93.

4. Leaver 1985: 95.

from Bach. It aims to test whether his insights can be substantiated exegetically from the books of Chronicles.

The books of Chronicles often mention, or allude to, liturgical music at the temple in Jerusalem. It is dealt with in 1 Chron. 6.31-47 (6.16-32);[1] 9.14-16, 33; 15.1-16, 43; 23.2-5, 25-32; 25.1-31; 2 Chron. 5.11-14; 7.1-6; 8.12-15; 20.18-30; 23.12-13, 18; 29.25-30; 30.21-22; 31.2; 34.12-13; and 35.15. The institution of the temple choir by David and its patronage by his successors, the organization and status of the musicians, the instruments for its performance, and the place of music in the service at the temple—all these matters are covered in the narrative. There is thus a considerable amount of material on choral music in Chronicles.

Since all this material, none of which is found in Samuel and Kings, has been added by the Chronicler,[2] it would appear that he had a special interest in choral music. Some scholars have indeed deduced from this that he may have been a musician who wished to promote his own profession.[3] Yet, while this could possibly be the case, it is plain that the Chronicler was not interested in sacred song by itself but rather as part of the total system of worship at the temple.

In this study I shall examine the reasons for the Chronicler's portrayal of sacred song as a part of the sacrificial worship at the temple. Broadly speaking, two matters will be covered. First I shall investigate the location and function of sacred song within the sacrificial ritual. Secondly, I shall investigate the Chronicler's understanding of its theological significance as shown by its interpretation in the light of the priestly ritual system as codified in the Pentateuch. The purpose of this investigation is to discover why the Chronicler insists that the performance of sacred song was synchronized with the presentation of the regular public burnt offering as prescribed in the law of Moses.

---

1. Where the Hebrew differs from the English tradition for numbering of verses, I shall quote according to the English text but will include the Hebrew reference in brackets, if it is significant for the argument.

2. The term 'Chronicler' is used in this study merely to designate the author(s) of Chronicles. Furthermore, while all secondary literature on Chronicles will be cited by author, date and page, citations of commentaries will be distinguished by an asterisk prefixed to the date (e.g. Rudolph *1955).

3. E.g. Driver (1913: 519), Eissfeldt (1965: 539), Pfeiffer (1941: 797). This identification is, however, regarded as most unlikely by Braun (*1986: xxxi).

Previous Studies

In keeping with the preoccupation of modern scholarship with questions of historical development, most of the work on the choral service in Chronicles has dealt with historical matters. Generally speaking, five topics have attracted attention. First, there has been considerable discussion on whether Chronicles is in fact historically correct in presenting David as the organizer of the choral service in Jerusalem.[1] Secondly, scholars have explored the related question of the history and development of the three musical guilds which we find described in 1–2 Chronicles.[2] Thirdly, in attempting to unravel the various sources and layers of redaction in Chronicles, some critics have considered whether the passages on the singers were original or added by a later redactor.[3] Fourthly, the duties of the singers and their relation to their fellow clergy have been investigated in studies on the development of the Levites as a subordinate class within the clerical hierarchy at the temple in Jerusalem.[4] Lastly, much work has been done by many scholars on the origin, nature and use of the various musical instruments mentioned in Chronicles and elsewhere in the Old Testament.[5] Apart from passing references in commentaries and in studies on other matters, no one has yet investigated these texts systematically to discover what they have to say about the nature of sacred song, its place in the total sacrificial ritual, its ritual function, and the ritual purpose of its performance.

1.   So, for example, while Pfeiffer (1941: 798-801) holds that liturgical music developed mainly in the postexilic period, Albright (1942: 125-29) argues for its Davidic origin.

2.   While Gese (1963) (building on the earlier work of Köberle [1899] on the history of the temple song and of von Rad [1930: 98-115] on the identification of the singers in Chronicles with the Levitical bearers of the ark) outlined the possible stages in the development of the three musical guilds in the postexilic period, Mowinckel (1922: 14-22; 1967: II, 53-58) argued that the postexilic singers developed from the pre-exilic guilds of cult prophets.

3.   See Noth 1943: 110-22, followed by Rudolph (*1955: 1-5), Willi (1972: 194-204), Braun (*1986: xxxi) and Throntveit (1987: 6).

4.   See the summary of the generally accepted position by de Vaux (1961: 388-92) as well as the dissertation by Zalewski (1968: 233-378).

5.   See Stainer 1879; Graetz 1881; Weiss 1895; Wellhausen 1898; Gressmann 1903; Finesinger 1926; Sellers 1941; Kolari 1947; Wohlenberg 1967; Sendrey 1969; Sendrey 1974: 77-278; Keel 1978: 335-52; Eaton 1984[a]; Jones 1986; Jones 1987.

This lack of attention is surprising, because there is a general consensus on the centrality of the cult and the prominence of liturgical
song in Chronicles.[1] It would seem, then, that sacred song figured
prominently in the theology of the cult as developed in Chronicles.
But why was this so?

It has been argued that the description of the choral music in
Chronicles merely reflected the pattern of worship at the temple when
the book was written.[2] That explanation, however, begs the question,
since it does not consider why liturgical song became so important in
the postexilic era, despite the lack of any apparent authorization for it
in the cultic traditions of the Pentateuch.

The prominence of temple music has also been attributed to the
apologetic concerns of Chronicles. If, as some claim, the book was
written either by a Levite or in defence of Levitical claims, these passages could be taken to legitimize the gradual advancement of the
Levitical musicians during the postexilic period. Their increased
involvement in the cult could then have resulted in a claim for higher
status over against the priesthood with its entrenched position of
power.[3]

In his examination of this interpretation, A.C. Welch (1939: 56-73)
denies that this was so. He argues, first, that in 5 of the 22 passages
which refer to the performance of sacred music in the cult there is no
reference to the status of the musicians as Levites (1 Chron. 13.8;
15.28; 2 Chron. 15.14; 20.28; 23.13). Secondly, the musicians are at
times clearly distinguished as a separate group from their fellow
Levites (1 Chron. 15.16-24; 16.1-6, 7, 37-40; 23.5; 25.1-31; 2 Chron.
35.15). Thirdly, even though the musicians are sometimes merely
designated as Levites (2 Chron. 29.25, 30; 30.21; 31.2; 34.12), they,
like all Levites, are clearly subordinated to the priests in their performance of praise (1 Chron. 23.28-32; 2 Chron. 5.11-13; 7.6; 8.14).
Welch (1939: 62) therefore concludes that the author of Chronicles
has no special interest in the status of the musicians as Levites or in

---

1.   Eissfeldt (1965: 537) sums up this consensus by speaking of the Chronicler's
'pronounced love for everything cultic, and particularly for cultic singing and the
Levites'.

2.   See Rudolph *1955: xv; Myers *1965[a]: 121; Ackroyd *1973: 183; Coggins
*1976: 163. But note the remarks of Köberle (1899: 83-84) about the lack of evidence
for this assumption.

3.   See von Rad 1930: 98-115.

the association of all the Levites with sacred song, but rather in temple music as part of the sacrificial worship.

Welch thus focuses attention away from the status of the temple musicians to the function of sacred song in the sacrificial cult. He claims that the sacred song which accompanied the main ritual at the temple, made its purpose and meaning clear (1939: 107). The singers then provided the spoken liturgy which accompanied the sacrifical enactment. Welch, however, does not develop this decisive insight. It has been left to others to explore some aspects of this connection between sacred song and sacrificial ritual.

First, W. Rudolph (*1955: 293) notes that in 2 Chron. 29.25-30 the performance of sacred song by the Levites coincides exactly with the presentation of the burnt offering by the priests. He, however, fails to inquire why the coincidence of these two aspects of the same ritual was of such importance as to warrant such exact elaboration. G. von Rad (1957: 365-66) suggests that this correlation of the two prevented an over-emphasis on either the material or the spiritual aspects of temple worship, since both together produced a single cultic enactment. More recently, H.G.M. Williamson (*1982: 127) has claimed that the role of the Levitical songs is set out summarily in 1 Chron. 16.4, where 'invoke' is said to refer to psalms of lament, 'thank' to psalms of thanksgiving, and 'praise' to the hymns of the psalter. All these were 'linked with appropriate forms of sacrifice, in which the Levites were thus guaranteed a role'. He does not, however, explore the reasons for this linkage.

The second attempt to explain the ritual function of sacred music and song in temple worship derives from some remarks by von Rad (1957: 348, 351). He argues that, for the Chronicler, public worship consisted almost entirely of praise and thanksgiving, which accounts for the great joy so frequently mentioned in his accounts of religious celebrations. This point is picked up and developed by Rudolph (*1955: xv). In his opinion, the Chronicler not only put greater emphasis on celebration than on atonement in worship; he also promoted the praise of the LORD as the supreme task of his people who thereby rejoiced in his gracious presence with them. While H.D. Hummel (1979: 631-32) agrees on the importance of celebration with sacred song in Chronicles, he is wary of any attempt to separate praise and joy from sacrificial atonement. Rather, he asserts that the penitential and the celebrative aspects of the cult are two sides to the same joy of God's people in his

Torah. Yet he does not consider why the praise of God by the choir
was associated so closely in Chronicles with the sacrifical ritual in the
temple at Jerusalem.

The third explanation of the ritual function of sacred music is given
by S. Mowinckel (1967: II, 53-58). He argues that the guilds of singers
not only originated from the cult prophets in the pre-exilic period, but
also took over their function at the temple in the postexilic period. By
virtue of their *ex officio* inspiration they interceded for the people and
delivered the LORD's answer to their prayers in public worship.
Generally speaking, this explanation has received widespread, if at
times qualified, acceptance.[1] D.L. Petersen (1977: 62), however, maintains that Mowinckel's position cannot be sustained, since according to
the generally accepted analysis by von Rad and Gese of the development of the music guilds, prophetic attributes were ascribed to the
singers only in the last stages of the tradition. The assignment of prophetic attributes and functions to the Levitical singers was therefore
most probably an innovation by the Chronicler and his compatriots.
At the end of his survey of the evidence Petersen concludes that the
book of Chronicles uses prophetic titles to describe the prophetic
authority and activity of the singers in the ritual performance of
worship at the second temple (1977: 85, 87). He does not, however,
consider how the singers functioned as prophets within the cult.

While Rudolph (*1955: 170-71) believes that the singers developed
historically from the pre-exilic cult prophets, he is wary of interpreting their prophetic activity too broadly. The singers did not act
generally as prophets, as Welch (1939: 90) seems to imply, but only in
their function of singing psalms to musical accompaniment. The singing
of these sacred songs in the cult was a form of prophetic proclamation. Yet, even though Rudolph clearly understands the ritual liturgical
song as prophetic proclamation, he does not investigate how it could
function thus within the sacrificial ritual at the temple.

A fourth rather tentative, and yet potentially promising, proposal
for the interpretation of the ritual function of liturgical song derives
from Rudolph. He maintains that 2 Chron. 5.11b-13a was inserted to
show that sacred song invoked the LORD's glory (*1955: 211) and

---

1. E.g. von Rad 1930: 113-15; Rudolph 1955: 171; Johnson 1962: 69-74;
Williamson *1982: 166.

effected its entrance into the newly dedicated temple (p. xxii). Yet he fails to develop this rather decisive insight.[1]

His observation is taken up in passing by G. Mayer (1986: col. 437). He agrees that, according to Chronicles, music and singing evoked the divine presence. He maintains, on the one hand, from 2 Chron. 29.31 and 30.22, that there was an open slot in the festal liturgy of the postexilic period, where thank-offerings could be presented by the members of the congregation. These were accompanied by the hymnody of the temple singers. Yet, on the other hand, he also argues from 1 Chronicles 16 that the Chronicler deliberately dissociates sacred song from sacrifices and the priesthood by his description of David's institution of the choral service before the ark at Jerusalem. So, while both Rudolph and Mayer agree that the purpose of cultic hymnody was to evoke the divine presence, they do not investigate how this was accomplished regularly through its combination with the sacrifical ritual at the temple.

There have been three attempts to draw together at least some of these points into a more comprehensive synthesis. The first comes incidentally from S. Zalewski (1968: 233-378) in his doctoral dissertation on the cultic officials in Chronicles. He notes that the frequent mention of singers in Chronicles indicates their importance in the cultic service at the temple (p. 296). There they were directly engaged with the priests in the daily ritual of sacrifice. Both 'minister' (*šērēt*) at the temple and are involved in the 'service' (*ʿbôdâ*) of the LORD's house (pp. 306-307). Like the priests with their trumpets, whose function was determined by Moses in Num. 10.1-10, the singers with their musical instruments served to call the LORD to remember his people (1 Chron. 16.4); they reminded him to protect his people and save them (pp. 307-308). The use of the verb *hizkîr* in 1 Chron. 16.4, derived as it is from Num 10.9-10, shows that the choral service had the same ritual function as the blowing of the trumpets over the sacrifices on the altar.

By singing psalms of thanksgiving and praise, the members of the temple choir were to recall the acts of God in the past and 'evoke the repetition of those acts in the present' (Zalewski 1968: 308). The singers prophesied through their performance of inspired psalmody in the liturgy sung at the temple (pp. 308-10). The singing of these

---

1. Cf. Koch 1961: 541; Becker *1988: 24.

psalms in their prescribed context had prophetic power (p. 305). In their performance of psalmody within the sacrificial cult, the singers then functioned, to some extent, ritually both as prophets and priests (p. 309).

Zalewski also observes that both the priests with their trumpets and the singers with their instruments together evoked the presence of the LORD's glory at the dedication of the temple in Jerusalem, as described in 2 Chron. 5.11-14 (1968: 357). Moreover, by his arrangement of 2 Chron. 5.11-14 and 7.1-6 the Chronicler highlights the connection between the appearance of the LORD's glory and the involvement of the Levitical singers in the sacrificial ritual at the temple. He deliberately introduces the activity of the orchestra and choir both before and after the consumption of the burnt offerings by fire from heaven, even though his *Vorlage* did not mention the singers and their activity at this ritually decisive moment (pp. 373-74). The singers thus ensured a successful outcome from the performance of the sacrificial ritual for God's people (pp. 344-45).

The second attempt to describe the ritual function of the choral service comes from A. Arens (1961: 34-54), in his liturgical-historical monograph on the origins in the Old Testament of the Christian practice of reciting the psalms in the daily office. In this study, the perceptive liturgical and theological insights of which are weakened by the author's dubious historical judgments about the origins of the choral service in the Mosaic period, the reasons for the singing of psalms in the regular worship at the temple come under discussion. Arens notes that, in presenting David with Moses as a founder of Israel's worship in Jerusalem, the Chronicler deliberately coordinates the performance of praise with the presentation of the sacrifices there (pp. 34-38). 2 Chron. 5.11-14 and 7.1-3 show that the purpose of praise was to produce the LORD's advent in Israel's worship and to respond to it (pp. 45-46; cf. 49). The singers ensured Israel's survival in a hostile world, as is shown in 2 Chron. 20.1-30, by securing the LORD's intervention against their enemies through the performance of sacred song (pp. 50-51). They functioned as prophets by praying for the people and delivering inspired oracles to them during the singing of their psalms, while they also acted as priests by offering praises together with the people during the presentation of the sacrifices at the temple (pp. 51-54). Even though none of these points is developed at length, since they are merely incidental to his main concern with the use of the psalms in Israel's daily worship, he does indicate in broad outline why the choral service was combined with the sacrificial ritual at the temple.

The third and most recent attempt to explain why the performance of praise was presented in Chronicles as an integral part of the divine service at the temple comes from J. Hausmann (1987) in an article on 1 Chron. 16.8-36 about divine worship as praise of God. She claims that this composite psalm explains what is meant by 1 Chron. 16.4, so helping us to understand the function of liturgical song in Chronicles (1987: 86). By praising God for his past acts of salvation, the singers sought to move him to save his people once again. Such praise anticipated the salvation which it hoped for (p. 87; cf. 89, 90). This praise occurred regularly within the context of the cult. There it was always coupled with sacrifice, just as the Levites were always associated with the priests. The singers thanked God for his acts of salvation, culminating in the establishment of the cult at Jerusalem, as well as for his atoning activity through the sacrificial ritual enacted there (pp. 89-90). For Chronicles, worship was so essentially praise of God that sacrifice could not be thought of without praise. Apart from the activity of the temple orchestra and choir, the cult and its sacrifices were incomplete and ultimately irrelevant. Sacrifice, therefore, was complemented by praise.

The book of Chronicles shows that the choral service of the Levitical singers was connected ritually both with the presentation of the public burnt offering (1 Chron. 16.39-40; 23.30-31; 2 Chron. 8.12-14; 23.18; 29.20-30; 31.2) and with the presentation of private thank-offerings (2 Chron. 7.4-6; 30.21-22; 31.2). This could hardly be ritually accidental, or theologically insignificant. Yet my research into the ritual function of liturgical song has shown that this combination has not attracted much attention from scholars. Apart from some incidental suggestions and passing observations, no scholars, except Zalewski, Arens and Hausmann, have yet examined what Chronicles has to say about the function and significance of liturgical song within the sacrificial ritual at the temple. That is the aim of this project.

Methodology

This study will explore the ritual function and significance of liturgical song by the exegesis of the relevant passages from Chronicles. Its

methods are largely conventional. There are, however, three matters
of methodology which merit some comment, since they depend on
certain literary, ritual and genetic presuppositions about the texts
from Chronicles.

Literary Analysis

I intend to undertake a ritual analysis of the choral service as
presented in the books of Chronicles. In doing this, I shall deal with
the canonical text of Chronicles and assume that it was composed in its
present form somewhere between 400 and 350 BC.[1] The exegesis of it
will be largely synchronic, with an emphasis on the literary analysis
of the various units in their context. Since such historical matters as
the origin of the singers and the development of text in Chronicles are
not under consideration, they will be touched on only in passing in so
far as they are relevant to the argument.

The basic presupposition of this study, therefore, is that the two
books of Chronicles form a separate, unified work of literature. Now
this is by no means self-evident. The unity and extent of Chronicles
has indeed been contested, and that from three angles. First, since the
work of Zunz (1832), it has been treated as part of a larger historical
work which also included Ezra and Nehemiah. This has, however,
been called into question by S. Japhet (1968) and H.G.M. Williamson
(1977: 5-70), who both argue for its separate identity. While some
scholars have not been convinced by their case,[2] that position is adopted
here in this study, though, strictly speaking, my findings should not be
significantly affected even if Chronicles is viewed not as an
independent work but as part of a larger history by the Chronicler.

Secondly, the genealogical preface in 1 Chronicles 1–9 has often
been regarded as a later addition to the original text.[3] The arguments
for this position have, however, been successfully countered by

1.   See Williamson *1982: 15-17; 1977[a]: 83-86. In his recent summary of the
main options for dating Chronicles Throntveit (1987: 97-107) argues for 527–515 BC
as the date for its original form. He can, however, sustain this only by postulating a
later Levitical redaction which inserted 1 Chron. 1–9, 23–27 and 29.1, 9.

2.   E.g. Clines 1984: 9-12; Haran 1985; Blenkinsopp 1988: 47-54. Throntveit
(1982) and Talshir (1988) have also questioned the validity of their linguistic arguments without rejecting their conclusions.

3.   E.g. Welch 1935: 185-86; Freedman 1961: 441; Cross 1975; Newsome
1975: 215.

M.D. Johnson (1969: 44-55), H.G.M. Williamson (1977[a]: 71-82) and W.L. Osborne (1979: 19-95). They have demonstrated that there is a similarity in terminology, subject matter, thought and purpose in both parts. While I accept their findings, they are not altogether essential to my case, which rests on the present canonical text.

Thirdly, since the last century some scholars have regarded this or that mention of the singers as a secondary addition. In *The Chronicler's History* (1987: 31-40), M. Noth claimed that many of the references to the singers were not original.[1] His influential proposals have, however, been called into question and rejected in most cases by Williamson (*1982: 14-15; cf. Williamson 1979). Like Williamson, I hold that they are most probably original, and I shall show why in each instance. Yet, even if they were not original, my case would still stand, albeit in a modified form. The present books of Chronicles would then show us what a later editor, rather than the Chronicler, understood to be the function and significance of the choral service.

Ritual Analysis

In his famous *Prolegomena to the History of Israel* (1885), J. Wellhausen notes that the Chronicler's evident interest in the cult with its ceremonies, appurtenances and personnel led to a complete reinterpretation of the material taken from Samuel and Kings. This interest in ritual is most obvious in his portrayal of David. With withering scorn Wellhausen sums up the Chronicler's depictment of him (1885: 182):

> See what Chronicles has made out of David! The founder of the kingdom has become the founder of the temple and the public worship, the king and hero at the head of his companions in arms has become the singer and master of ceremonies at the head of a swarm of priests and Levites. . . Just as the law framed by Ezra as the foundation of Judaism was regarded as having been the work of Moses, so what upon this basis had been

---

1.   While Noth rejects 1 Chron. 6.31-48; 15.4-10, 16-24; 16.5-38, 41-42; 23.3–25.31; 2 Chron. 5.11b-12a, 13a; 8.14-15; 23.18; 35.15, he accepts as original 1 Chron. 15.27-28; 16.4; 2 Chron. 7.6; 29.25-30; 30.21-22; 31.2; and 34.12-13. Noth does not always give the reasons for his judgments, which seem to be based mainly on the earlier commentary of Rothstein and Hänel (*1927). His judgments have been accepted in most cases by Rudolph (*1955). Since Rudolph always gives the reasons for his judgments, I shall interact mainly with him. Willi (1972: 194-204) goes further than both these scholars in regarding all references to the singers as secondary.

developed after Moses—particularly the music of the sanctuary and the
ordering of the temple personnel—was carried back to King David, the
sweet singer of Israel, who had now to place his music at the service of
the cultus, and write psalms along with Asaph, Heman, and Jeduthun, the
Levitical singing families.

His attack was so successful that those scholars who since then endeav-
oured to rehabilitate the Chronicler's reputation have found it necessary to defend him against the charge of ritualism.[1] Yet none has
taken up Wellhausen's observations and examined the Chronicler's
ritual concerns positively in their own right. It will not do merely to
ascribe them to the taste of the postexilic period, as Wellhausen did;
some attempt must be made to show why ritual was so important for
him and his audience that it figured prominently in his history.

Even though ritual has always been a subject of theological study as
part of liturgics within the Christian tradition, this has had little influence on the study of ritual in the Old Testament, except in tracing
either the continuity or discontinuity between Jewish and Christian
worship. Where ritual has not been dismissed as of little value or
treated as an allegorical charade, it has been examined technically and
symbolically in the tradition derived from the rabbis[2] or else historically in terms of its genesis and development.[3] In recent times some
eminent Jewish scholars have combined these two approaches with
remarkable success.[4]

Yet the decisive stimulus for a change in attitude to the nature of
ritual among some Old Testament scholars and for the use of new
methods of ritual analysis on the ritual texts of the Old Testament has
come from the British school of social anthropology. In their studies
of traditional societies, these anthropologists have shown how those
societies structured themselves socially, and how they constituted their
world symbolically through the performance of certain rituals that
therefore embodied their basic values and uncontested convictions.
V. Turner (1957, 1967, 1968, 1969[a], 1974) has been the most influential
of these scholars.

The most immediate and direct influence on the study of ritual by
Old Testament scholars has come through the book *Purity and Danger*,

---

1. E.g. Rudolph *1955: xxi; Williamson *1982: 30-31.
2. E.g. Kurtz 1862.
3. E.g. Rendtorff 1967.
4. See especially Haran 1978 and Milgrom 1970, 1976[b], 1983.

by M. Douglas (1966). As part of a wider study she analysed how the categories of clean and unclean were used ritually in Leviticus to structure Israelite society within its symbolic cosmos (pp. 41-57). Her basic notions on the function of ritual were taken up by G.J. Wenham in his commentaries on Leviticus (1979) and Numbers (1981). Since then, the work of Douglas and her fellow social anthropologists, as well as the studies on ritual done by scholars from many different disciplines,[1] have influenced the examination of various rites and ritual systems in the Old Testament.[2]

This study stands within that trend. It has been stimulated by Turner's insights into the nature and interpretation of ritual, insights such as the role of foundational charters in authorizing a ritual, the creative power of ritual and its symbolism to constitute communities and affect its participants at all levels of their being, the multivocal nature of ritual symbolism which condenses the underlying values and beliefs of traditional societies in terms of certain basic polarities, and the interaction of each ritual symbol with the symbols adjacent to it in time and space within the total ritual system which serve to elucidate its sense.[3] Generally speaking, my approach approximates Turner's three suggested modes of interpretation by considering the choral service exegetically in Chapters 2 and 5, positionally in Chapter 3, and operationally in Chapter 4.[4] Yet it differs from the anthropological approach found in Turner by concentrating on the theological rather than the social significance of sacred song.

While Turner and his disciples hold that a society constitutes itself with the status of its members and its place within the cosmos by the performance of ritual, the Chronicler goes much further than that; he believes that through the enactment of right ritual God maintains Israel as his people, confers the status and benefits due to each of them, and assigns them their proper role in the divinely created cosmic order. Since I am interested in the Chronicler's belief in divine activity in and through the sacrificial ritual, I shall not interact with the ideas

1. For a succinct summary of the various ways of interpreting ritual, see Grimes 1982a, 32-33.

2. See particularly the essays of Leach (1976) and D. Davies (1977) on the interpretation of the sacrifices, as well as the dissertations by Wright (1987), Kiuchi (1987), Jenson (1992) and Gorman (1990).

3. See Segal 1983 for a succinct summary of Turner's theory of ritual.

4. For these terms, see Turner 1969[a]: 17, 81-82; 1969[b]: 11-13.

of Turner by reconstructing the social context of sacred song, but rather attempt to discover the Chronicler's understanding of its theological role within the sacrificial ritual by an exegesis of the texts on it. My basic presupposition is that, since the Chronicler was obviously interested in the ritual performed at the temple in Jerusalem, that interest informed his selection of material and its arrangement in his history.

Inner-Biblical Exegesis
There has been, recently, a growing interest in discovering how later biblical authors reinterpreted and reapplied earlier biblical texts which were regarded by them as authoritative. From this we may determine how certain texts were gradually canonized, as well as what methods were used to interpret them. While much of this work is by its very nature rather specialized and limited in scope, some of its results have been drawn together more comprehensively by M. Fishbane in *Biblical Interpretation in Ancient Israel* (1985) and in the summary essays by various authors in *Scripture Citing Scripture* (Carson and Williamson 1988).

Some work has also been undertaken on this topic in Chronicles. This is not at all surprising, since Chronicles includes much of Samuel and Kings, cites the writings of certain prophets as its sources, and frequently notes that some matter is in accord with the law of Moses. Whereas T. Willi (1972), followed in part by P.R. Ackroyd (1977), has treated all the original material in Chronicles as an exegesis of Samuel–Kings,[1] J.R. Shaver (1984) has analysed the Chronicler's use of Pentateuchal legislation on cultic matters, and Fishbane (1985) has examined his exegesis of legal material from the Pentateuch. P. Welten (1979) has argued that Psalm 132, which is partially quoted in 2 Chron. 6.41-42, has influenced the composition of the narrative from 1 Chronicles 13 to 2 Chronicles 7, and J. Hausmann (1988) has studied the reinterpretation of the psalms in 1 Chron. 16.8-36.

---

1.   While scholars like Willi have generally assumed that the text of Samuel used by the Chronicler was identical with our present MT, the work of Cross (1964) and his students Lemke (1963, 1965), Ulrich (1978), McCarter (1980, 1984) and McKenzie (1985) has shown that it was in fact closer to 4QSam[a] and the LXX. Divergences from the MT cannot therefore automatically be regarded as instances of the Chronicler's exegesis.

Much of this work has been summarized by Williamson (1988). In this essay he also argues for the validity of the five principles of interpretation which Clines (1981) had deduced from Nehemiah 10. Williamson concludes that the Chronicler not only clearly distin-- guished between a text and its exegesis (1988: 31) but also regarded the written law as more authoritative for religious practice than written prophecy (p. 35) and written prophecy as more authoritative than narrative history (p. 34).

In this study I shall show how the Chronicler not only uses earlier texts, overtly or covertly, to establish a particular point of ritual and to elucidate its sense, but also reinterprets them in a new way through his additions and changes to the text from Samuel–Kings. I therefore presuppose that the Chronicler had at his disposal much, if not all, of the present texts of Samuel–Kings, the Pentateuch, and Psalms 96, 105, 106 and 132.

Approach and Presentation

The basic contention of this study is that the Chronicler included all the material on the origin, organization and work of the temple singers in his narrative because he wished to show that the singers were to announce the LORD's acceptance of his people and to proclaim his gracious presence with them by the performance of their choral music during the presentation of the public burnt offering.

In Chapter 2 I shall investigate the divine institution and royal establishment of sacred song as part of the sacrificial ritual at the temple in Jerusalem. This will be followed in Chapter 3 by an analysis of the ritual components of the LORD's song in terms of its verbal content, location, times, instruments and performers. Chapter 4 explains the function of sacred song as determined by its place within the total sacrificial ritual, and Chapter 5 draws out its theological significance as the proclamation of the LORD's presence in the sacrificial ritual and as the prophetic announcement of the LORD's acceptance of his people. Chapter 6 will conclude the study, summarizing the findings.

Chapter 2

THE RITUAL INSTITUTION OF THE LORD'S SONG

The Foundational Charter for Sacred Song

In their analysis of ritual B. Moore and N. Habel (1982: 94) claim that, where ritual acts are linked with foundational myths or legends, these foundational stories which give the charter for the ritual action are a key component in the interpretation of that ritual. The stories in Chronicles about the organization of choral music by David and Solomon fulfil that function; they give the charter for its performance by the musicians and so help to establish its significance.

These foundational stories serve a twofold purpose. On the one hand, they show the origin of choral music. In this the Chronicler differs from modern historians by holding that the nature and significance of this institution was given embryonically in its divinely authorized foundation by David and Solomon rather than as a result of its gradual historical development. For him, the key to the understanding the choral rite lay in its establishment by David and Solomon. On the other hand, these foundational stories set ritual precedents for the proper enactment and permissible development of temple music. There was therefore room for innovation in some areas, but it had to be on the foundation set by the initial charter, if its performance was to be legitimate and effectual.

The central figure in these foundational stories is David. The Chronicler, in fact, regards him as the second great cult founder after Moses. David not only instituted the choral rite and established the temple choir but also planned the temple and organized the orders of clergy to officiate there. In doing this, he did not, however, supplant Moses but rather supplemented his work.

In an article entitled 'Moses and David as Cult Founders in Chronicles', S.J. De Vries (1988) has shown how the Chronicler compares and contrasts the roles of Moses and David as cult founders by using two sets of formulations. First, there is 'the authorization formula' which defines what is absolutely obligatory in worship and bases ritual practice on the authority of Moses and his law.[1] Then there is 'the regulation formula', which refers to the ritual statutes for the administration of the cult as arranged by David and his successors.[2] These statutes were either contained in the Pentateuch[3] or in the instructions of David given in 1 Chronicles 23–26 and 28.[4] David is therefore presented in Chronicles both as the heir of Moses in enacting his ritual legislation and as a second Moses in establishing the worship at the temple in Jerusalem. His successors stood in his shoes. Just as David had implemented the law of Moses, so his true heirs from Solomon to Josiah implemented the law of Moses as well as David's ritual legislation.[5]

The Chronicler held that, just as Moses had founded the sacrificial cult, so David founded the choral rite. It was his great innovation in ritual matters. He was its founder, and his successors were its patrons. In founding it, he determined its character and purpose. This chapter will therefore examine the role of David and his successors as patrons of choral music at the temple.

---

1. See 1 Chron. 6.49 (6.34); 15.15; 16.40; 28.19; 2 Chron. 8.13; 23.18; 30.5, 18; 31.3; 35.6, 12.

2. See 1 Chron. 15.13; 23.31; 24.19; 2 Chron. 4.7, 20; 8.14; 23.18; 29.15, 25; 30.6, 12, 16; 35.4, 10, 13, 15, 16. 1 Chron. 6.32 (6.17) should be added to his list.

3. 1 Chron. 15.13; 23.31; 24.19; 2 Chron. 29.15; 30.5, 12, 16; 35: 13, 16.

4. 1 Chron. 6.32 (6.17); 2 Chron. 8.14; 23.18; 29.25; 35.10, 15; cf. 2 Chron. 4.7, 20. Wright (1991: 231-37) calls these 'Davidic assignment formulas' and shows how they authorize the placement of clergy in their positions of authority as determined by David in 1 Chron. 23–26.

De Vries (1988: 630-31) claims that in 2 Chron. 35.4 the 'writing' ($k^e t\bar{a}b$) of David refers to the injunctions in 1 Chron. 23–26, which are implemented by the 'writing' ($mikt\bar{a}b$) of Solomon as reported in 2 Chron. 8.12-15.

5. As de Vries maintains (1988: 639), Josiah's anachronistic command that the Levites place the ark in Solomon's temple and assume other duties in 2 Chron. 35.3 is probably meant to indicate that what David had begun with the transferral of the ark in 1 Chron. 15 had now come to its full fruition.

The Divine Institution of Sacred Song

The people of Israel could not worship the LORD as they pleased but only with the rituals ordained by him. That is the first and perhaps most fixed principle of worship in Chronicles. Through Moses the LORD had commanded that Israel implement his statutes and ordinances for them (1 Chron. 22.12-13).[1] Among these were the statutes by which he instituted and regulated their worship. Such statutes prescribed when, where and how the Israelites were to 'seek' him.[2]

These liturgical regulations centred on the ritual process of sacrifice. The proper procedure for its performance was commanded by the LORD (1 Chron. 16.40; 2 Chron. 31.3) and set down in the law of Moses (1 Chron. 6.49; 2 Chron. 8.13; 23.18). The law not only prescribed the agents, places, times, materials and pattern for its performance but also determined its ritual function, which was to make atonement for Israel (1 Chron. 6.49). If the sacrificial ritual was to make atonement for Israel, it had to be performed according to the law, which, for the Chronicler, consisted mainly of ritual legislation.[3] This applied to all important aspects of worship which were therefore regulated by ritual statutes.[4]

Now this insistence on the conformity of Israel's worship with the prescriptions of Moses could conceivably be the mark of a reactionary conservative, bent on restoring the worship at the temple to its imagined former splendour. But that could hardly be, since the Chronicler was well aware that the worship at the temple under the monarchy only

---

1. Von Rad (1930: 38-63) has refuted the claims of Rothstein and Hänel (*1927) that the Chronicler bases his work on P by showing his dependence on both P and D.

2. The Chronicler uses the verb dāraš and its synonym biqqēš in this sense. In obedience to his law (2 Chron. 31.21) the LORD was to be sought first at his altar in Gibeon (1 Chron. 21.30; 2 Chron. 1.5) and then in Jerusalem (2 Chron. 11.16), as well as at his ark (1 Chron. 13.3; 15.13). There he could be sought and found through the presentation of sacrifices (2 Chron. 1.5-6; 11.16; cf. 2 Chron. 25.15) and prayer (2 Chron. 7.14) at holy times such as the Feast of Passover (2 Chron. 30.19) and a duly constituted fast (2 Chron. 20.3-4). For a further analysis of these terms in Chronicles, see Schaefer 1972: 54-67.

3. See Kellermann 1988.

4. See the use of kammišpāṭ in 1 Chron. 6.32 (6.17); 15.13; 23.31; 24.19; 2 Chron. 4.7, 20; 8.14; 30.16; 35.13. From his examination of these passages, Carr (1972: 173-76) concludes that the term is used to describe the divinely prescribed pattern for ritual service; cf. Fishbane 1985: 208-13; de Vries 1988: 627-31.

rarely approached his high ideals for it. It more likely stemmed from his desire to defend the legitimacy of worship at the second temple by appeal to authoritative tradition with its claims of divine legislation. Yet the legitimation of worship by recourse to ancient tradition was not an end in itself. Rather, for Chronicles, the sacrificial ritual was to be conducted according to its divine institution, so that it would, as the LORD had promised, be effectual in mediating his gracious presence and blessing to his people.

The reason for this interest in the divine institution of the sacrificial cult is clear. Worship was effective and beneficial only as long as it was performed in accordance with divine law. In fact, its divine institution empowered it, so that, by its enactment, the LORD himself received his people, like a king his petitioners, and acted in their favour. Hence, the LORD was with those who worshipped him as he had directed (2 Chron. 13.10-12). Where the law, which instituted and regulated worship, was not implemented and taught by the priests, the true God was absent from his people (2 Chron. 15.2b-3). One could therefore seek the LORD and worship him only as he had determined (2 Chron. 7.12-16). Such orthodoxy led to success (1 Chron. 22.13; 2 Chron. 31.21); it resulted in possession of the land (1 Chron. 28.8; 2 Chron. 33.8), just as failure to worship him correctly resulted in dispossession from the land and the destruction of the temple (2 Chron. 7.19-22).[1]

This principle is exemplified most clearly by the stories in 1 Chronicles 10–16. Saul and his family were exterminated, because he failed to 'seek' the LORD. Instead, he disobeyed the command of the LORD and consulted a medium (1 Chron. 10.13-14). In contrast to this, David 'sought' the LORD by attempting to bring the ark to Jerusalem (1 Chron. 13.1-3). Yet, even though he rightly sought the LORD where he was to be found,[2] he failed, and Uzzah died, because he did not seek him in the right way (1 Chron. 15.13). However, once he transported the ark and attended to it as prescribed, he was successful. As a result he conferred blessing to all Israel (1 Chron. 16.2-3)

1. Since von Rad (1957: 349) fails to appreciate the importance of the divine institution of Israel's worship in Chronicles, he speaks rather dismissively of a formal and external reference to the correspondence of a certain cultic usage with a canonical ritual regulation.

2. See Exod. 25.21-22; 30.6, 36; Num. 7.89; 17.19, which speak of the ark as the place where God meets with Moses and speaks to him.

and his own household (1 Chron. 16.43).

Now this insistence on the correct performance of divinely ordained ritual seems to be contradicted by the description in Chronicles of the foundation of sacred song by David. Despite the lack of reference to choral music in the Pentateuch, David not only established it before the ark in Jerusalem but also prescribed its performance during the presentation of the burnt offering, first at Gibeon (1 Chron. 16.40-41), and then at Solomon's temple in Jerusalem (1 Chron. 23.30-31). Even though this major innovation in that central rite seems to lack divine sanction, the Chronicler speaks about the proper arrangement for the choir, the proper procedure for its performance, and the proper function of its ministry, as if it were equivalent in status to the sacrificial ritual (1 Chron. 6.32; 23.31). How then could this innovation be justified?[1]

The Chronicler deals with this problem in two ways. First he affirms the prophetic institution of the choral rite. Secondly, he supports this prophetic innovation by the exegesis of three pieces of ritual legislation in the Pentateuch.

In the story of Hezekiah's restoration of the worship at the temple, the Chronicler claims in 2 Chron. 29.25 that the choral rite was in fact authorized by the LORD:

> He (Hezekiah) stationed the Levites in the house of YHWH with cymbals, harps, and lyres according to the commandment of David and of Gad the king's seer and of Nathan the prophet; for the commandment was by YHWH[2] through his prophets.

The Lord did not institute the ritual performance of sacred song in the law of Moses but rather through his commandment to David. Yet, unlike Moses, David was not himself the direct recipient of the

---

1. As far as I can establish, no modern scholar has considered this question, even though in *b. 'Arak.* 11a-11b the rabbis had discussed the related question of whether liturgical song was obligatory for the presentation of the burnt offering.

2. The formulation of this point is rather puzzling in the MT with its repetition of *b*e*yad*. As it now stands, the phrase seems to be used here in two different ways: with *b*e*yad YHWH* it means 'under the authority/control of the LORD', while *b*e*yad n*e*bî'āyw* means 'through his prophets'. Rudolph (*1955: 296) wrongly assumes that both phrases bear the same sense. Since a commandment cannot be given through the mediation both of the LORD and of his prophets, he proposes that we read *b*e*yad dāwîd* instead. The phrase, however, is also found in 1 Chron. 29.12, which speaks about the LORD's possession and disposal of stength and power to humans.

LORD's instructions; they came to him through the prophets Gad and Nathan. This authorization of sacred song through two prophets gave the decree added significance and weight; it was, in fact, the only aspect of the ritual at the temple which had been ordained through the prophets. They not only authorized choral music but also prescribed the location of the musicians in the temple, the instruments for it, and its performance by the Levites during the presentation of the burnt offering.

The choral rite was thus instituted by the LORD through his prophets and organized by his royal deputy David. Its divine origin was confirmed by the advent of the LORD with his glory into the temple during the song of thanksgiving as recorded in 2 Chron. 5.11-14, which serves as the foundational story for it in Chronicles. Yet the Chronicler does not appear to have been entirely satisfied with the prophetic commandment and the divine confirmation of it by a theophany as a sufficient basis for this innovation in the sacrificial ritual. He therefore presents a theological rationale for the choral rite based on an exegesis of selected passages from the Pentateuch. These passages do not, however, explicitly mention choral music, but rather give certain divine directions which, according to the Chronicler, were properly implemented by the performance of sacred song in the sacrificial ritual.

The first of these is Deut. 10.8 with its associated legislation in Deut. 18.5. In his decree about the transportation of the ark to Jerusalem in 1 Chron. 15.2, David repeated the substance of these two passages.[1] He realized that he had not sought the LORD in the right way in his initial attempt to transfer the ark (1 Chron. 15.13).[2] On the basis of Deut. 10.8, he therefore decreed that the Levites should carry the ark on their shoulders (rather than in a cart) and minister to the LORD as they had been chosen to do.[3]

---

1.   While Rothstein and Hänel (*1927: 273, 309), in keeping with their assumption that Chronicles used P rather than the whole Pentateuch, propose that David alludes to Num. 1.48-50 and 3.5-37, von Rad (1930: 99) demonstrates that it paraphrases Deut. 10.8 and 18.5.

2.   The suffix on *dᵉrašnuhû* in 1 Chron. 13.3 and 15.13 is, it seems, deliberately ambiguous. It could refer either to the ark or to the LORD. See Curtis and Madsen *1910: 214.

3.   Only if the connection of this passage with Deut. 10.8 and 18.5 is disregarded could it be argued, as Welch does (1939: 67), that the Levites ministered to the ark rather than the LORD.

The Levites were given two discrete and yet complementary tasks by David in 1 Chron. 15.2: the transportation of the ark, and ministry to the LORD. On the face of it, the mention of ministry to the LORD seems out of place in a discussion on the correct way to move the ark to Jerusalem. The phrase could hardly have come in here by accident with the first part of Deut. 10.8, since the Chronicler deliberately excludes what he considers irrelevant—for example, the duty 'to bless in his name', which, for him, was the responsibility of the priests rather than the Levites (1 Chron. 23.13; 2 Chron. 30.27). He also deliberately recalls Deut. 18.5 by his mention of the divine election of the Levites and the perpetuity of their ministry. This ministry, which the Levites were to perform for the LORD, is explained in 1 Chronicles 16. The Levites were to 'minister' regularly to the LORD before the ark of the covenant (1 Chron. 16.4, 37) as well as at the tabernacle in Gibeon (1 Chron. 6.32). This was accomplished by 'proclaiming', 'thanking' and 'praising' him (1 Chron. 16.4; cf. 2 Chron. 8.14; 31.2). Their ministry to the LORD was therefore the ministry of song (1 Chron. 6.32).

The argument which is implied here in Chronicles is as follows. The temporary responsibility of the Levites for the transportation of the ark was part of a larger and more permanent duty to minister to the LORD who sat enthroned above it and met with his people there. This ministry, which was performed 'in' or 'with the LORD's name' (Deut. 18.5, 7), was carried out by the Levites as they proclaimed that name to the people in songs of praise. So then, while liturgical song was not explicitly instituted in the Pentateuch, it was held to be included in the commission of the Levites by the LORD to minister in his name.[1]

Num. 10.10 was also used by the author of Chronicles to provide a theological basis for the choral rite. It comes at the end of a section which contains the divinely given regulations for the use of the holy trumpets by the priests. The whole section on the trumpets in 10.1-10 is enclosed by the description of the cloud, by which the LORD tabernacled with his people (Num. 9.15-23) and led them as his army stage by stage with his ark to their destination (Num. 10.11-36). The trumpets are therefore associated thematically with both the LORD's presence and the ark.

---

1. Interestingly, Rabbi Judah hands on a similar argument from Rabbi Samuel based on Deut. 18.7 and 10.8 in *b. 'Arak.* 11a.

Apart from the practical function of communicating information for assembly and movement (Num. 10.1-8), the trumpets served a common ritual function in two different and yet related contexts. In war they were blown before the army as it went into battle, so that Israel would be 'remembered' and given victory by the LORD; in the cult they were sounded over the burnt offerings and peace offerings, so that they would serve to bring the people to the LORD's 'remembrance' and him to their 'remembrance'.[1]

1 Chron. 16.4 states that David appointed the Levitical choir to 'proclaim'[2] the LORD, the God of Israel. The term is noteworthy for its singularity. Nowhere else is the *hiphil* of *zākar* used in Chronicles as a synonym for thanking and praising the LORD in the context of liturgical song. By itself, the function of this reference is unclear because it seems to add nothing to the other two verbs which stand in apposition with it.[3]

Rothstein and Hänel (*1927: 287) propose two possible explanations for the occurrence of this term in 1 Chron. 16.4. The first of these takes its cue from the title *leʰazkîr* in Psalms 38 and 70. There, as in Isa. 66.3, the *hiphil* of *zākar* is used as a denominative for the presentation of a memorial offering (*'azkārâ*). *hazkîr* would then refer to those songs which were sung during the presentation of the memorial offering in the sacrificial ritual. This proposal, however, is rather unlikely, since sacrifices were at that time presented at the altar in Gibeon rather than before the ark in Jerusalem.[4]

---

1.   The sounding of trumpets was one of the four memorials instituted by God with an accompanying promise of grace. The other three were the blood of the Passover (Exod. 12.14), the breastplate of the high priest (Exod. 28.12, 29) and the ritual at the tabernacle financed by the levy for the census (Exod. 30.16). Apart from the Passover, all these were to be performed for Israel by the priests in 'the LORD's presence'.

2.   Eising (1980: 74) concludes that the *hiphil* of *zākar* can be best translated by 'extol' or 'proclaim'. It is used for the pronouncement of the holy name (Ps. 20.8; Isa. 26.13; 48.1; 62.6; Amos 6.10) with a recitation of his characteristics and achievements (Ps. 71.16; 77.12; Isa. 63.7).

3.   Without giving any reason for his judgment, Williamson (*1982: 127) limits this to invocation through psalms of lament, which is to be distinguished from 'thanking' through psalms of thanksgiving and 'praising' through hymns.

4.   See also Rudolph (*1955: 120). This is not a compelling argument, as Curtis and Madsen (*1910: 220-21) show: 'Since the Chronicler represents that no regular sacrifices were made in Jerusalem at this time. . . it may be inferred that these Levites

Their second, preferred, explanation is that the use of *hazkîr* was meant to recall the function of the trumpets in Num. 10.9-10. The Chronicler, then, associated the work of the singers in thanking and praising the LORD with the work of the priests in sounding their trumpets in 1 Chron. 16.6. By this allusion he did not imply that only the priests 'proclaimed' the LORD, while the Levites thanked and praised him,[1] but that the Levites combined with the priestly trumpeters in proclaiming him. In fact, 'the singers fulfilled the same function as the trumpet' (Zalewski 1968: 308). This combination of trumpets with sacred song was so important for the Chronicler that he never mentioned the use of trumpets in worship apart from the performance of the other temple instruments (1 Chron. 13.8; 15.17-24, 28; 16.4-6; 2 Chron. 5.12-13; 7.6; 20.28; 23.13; 29.26-28). The singing of the LORD's song to instrumental accompaniment was therefore regarded as an extension of the priestly mandate to sound the trumpets over the public sacrifices.

Now it may be, as Zalewski (1968: 309-10) claims, that the Chronicler thereby ascribed some priestly attributes and functions, if not priestly status, to the Levites. But it seems that his intention was rather to justify the place of liturgical song in the sacrificial ritual by connecting it with the blowing of trumpets over the sacrifices, for the trumpets were, after all, the only musical instruments explicitly ordained by the LORD for worship.[2]

The argument of Chronicles would then run as follows. By sounding the trumpets the priests were to proclaim the LORD's presence and announce that he had come to the aid of his people. But the trumpets could not by themselves announce the LORD's presence. Indeed, how else could his presence be announced but by mention of his name, which was his 'mode of remembrance' (Exod. 3.15)? The trumpet was therefore supplemented by the instruments used to

were to conduct the musical liturgy before the ark at the same time that the offerings were being made on the altar at Gibeon with the corresponding musical service. The two priests also (v. 6) sounded the two silver trumpets as if present at the burnt offerings. . . '

1.   *Contra* Rothstein and Hänel *1927: 287. Rudolph (*1955: 120) rightly asserts that the command in 1 Chron. 16.4 excludes this interpretation.

2.   In *b*. '*Arak*. 11b Rabbi Abin also bases his argument for the obligatory performance of liturgical song with the free-will offerings of the community on Num. 10.10.

accompany those sacred songs which were sung to introduce the LORD by name. The whole temple choir, which consisted of priestly trumpeters and Levitical musicians, thus announced the LORD and proclaimed his presence. The divine command of Num. 10.10 was thereby fulfilled by David through the institution of the choral rite.

The third theological justification from the Pentateuch for sacred song is given in 2 Chron. 23.18. There the Chronicler says that the priests and the Levites were divided into groups 'to offer up the burnt offerings of the LORD according to the written record in the law of Moses with rejoicing and song, as David had directed'. As the MT indicates in its punctuation, the last phrase is resumptive; it refers to the whole subordinate clause rather than just to the preceding phrase. The passage then seems to imply that the law had ordered the burnt offerings to be presented with singing.

Yet the matter is not quite as straightforward as that. We have here a combination of the formula for divine authorization with the formula for ritual regulation.[1] Since, as Williamson (1988: 28-31) has shown, *kakkātûb* is used to qualify only what immediately precedes it, 2 Chron. 23.18 creates a contrast between the clear command in the Pentateuch to present burnt offerings to the LORD and the directive of David to do so with songs of rejoicing. Now this directive is itself based on the exegesis of certain passages in the Pentateuch. While it could possibly recall Num. 10.10 with its mention of trumpets sounded over the sacrifices 'on the day of Israel's rejoicing', it seems rather to allude to those places in Deuteronomy (e.g. 12.6-7, 11-12, 18; 16.10-11; 26.11 and 27.6-7) where the Israelites are told to present their sacrifices at one chosen sanctuary and to rejoice there in the LORD's presence.

2 Chron. 23.18 should most likely be taken together with 1 Chron. 15.16 and 2 Chron. 29.30. In 1 Chron. 15.16 David commands the chiefs of the Levites to appoint the Levitical choir to raise music and song for rejoicing during the transportation of the ark to Jerusalem. The same point is made in 2 Chron. 29.30, where the psalms of David and Asaph are said to have been performed during the presentation of the burnt offering to produce rejoicing (*'ad-lᵉśimḥâ*).[2] The choral rite

---

1.   See de Vries 1988: 629.

2.   The sense of this is not that they praised the LORD 'with gladness', as the phrase is usually translated (e.g. RSV), but that they praised him 'until there was rejoicing'. The compound preposition *'ad-lᵉ* before a substantive is, as Polzin shows

was therefore instituted to create rejoicing, first during the transferal of the ark, and then during the presentation of the public burnt offerings, as God had commanded in Deuteronomy.

The question arises whether this was what was intended by the instruction to rejoice in Deuteronomy. There are, in all, three ways of taking this instruction. First, it could prescribe the attitude to be taken by the people. Yet that is hardly possible, for attitudes cannot be enforced. Nor does it fit the context of these passages, which have to do with matters of ritual such as the presentation of sacrifices and the consumption of the sacrificial meal. Secondly, it could refer to the eating of the sacrifices with one's guests, since eating and rejoicing are mentioned together in Deut. 12.7, 18 and 27.7. While this is more likely, it is called into question by the claim in Deut. 28.47-48 that, since Israel did not serve the LORD 'with rejoicing and goodness of heart', she would have to serve her enemies in hunger, nakedness and poverty. It is rather unlikely that Israel failed to indulge in feasting at her festivals. Thirdly, rejoicing could refer to the performance of sacred song together with the presentation of the sacrifices.[1]

Whatever the case, the Chronicler in 2 Chron. 23.18 understood the command to rejoice in Deuteronomy as an instruction to perform liturgical song. Even if Deuteronomy refers to the rejoicing at a sacrificial banquet, the Chronicler speaks about rejoicing during the presentation of burnt offerings, which were not eaten, rather than the peace offerings, which were eaten. This was made possible exegetically by the identification of rejoicing in Deuteronomy with music and song, as in Pss. 100.2; 137.3; Isa. 16.10; 30.29; 51.3; and Jer 33.11, and by the understanding of service in Deut. 28.47 as the performance of the sacrificial ritual. So then, by the equation of rejoicing with liturgical song, the Chronicler laid the third theological foundation for the place of choral music in the sacrificial cult. The divine command to rejoice in his presence was to be fulfilled through the performance of sacred song which created joy in the hearts of the people and articulated it for them.

(1976: 69), used in Chronicles instead of l^e or *'ad* to signify a spatial or temporal limit. Here it is used to signify extent and degree (see BDB, 725), or perhaps even purpose.

1.   Deut. 28.47 may also have influenced the development of liturgical song in the postexilic period. It was used much later by Rabbi Mattenah in *b. 'Arak.* 11a to argue that the sacrificial ritual required liturgical song.

The Chronicler implies that the sacrificial ritual at the temple in Jerusalem had to be conducted in conformity with the divine legislation which instituted it, if it was to perform its divinely given function of mediating the LORD's presence and blessing to his people. Choral music was an important part of the sacrificial ritual. Even though it was not commanded by Moses, the Chronicler claims that it was instituted by David in fulfilment of the LORD's commands to him through the prophets Gad and Nathan. This, however, was not a disruptive innovation but was entirely consistent with the letter and spirit of the Mosaic tradition. The institution of the choral rite indeed fulfilled three of the divine commands in the law: the instruction in Num. 10.10 for the priests to proclaim the LORD at the altar, the commission in Deut. 10.8 and 18.5 of the Levites to minister in his name, and the injunctions in Deuteronomy for all Israelites to rejoice in his presence. So, since liturgical music was divinely authorized and consistent with the pattern and purpose of the sacrificial ritual, it was both legitimate and effectual.

David's Organization of Sacred Song

Organizational Terminology

The Chronicler claims that David organized the choral rite as part of his scheme to adapt the traditional ritual of sacrifice for the temple at Jerusalem. A range of technical terms are used to clarify the nature of his project as well as its theological basis. These are mainly derived from traditional sacral language which is reworked and reapplied to describe the work of David as the patron of temple worship. Since this terminology has not yet been adequately analysed, I intend to investigate the chief terms for it, before undertaking an examination of the texts on the organization of temple music.

Chief among these terms is the verbal root *'āmad* with its derivatives.[1] Chronicles uses its *hiphil* for the appointment of personnel to their offices within the cult (1 Chron. 6.31; 15.16, 17; 2 Chron. 8.14;

---

1.   There is no precedent for this in the Pentateuch apart from the use of *'āmad* in the *qal* as a cultic term in Deut. 4.11; 10.8; 18.7; 19.17. Already Curtis and Madsen (*1910: 32) had noted that in Chronicles, Ezra and Nehemiah its *hiphil* meant 'appoint' rather than 'station' as in earlier books. Yet, as Braun (*1986: 90) remarks, the lexica do not adequately reflect the corresponding shift in meaning for the *qal*, which in Chronicles often means 'to stand to function as one has been appointed'.

11.15; 20.21; 23.19; 29.25; 31.2; 35.2). The verb usually governs one of several prepositions: *'al* for the position to which a person is appointed, or its responsibilities (1 Chron. 6.31 [6.16]; 2 Chron. 8.14; 31.2; 35.2), *b^e* for the instruments given for the performance of the designated task (1 Chron. 15.16), and *l^e* with an infinitive construct to define the purpose of the appointment (1 Chron. 15.16, 19, 21; 2 Chron. 8.14; 31.2). The appointed place for that person within the temple is called his *'ōmed* (2 Chron. 30.16; 35.10; cf. 34.31), which determines his *ma'ªmād*, his position and task within the clerical hierarchy (1 Chron. 23.28; 2 Chron. 35.15; cf. 2 Chron. 9.4).[1] The person who has been duly appointed 'stands' in his appointed position and functions there according to the terms of his appointment.[2]

Such appointments, however, had to be made in due order, so that the right people were chosen for the right positions. Now this process of appointment could proceed in one of two ways. On the one hand, the king could arrange a census, as David had done with such disastrous consequences, to provide the raw data for organization (1 Chron. 21). On the other hand, he could proceed less bureaucratically, along traditional tribal lines, together with the heads of families and clans. This was the method employed by David in 1 Chronicles 23–26. He modelled his reorganization of the cult on the procedure for the arrangement of the Israelite camp in Numbers 1–4 and for the division of the land in Numbers 26 and Joshua 13–19.

This process of sacral organization is described by the verb 'allot' (*ḥālaq*) and its noun 'allotment' (*maḥªlōqet*). These words, which once described the apportionment of land to the tribes by the casting of lots in the book of Joshua,[3] are re-employed in Chronicles for the establishment of positions within the temple and the allotment of personnel to them from the tribe of Levi, the one tribe without a divine allotment of land.[4] Just as God had once apportioned land to his people for their

1. See Ringgren 1987: col. 203 and de Vries 1989: 196.
2. *'āmad* in the *qal*. See 1 Chron. 6.32, 33, 39 (6.17, 18, 24); 23.30; 2 Chron. 5.12; 7.6; 29.11, 26; 30.16; 35.5, 10.
3. See the use of the verb in Josh. 13.7; 14.5; 18.2, 5, 10; 19.51; and of the noun in Josh. 11.23; 12.7; 18.10.
4. See the use of the verb in 1 Chron. 23.6; 24.3, 4, 5; 2 Chron. 23.18; and of the noun in 1 Chron. 23.6; 24.1; 26.1, 12, 19; 28.13, 21; 2 Chron. 5.11; 8.14; 23.8; 31.2, 15, 16, 17; 35.4, 10. The noun is also used for the divisions of the army on active duty in 1 Chron. 27.1–28.1.

livelihood via Eleazar and Joshua (Josh 14.1; 19.51), so David and his chief priests apportioned the positions at his temple to the priests and Levites (1 Chron. 24.3-6, 31). They thereby entered their inheritance.

Since this organization involved the creation of sacral offices, appointment to them occurred by the casting of lots (1 Chron. 24.5-18; 25.8-31; 26.13-18). While the procedure for such appointment by lots remains uncertain, its purpose is not; by this device God himself appointed his servants to their positions of responsibility. David did not then promote his own candidates. Nor did he decide the eligibility of the candidates for office. To be sure, he did call an assembly of all priests and Levites and so established the total number of candidates for office (1 Chron. 23.2-3).[1] But the heads of the respective families were involved with their members in actual process of allotment (1 Chron. 24.5-6, 31; 25.8; 26.12-13). Thus God himself made the appointments through his authorized representatives.

Now, if the verb *ḥālaq* denotes the sacral manner of appointment by the casting of lots, its noun *maḥᵃlōqet* describes the organizational unit, the allotted group to which the Levites are appointed. Since the priests had 24 families with their leaders (1 Chron. 24.4), they were organised into 24 such 'groups' (1 Chron. 24.7-18). The Levites were similarly divided into their respective 'groups', though their number is uncertain (1 Chron. 23). Likewise, despite the confused state of the genealogical data in 1 Chron. 26.1-11, there were clearly 24 'groups' of gatekeepers (26.17-18).

The group of people on duty at the temple on any given occasion was called a *mišmeret*, that is, a watch.[2] This term is again traditional. It comes from Numbers, where it denotes the duty of the Levites to act as guards in protecting the tabernacle and its furnishings.[3] While the word still retains this sense in Chronicles in

---

1.   Curtis and Madsen (*1910: 260) rightly note that 1 Chron. 23.2 is the heading for 1 Chron. 23–27, where, in reverse order to the heading, David first organizes the Levites and priests (23–26) and then his princes (27). As Wright (1991: 230-31) has shown, the use of *'āsap* here distinguishes this briefing from the formal convocation of Israel as a nation in 28.1, where *qāhal* is used; cf. Williamson 1979ᵃ: 265.

2.   This term is probably secular in origin. It was used for the protection of a palace, as in 1 Chron. 12.30, or a city, as in Neh. 7.3, by a rostered system of guards; cf. BDB, 1038.

3.   See the analysis of the term by Milgrom (1970: 8-16); cf. Milgrom and Harper 1986.

connection with the activity of the gatekeepers at the temple (1 Chron. 9.23, 27; 26.12), it has been extended semantically to include the ritual duty of the priests and singers. As such it refers to the clergy on duty, their place of service and their duties there.[1]

Three things stand out from this examination of the terms used by the Chronicler to describe the appointment of people to new positions within the temple apparatus. The procedure for the appointment of the clergy by the combination of hereditary eligibility with the casting of lots is shown to be in harmony with the traditional methods of sacral organization in the Pentateuch. While David created the new clerical positions for the temple, they were not filled by him but by God, through the manipulation of lots by the parties involved. By describing this system of divine appointment with its relative independence from royal control, Chronicles establishes a precedent for all subsequent appointments to positions at the temple.

The Process of Organization by David

The Chronicler outlines the four stages in David's organization of the choral rite in five interrelated sections. The initial summary of his project in 1 Chron. 6.31-47 (6.16-32) is followed by his arrangement of the choir for the transferral of the ark in 15.16-24. Then comes his arrangements for a provisional two-part service at Jerusalem and Gibeon in 16.4-42. After that we read how David fixed the number of singers and their duties in 23.2-5, 30-31 as part of his major plan for the reorganization of the Levites for temple service. Lastly, there is his organization of the temple choir with its three guilds and twenty-four watches in 1 Chron. 25.1-31.

The Initial Summary in 1 Chronicles 6.31-47. The first mention of David's institution of the choral rite in 1 Chron. 6.31-47 comes at the focal point of the Israelite genealogies which comprise 1 Chronicles 2–8.[2] There the genealogies of the three heads of the musical guilds have the following introduction in 6.31-32 (6.16-17):

---

1.   See (a) 1 Chron. 25.8; 26.12; 2 Chron. 31.16-17; 35.2; (b) 2 Chron. 7.6; 35.2; cf. Neh. 12.9; (c) 2 Chron. 8.14; 35.2; cf. Neh. 13.30.

2.   See Williamson *1982: 68. Johnstone (1986: 127-29) argues that the genealogies were arranged chiastically so as to centre on the tribe of Levi with its musical and sacrificial duties.

A   Now these are the men whom David *appointed* over the song.[1]
B   In *YHWH's house*[2] after the deposition of the ark,
C   they were ministers[3] in song before the tabernacle of the tent of meeting
B′   until Solomon's construction of *YHWH's house* in Jerusalem.
A′   They *stood* for their service according to their ritual statute.

These two verses form a simple chiastic pattern with its outer focus on David's institution of sacred song and its inner focus on the ministry of song at Gibeon.

The account in 1 Chron. 6.31-47 of the institution by David of the choral service makes six points which are worth noting. First, David appointed the personnel for the temple choir. They were divided into three guilds. Each of these guilds with its leader and its members was taken from one of the three main Levitical clans which were entitled to be involved in the ritual at the temple. Secondly, he appointed three leaders for the arrangement and performance of sacred song. This song is defined more closely as 'the song in the LORD's house', that is, songs set to be sung at the temple. Thirdly, by the performance of choral music at the temple, the musicians 'ministered' to the LORD, like courtiers at the palace of a king. Since they were appointed to stand in the LORD's service, their ministry proceeded according to the ritual statute for their performance of sacred song. They therefore attended to the LORD and administered his business. Fourthly, the choir was divided into two parts for two separate locations.[4] Sacred song was performed at the site of the ark in Jerusalem, anachronistically

1.   The use of *'al y^edē* with an impersonal object is unusual. Its only parallel is in 2 Chron. 29.27, where it refers to the position of the trumpets in the orchestra. This prepositional phrase with personal objects means 'under the control of' or 'beside' in 1 Chron. 25.2, 3, 6; 2 Chron. 23.18; cf. Ezra 3.10. Here it describes either the control of the song by the leaders (Keil *1870: 90) or else their location beside the choir as it performed the song (cf. BDB, 391).

2.   The Masoretic accentuation indicates that *bêt* is an accusative of place, not a genitive, as preferred by Rudolph (*1955: 56).

3.   The periphrastic construction indicates continuing activity; cf. GKC §116r; Holl, 78.

4.   While Keil (*1870: 90) argues that the choral service was held only at Jerusalem by identifying the tent of meeting with the tent David had erected for the ark, and Rudolph (*1955: 56) locates the performance of song at Gibeon by overruling the locative sense of *bêt YHWH* in 6.16, Goettsberger (*1939: 68) and Becker (*1986: 35) rightly argue that the choral service was performed both at Jerusalem and at Gibeon. This agrees with the data in 1 Chron. 16.4-6, 37-42.

described as the LORD's temple, as well as at the tabernacle in Gibeon. Fifthly, this arrangement began after the ark had been deposited in Jerusalem and lasted until Solomon had completed the construction of the temple. It was therefore a preliminary arrangement which was later superseded by the services at Solomon's temple. Lastly, and by inference from the context, the ministry of the singers was connected with, and yet distinguished from, the work of their fellow Levites as well as the priests. This is not only indicated by the location of this section on the musicians between the Levitical genealogies in 6.1-30 and the list of Levitical towns in 6.54-81, but also by the material on the Levites and priests which follows it in 6.48-53.[1] The service of song was thus connected with, and yet differentiated from, the general duties of the Levites at the temple as well as the rite of atonement performed by the priests.

We have here then a preview of the institution by David of sacred song. As part of 1 Chron. 6.31-49, which introduces the central theme of temple worship, 6.31-32 not only gives prominence to the place of liturgical song in it, but also serves to connect the various steps taken by David in planning the choral rite with its actual establishment by Solomon.

The Creation of a Choir for the Transferral of the Ark in 1 Chronicles 15.16-24. The Chronicler held that the first stage in David's organization of temple music began with the transferral of the ark to Jerusalem. Since the Levites were to minister to the LORD before the ark, besides transporting it as prescribed in Deuteronomy (15.2), David arranged for the creation of a Levitical orchestra and choir.

Because the appointment of the singers in 1 Chron. 15.16-24 occurs after they had apparently begun their march, and so seems to disrupt the narrative flow from 1 Chron. 15.15 to 15.25-28 many scholars regard it as a secondary intrusion.[2] Williamson (*1982: 121-22, 124-26) counters this by noting that 15.26 rather than 15.25 continues the narrative from 1 Chron. 15.15. Moreover, by its repetition of *śimḥâ*,

---

1.   There is a further striking formal grammatical link between 6.31-47 (6.16-32) and 48-49 (6.33-34). The two disjunctive participial clauses in 6.48 and 49 follow grammatically from the participial clauses in 6.33, 39, 44(?). These in turn depend on the *waw* consecutive sequence in 6.31-32.

2.   See Rothstein and Hänel *1927: 304-12; Noth 1943: 116; Rudolph *1955: 115; Myers *1965ᵃ: 111-12; Braun *1986: 187-88.

15.25 forms an inclusion with 15.16. The Chronicler is less interested in chronological continuity than in organizational procedure. The literary integrity of 1 Chron. 15.1-25 also argues against the interpolation of this section. In 15.1-2 David declares programmatically that the Levites were both to carry the ark and to minister to the LORD. The organization of these two tasks is then dealt with separately. First, the arrangements for the transportation of the ark are described in three parts: the assembly of the Levites in their six groupings (15.4-10), David's instruction to them and the priests about the carrying of the ark (11-13), and the fulfilment of that instruction (14-15). Secondly, the parallel arrangement of the musical ministry is also covered in three parts: the command to appoint the choir for the purpose of rejoicing (v. 16), the appointment of the choir in fulfilment of that command (17-24), and the transferral of the ark with rejoicing as had been commanded (25). 1 Chron. 15.1-25 is therefore a literary unit which describes the involvement of the Levites in the twofold task of transporting the ark and performing the ministry of song to the LORD.

The account of the choir's creation falls into two parts; the command given in 15.16, and its fulfilment in 15.17-24:[1]

> v. 16   Then David told the chiefs of the Levites to appoint their kinsmen, the musicians, with musical instruments—harps, lyres and sounding cymbals[2]—to raise[3] (their) voices[4] for rejoicing.[5]

---

1.   This interpretation hinges on the assumption that *wayyaʿᵃmîdû* in v. 17 governs the infinitives in 19 and 21 and that all the names listed in vv. 17-24 are its objects.

2.   Grammatically speaking, *mašmîʿîm* could belong to the three preceding instruments (Bertheau *1854: 156) or to *ʾᵃhêhem* (Rothstein and Hänel *1927: 276) or, despite the Masoretic punctuation, to *mᵉṣiltayim* (Keil *1870: 148). Zalewski (1968: 283-87) notes that *hišmîaʿ* does not usually describe the playing of music, but rather the sounding of the cymbals by themselves (1 Chron. 15.19; 16.5) or else with the trumpets (1 Chron. 15.28; 16.42). It therefore most likely qualifies the cymbals here.

3.   An infinitive of purpose (Keil *1870: 148) rather than infinitive of means (Curtis and Madsen *1910: 217) or gerundal infinitive (Rothstein and Hänel *1927: 276).

4.   Taking *bᵉqôl* as an instrumental object (cf. BDB, 90; GKC §119q).

5.   The occurrence of *ʿad-lᵉśimḥâ* in 2 Chron. 29.30 weighs against the removal of the preposition before *śimḥâ* as dittography under the influence of the LXX (*contra* Curtis and Madsen *1910: 217; Rudolph *1955: 116).

v. 17   So the Levites appointed Heman, the son of Joel; Asaph, the son of
          Berechiah, one of his kinsmen; and Ethan, the son of Kushaiah, one of
          their Merarite kinsmen;

v. 18   and second in rank[1] with them their kinsmen Zechariah,[2] Ja-aziel,[3]
          Shemiramoth, Jehiel and Unni;
          Eliab, Benaiah, Ma-aseiah, Mattithiah, Eliphelehu, Mikneiah, Obed-edom
          and Je-iel,[4] the gate-keepers

v. 19   (the singers[5]—Heman, Asaph and Ethan to sound[6] with bronze cymbals;

v. 20   Zechariah, Azi-el, Shemiramoth, Jehiel, Unni, Eliab, Ma-aseiah and
          Benaniah [to perform][7] according to the Alamoth[8] with harps;

1.   *hammišnîm*, a rare plural form with only two other disputed occurrences in
1 Sam. 15.9 and Ezra 1.10, could mean either second in rank or second in command.
Since a large number of people are listed, the former is the sense here, while the latter
occurs in 1 Chron. 16.5; cf. 1 Chron. 5.12; 2 Chron. 28.7; 31.12.

2.   The MT adds 'Ben', which is absent in the LXX.

3.   Ja-aziel is also called Azi-el (15.20) and Je-iel (16.5).

4.   The LXX adds Azaziah. While this name could have been taken from 15.21, I
would argue that the name originally came after Je-iel or before Obed-edom but was
excluded by the same editor who left out the *wᵉ* before Eliab in order to construct two
groups of eight, the first of them pure musicians and the second of them musicians
doubling as guardians of the ark.

5.   While 'singers' could refer only to the three heads of guilds, I take it as a
summary heading for all the choristers in vv. 19-21.

6.   Since the infinitives here and in v. 21 follow the main verb, they need not be
construed modally with the force of finite verbs, as Kropat (1909: 24) does.

7.   While Rothstein and Hänel (*1927: 278) believe that *lᵉnaṣṣēah* in v. 21 refers
to all the people mentioned in vv. 19-21, I hold that, since, like *lᵉhašmîaʻ* in v. 19, it
is governed by the main verb in v. 17, it refers only to the people in vv. 20-21.
Hence its insertion here in this translation. Its sense, however, is not entirely certain.
According to the analysis by Anderson (1986), its root has five senses, one of which
is 'to supervise' or 'lead'. While the verb can be used for leadership over others by
foremen in the construction and repair of the temple (2 Chron. 2.2, 18 [2.1, 17];
34.12, 13; Ezra 3.8, 9), or by the priestly trumpeters in war (1QM 8.1, 9, 12; 9.2;
16.6), it can also describe the work done at the temple by the Levites (1 Chron. 23.4)
and the performance of stringed music (1 Chron. 15.21; cf. 2 Chron. 34.12 as well
as term *lamᵉnaṣṣēah* in Hab 3.19 and 55 psalms). Since the musicians in 1 Chron.
15.19-21 did not supervise the music but rather performed it, it is probably a musical
term in 15.21 (cf. Seidel 1989: 185, 279 n. 23).

8.   In his analysis of the psalm titles in the light of a text from Ugarit, Seidel
(1983) has confirmed that *ʻal* indicates the mode or melody of the psalm. Yet neither
he nor anyone else has yet satisfactorily explained the terms in 15.21 and 22. The
traditional view, reaffirmed by Delekat (1964: 292), is that *ʻal-ʻᵃlāmôt* referred to the
soprano voice, while *ʻal-haššᵉmînît* was the tenor part; that is unlikely, since the harp
probably produced a deeper sound than the higher, sweeter lyre.

v. 21   Mattithiah, Eliphelehu, Mikneiah, Obed-edom, Je-iel and Azaziah to perform according to the Sheminith with lyres);

v. 22   Chenaniah, the leader of the Levites in transportation[1] as instructor[2] in
transportation, because he was a skilled man;

v. 23   Berechiah and Elkanah as gatekeepers for the ark;

v. 24   the priests Shebaniah, Joshaphat, Nethanel, Amasai, Zechariah, Benaiah
and Eliezer as trumpet-players in front of the ark of God;
Obed-edom and Jehiah as gatekeepers for the ark.[3]

The basic pattern of the long sentence in vv. 17-24 with its lists of
people and mass of organizational detail is apparent. A single verb in
15.17 is followed by lists of appointees to various positions in vv. 17-
18 and 22-24. This list of appointees is, however, interrupted by two
parenthetical infinitive construct sequences in vv. 19 and 20-21, which
specify the duties of various members of the choir.

The Chronicler shows that David did not organize the choir for the
transferral of the ark by himself, but rather ordered the chiefs of the
Levites to appoint suitable musicians. These organizers consisted of
the six Levitical chiefs as well as the two chief priests mentioned in
15.4-11. David therefore did not usurp their rights in sacral matters,
but paid due respect to them. He did, however, specify the instruments
which were to be used—harps, lyres and cymbals—as well as the
purpose of the performance, which was to stimulate festive rejoicing.

While the command of David is relatively easy to understand, the
description of its fulfilment in 15.17-24 contains some puzzling
features. The problems are obvious enough. First, does 'gatekeepers'
in 15.18 refer to the last two names, or to the names from Eliab to

---

1.   The primary sense of *maśśā'* here is 'transportation', as in 2 Chron. 35.3 and
Num. 4.15, 19, 24 and elsewhere. In Numbers it is a technical term for the duty of
the Levites to carry the ark and its furnishings (BDB, 672; *HALAT*, 604). See also
the use of *nāśā'* in 1 Chron. 15.2, 13, 15, 26, 27. Since the LXX interprets the term
musically, some scholars hold that it refers both to the transportation of the ark and to
the music of the singers (Rothstein and Hänel *1927: 278-80; cf. Petersen 1977: 63).
The ambiguity, however, probably arises, because, as Myers claims (*1965ᵃ: 110),
Chenaniah was in charge of the ceremonial procession for the occasion. 15.27 is then
best understood in the light of 15.22 by taking *haśśar. . . hamᵉśōrᵉrîm* as parallel to
śar-halᵉwiyyîm and emending *hammaśśā'* to *bammaśśā'*. He was therefore responsible for both the physical and musical 'transportation' of the ark.

2.   *yāśōr* is best taken as an active *qātōl* noun. See Rudolph *1955: 119; cf.
GKC §84ᵃ k.

3.   Most take this as a gloss based on 15.18. If this were so, the reason for its
insertion here rather than in 15.23 is not apparent.

Je-iel, or to all the names from Zechariah to Je-iel? Secondly, why are
the names Obed-edom and Je-iel/Jehiah mentioned twice, first in 15.18
as gatekeeper-musicians and then in 15.24 as gatekeepers for the ark?
Thirdly, why are Berechiah and Elkanah mentioned by themselves in
15.23 apart from Obed-edom and Jehiah in 15.24b, if both pairs of
men were gatekeepers for the ark? Fourthly, why are the gatekeepers
mentioned at all in this context? Fifthly, if Chenaniah is 'the chief of
the Levites', or even the director of the choir, why is he not mentioned earlier? Sixthly, why are the priests mentioned where they are,
if they are to blow the trumpets before the ark and so stand somewhere near the front of the procession? Lastly, what does 1 Chron.
15.22-24 have to do with David's command in 15.16?[1]

My proposed solution to these problems is that the present shape of
this piece is determined by two factors. First, it presents the fulfilment
of David's command to create a Levitical choir. This explains the
arrangement of names in descending rank in 15.17-18. This order
would, however, have been reversed in the procession. Secondly, the
list of people directly associated with the ark in 15.22-24 has in mind
the sequence of the procession for its transportation to Jerusalem.[2]
The repetition of the names of Obed-edom and Je-iel/Jehiah is thus not
the result of an intruded gloss but a literary device to indicate the
place of the choir at the rear of the procession.[3] The mention of these
two names suggests that musicians proceeded in pairs with the order
of rank reversed for the procession.

The procession would then be arranged in the following order:

---

1.   Rudolph (*1955: 124) claims that, since these verses have nothing to do with
David's command, they must be a later insertion.

2.   The idea that the processional order is given in 1 Chron. 15.16-24 comes
from Bertheau (*1854: 160), whose proposals influenced Keil (*1870: 150) and
Goettsberger (*1939: 123-24). Goettsberger also makes the helpful distinction
between the arrangement according to rank in vv. 17-18 and the arrangement according
to function in vv. 19-24.

3.   Zalewski (1968: 419-21) argues that the mention of the gatekeepers in 15.24
is a literary device to signal the inclusion of all the singers listed in 15.18 but in
reverse order. I differ from the proposed order given by Keil (*1870: 150) and
Goettsberger (*1939: 123-24) by locating the choir at the rear of the procession
rather than at its head.

1.	The Leader	Chenaniah
2.	The Gatekeepers	Berechiah and Elkanah
3.	Priestly Trumpeters	Shebaniah and Joshaphat
		Nethanel and Amasai
		Zechariah and Benaiah
		Eliezer
4.	Bearers of the Ark	Ark
5.	The Choir	
	a. Lyre players	Obed-edom and Je-iel/Jehiah
		(Azaziah) and Mikneiah
		Eliphelehu and Benaiah
	b. Harpists	Ma-aseiah and Benaiah
		Eliab and Unni
		Jehiel and Shemiramoth
		Zechariah and Ja-aziel
	c. Cymbal Players	Ethan, Heman and Asaph[1]

In this proposal I have made the following assumptions. First, that Azaziah, who is mentioned in 15.21 and included as the last of the musicians in the LXX, has been excluded from the MT in 15.18b because the editors assumed that there were eight musician gatekeepers in 15.17-18a, just as there were eight pure musicians in 15.18b. Hence the lack of a *waw* after Unni, which breaks the list into two groups of eight. Secondly, the order for the three heads of guilds in 15.17 and 19 echoes 1 Chron. 6.33, 39, 44, with its rubrics for their positions relative to each other. These rubrics were necessary, since all three guilds were involved, rather than just one, as was normally the case (cf. 1 Chron. 25). Thirdly, the primary sense of *hammišnîm* in 15.18 is 'those second in rank', rather than 'those second in command'. Fourthly, the pairing of the gatekeepers indicates that, apart from the three heads, the choir proceeded in pairs.

The advantage of this proposal is that it not only makes sense of the lists as they are arranged here, but also provides a possible solution to

---

1. This order resembles the arrangement of the two choirs for the dedication of the city walls in Neh. 12.31-42, which was as follows:

Right Choir (31)	Left Choir (38b, 40a)
Hoshaiah and Princess (32)	Nehemiah and Officials (40b)
Seven Trumpeters (33-35a)	Seven Trumpeters (41)
Ezra (36b)	(High Priest?)
Conductor Zechariah (35b)	Conductor Jezrahiah (42b)
Eight Musicians (36)	Eight Musicians (42)

three other problems in the text. First, if my proposal is correct, it
helps us understand the position of Chenaniah in 15.22 and 27b, which
has been the matter of some controversy.[1] The RSV, which represents
the consensus of many scholars, implies that he was the choirmaster.
But, if that were so, his position would usurp the authority of Heman,
Asaph and Ethan. It would have been created merely for the occasion.[2] Chenaniah, however, turns up later in 1 Chron. 26.29, where he
is not in charge of musicians but of Levitical officials with duties outside the temple. Chenaniah is described as *śar-halᵉwiyyîm bᵉmaśśā'* in
15.22. The problem here is the sense of *maśśā'*. In context, it could
mean either transportation or performance of music. Now, if Chenaniah
was the head of the procession, it would suggest that he arranged the
whole procession with the transportation of the ark and the performance of music. His brief would then have been to devise and execute
the ceremonies for the occasion, so that they would be ritually appropriate and properly coordinated.

Secondly, this proposal accounts for the mention of the gatekeepers
in 15.18, 23, and 24b. The Chronicler seems to have distinguished the
position of gatekeepers for the ark, mentioned only in 15.23 and 24,
from the earlier gatekeepers of the tabernacle (1 Chron. 9.17-26a) and
the later gatekeepers of the temple (1 Chron. 26.1-19). Theirs was a
temporary task which lasted for the duration of the procession. They
were to ensure that no unauthorized person touched the ark, as Uzzah
had previously done (1 Chron. 13.9). While the main responsibility for
this fell on the pair of guards who preceded the ark, it was also the duty
of those who followed it, in other words, Obed-edom and Jehiah, or
perhaps even all the musicians at the front of the choir, since *haššō'ᵃrîm*
could, by its position, refer to all the names in 1 Chron. 15.18.

Lastly, this proposal explains the presence of the priestly trumpeters
in what is otherwise largely a Levitical undertaking.[3] Normally two

---

1. See the recent discussion of his role by Petersen (1977: 62-64).
2. Apart from Neh. 12.46 (K), there is no record of a single choirmaster
coordinating the work of the three guilds.
3. Welch (1939: 65-66) and Rudolph (*1955: 115) consider that the mention of
the priests in 15.11 and 14 is intrusive, since they are not addressed in 15.12 and
play no part in the transferral of the ark. Zalewski (1968: 161-74) counters this by
arguing that, while Chronicles is mainly concerned here with the role of the Levites,
the priests are also mentioned because of their involvement in the playing of trumpets
(15.24, 28), the offering of sacrifices (15.26) and the insertion of the ark into the tent
(16.1).

priests with their trumpets preceded the army and the army of Israel in battle (Num. 10.9; 2 Chron. 13.12), but here the full complement of seven trumpeters with the full choir went before the ark in the LORD's triumphal victory procession with his army and people to his new place of residence in Jerusalem after his defeat of the Philistines (1 Chron. 14.8-16). They announced the advent of the heavenly King.

1 Chron. 15.16-24 thus contains David's command to the leaders of the Levites to arrange a choir for the transport of the ark, as well as the fulfilment of that command. Even though the arrangements were only for that occasion, the Chronicler implies that they set precedents for the subsequent organization of liturgical music with the delegation of responsibility for its arrangement to the Levites, the division of the musicians into three Levitical guilds, the choice of instruments used to accompany the song, and the association of liturgical music with the playing of trumpets by the priests.

The Provisional Arrangements for Liturgical Music in 1 Chronicles 16.4-6, 37-42. The second stage in David's organization of sacred song occurs after the placement of the ark in its tent in his palace (2 Chron. 8.11). After this had been accomplished, David inaugurated the regular performance of choral music in Jerusalem and Gibeon (1 Chron. 16.4-6, 37-42). The description of this comes within the account of the royal banquet to celebrate the successful transferrence of the ark. Significantly enough, it is flanked by reference to David blessing the people in 16.2-3 and his household in 16.43. David's act of blessing his people and his family after the presentation of burnt offerings and peace offerings is thus linked thematically with his institution of choral music. Moreover, the description of this rite itself encloses the account of the psalmody which he instituted in Jerusalem. That will be dealt with in Chapter 5.

v. 4   David commissioned some of the Levites as ministers before the ark of
         YHWH to proclaim,[1] thank and praise YHWH, the God of Israel:
v. 5   Asaph as chief;
         his deputy Zechariah,
         Je-iel, Shemiramoth, Jehiel,
         Mattithiah, Eliab, Benaiah, Obed-edom, and Je-iel with harps and lyres,
         while Asaph was to sound the cymbals;

1.   The *waw* here is explanatory; cf. GKC 154a n. 1 (b).

v. 6   the priests Benaiah and Jahaziel with the trumpets *regularly* before the ark of the covenant of God. . .

v. 37   There he left Asaph and his kinsmen before the ark of the covenant of YHWH to minister before the ark *regularly* according to the daily requirements;

v. 38   Obed-edom (and Je-iel) with their[1] sixty-eight kinsmen, that is Obed-edom, the son of Jedithun,[2] as well as Hosah, to be gatekeepers,

vv. 39-40   while before the tabernacle of YHWH at the high place in Gibeon the high priest Zadok and his fellow priests[3] were required to present[4] burnt offerings *regularly* to YHWH morning and evening on the altar of burnt offering, in accordance with all that was written in the law which YHWH had commanded to Israel;

v. 41   with them Heman, Jeduthun and the rest of those chosen and designated[5] by name were required to give thanks to YHWH, for his generosity is for ever;

v. 42   with them, that is Heman and Jeduthun,[6] were the trumpets and cymbals for those who sounded them[7] as well as the instruments for divine song; and the sons of Jeduthun were responsible for the gate.[8]

As indicated in the translation, this section falls into two parts with two different syntactical patterns. First, in the commission of David in 16.4-6, the verb *wayyittēn* is followed by a general object, 'some of

1.   The plural suffix on *'ᵃhêhem* suggests that the name Je-iel has dropped out of the MT. The LXX and other versions iron out the resulting problem by translating it as 'his kinsmen'.

2.   This is probably a marginal gloss which reminds the reader that according to 1 Chron. 15.18 Obed-edom was a musician as well as a gatekeeper. The spelling Jedithun occurs elsewhere only in Neh. 11.17, and Pss. 39.1; 77.1.

3.   Polzin (1976: 32) shows that *'ēt* is used emphatically here before a nominative case rather than as the object-marker for *wayya'ᵃzob*; cf. Kropat 1909: 2 and de Vries 1989: 150.

4.   For this use of the infinitive in a modal sense here and in v. 41, see Kropat 1909: 24; cf. GKC §114, 1.

5.   This Hebrew subordinate clause is absent from the LXX, which may indicate that it is a gloss.

6.   Another gloss to indicate that only these two had charge of the instruments.

7.   Since *lᵉmašmî'îm* refers only to the players of the cymbals and trumpets, it is not misplaced here as is felt by Rudolph (*1955: 128).

8.   While this may indeed be a later gloss under the influence of 16.38, the change from *lᵉšō'ᵃrîm* in v. 38 to *laššā'ar* argues against any harmonizing parallelism. It may reflect the tradition of 1 Chron. 9.19b-21 that there was a single guarded entrance to the tent of meeting.

the Levites', who are defined more specifically as singers and trumpeters in the two subsequent appositional lists. Secondly, its implementation in 16.37-42 begins with a *waw* consecutive main clause with two objects and is followed by four disjunctive nominal clauses, the first two with infinitives of obligation. The two parts are further linked by the catchword *tāmîd* in 16.6, 37 and 40.

There are in all four significant features in the Chronicler's account of David's initial institution of the choir. First, and most remarkably, he created a single service for sacred song in two parts, separated spatially in Gibeon and Jerusalem, yet coordinated temporally to coincide with the daily burnt offerings.[1] This coordination is highlighted by the repetition of the keyword *tāmîd*. By the time of Chronicles it had become almost exclusively a liturgical term for the regular daily and weekly performance of the sacrificial service. Thus David coordinated three things: the blowing of trumpets by the priests in Jerusalem, the performance of choral music in Jerusalem and Gibeon, and the presentation of the burnt offering at Gibeon. While Zadok and his associates offered the divinely instituted daily sacrifice to the accompaniment of liturgical music from the guilds of Heman and Jeduthun in Gibeon, the priests with their trumpets and the Asaphite musicians with their instruments praised the LORD in Jerusalem. This association is highlighted even more graphically by the use of the phrase *lidᵉbaryôm bᵉyômô* to describe the daily ministry of praise at Jerusalem in 16.37.[2] The term that was usually employed for the daily quota of sacrifices (Lev. 23.37; 2 Chron. 8.13; 31.16; Ezra. 3.4) is extended here and in 2 Chron. 8.14 to include the daily performance of praise by the musicians. Sacred song was thus regarded as a regular part of the sacrificial ritual.

Secondly, in this reformed order of service authorized by David, the priests with their trumpets supplemented the choral performance at Jerusalem (16.4-6), just as the musicians with their instruments supplemented the presentation of sacrifices by the priests (16.39-41). At Jerusalem, the priests, as commanded in Num. 10.10, joined with the musicians in proclaiming the LORD with their trumpets, as if the regular burnt offerings were in fact presented there. Together they

1. See Curtis and Madsen *1910: 220-21.
2. This idiom originally referred to the daily quota of work for servants (Exod. 5.13, 19) or daily quota of rations for dependants (Exod. 16.4; 2 Kgs 25.30; Dan. 1.5; cf. Neh. 11.23; 12.47).

performed their common ministry before the ark. At Gibeon the musicians cooperated with the priests in offering thanksgiving for the LORD's generosity, at the same time as the burnt offerings were being presented in their prescribed number and manner. Thus the choral rite came to consist of sacred song accompanied by both trumpets and the other musical instruments.

Thirdly, the responsibility for liturgical song is once again delegated to the three guilds of Levitical musicians under their heads. Now, however, since the ark has been transferred to Jerusalem, Asaph leads the singing there, while his two colleagues operate at Gibeon. There is nonetheless a change of name from Ethan to Jeduthun for the head of the third guild. The change is puzzling. While these may be two different names for the same person,[1] the change could reflect some development in the history of the guilds.[2]

Lastly, David not only determined which instruments were to be used in 16.5-6, but also made provision for their care in 16.42. Heman and Jeduthun were not only responsible for the care of the cymbals, harps and lyres used by their fellow musicians, but also for the storage of the trumpets. The inference is that, when they were not used, they were kept by them at Gibeon, because that was the site of the tabernacle and altar. They were perhaps also responsible for their maintenance and repair.

Thus in 1 Chron. 16.4-6 and 37-42 we find an account of the creation by David of the provisional choral rite, performed simultaneously at Jerusalem and Gibeon as part of the daily sacrificial ritual located at Gibeon. While the priests cooperated with the musicians in their praise of the LORD in Jerusalem, the musicians cooperated with the priests in the presentation of the daily burnt offerings at Gibeon. Within this general framework there was a division of responsibilities between the three musical guilds. As the guild of Asaph attended to choral music at Jerusalem, so the other two guilds offered thanksgiving to the LORD at Gibeon.

---

1. See Köberle 1899: 156-61 for a discussion of the possible derivation of Jeduthun as a name from Ethan by way of the musical ascription *lîdê-'ētān* (cf. Ps. 39.1).

2. See the influential analysis of Gese (1963) for an account of this historical development.

The Organization of the Musicians in 1 Chronicles 23.2-5, 30-31 and 25.1-31. The third stage in David's organization of liturgical music is set by Chronicles at the end of David's reign. It is included in his plan for the reorganization of the priests and Levites in 23.2–26.32 for worship at the temple of Solomon.[1] A consistent pattern, relevant to our discussion, emerges from the examination of this material. On the basis of the data from a census, David first fixed the total numbers of Levites for the four projected areas of work at the temple. Then, depending on their numbers and family affiliation within their three clans and subclans, he divided them into a fixed number of groups with their natural heads as leaders. Lastly, the roster for service and, in the case of the gatekeepers, the area of service was decided by the fall of the lots.

---

1.   While Noth (1943: 112-15) holds that the whole of 1 Chron. 23–27 was a massive insertion of material which gradually proliferated, Williamson (1979[a]) has argued for a single set of additions to the original work of Chronicles, which consisted of 23.3-6a, 6b-13, 15-24; 25.1-6; 26.1-3, 9-11, 19, 20-32. This original edition was governed by the list of duties in 1 Chron. 23.4-5 and arranged genealogically. In the secondary pro-priestly redaction, Obed-edom is mentioned as a gatekeeper and the 24 courses of priests and singers are appointed by lots rather than by David. While I accept his argument that two bodies of material have been combined in 1 Chron. 23–26, I am not persuaded that his secondary layer was added by a later redactor. I propose that it comes from the Chronicler himself, who combined two sources here with some of his own material. My reasons are as follows. First, Williamson's contrast between the organization by David and the appointment by allotment is overdrawn, since the verb *ḥālaq*, which is used for the organization by allotment in 24.3, 4, 5, is also found in 23.6 (cf. 2 Chron. 23.18), and its noun occurs in 23.6 and 26.1, 19, which are all part of his primary layer. Secondly, the list of holy times in 1 Chron. 23.30-31 is identical with the lists in 2 Chron. 2.4 (2.3) and 31.3 (cf. 8.12), which are unique to Chronicles. Thirdly, the use of *ma'ămād* in 23.28 and *'āmad* in 23.30 is consistent with their use elsewhere in Chronicles. Fourthly, 1 Chron. 23.13b seems to belong to the same strand of tradition as 1 Chron. 6.49; 2 Chron. 2.4; 13.11, which will be analysed in Chapter 4. Fifthly, since I hold that the references to Obed-edom as singer in 1 Chron. 15.21 and 16.5 and as gatekeeper in 1 Chron. 15.18, 24 and 16.38 stem from his dual ritual function rather than from two divergent traditions, there is no reason to exclude 1 Chron. 26.4-8 and 15 from the original draft of Chronicles. Lastly, since I also hold that the references to the priests in 1 Chron. 15.4, 11, 14 were necessary in anticipation of the appointment of the trumpeters in 15.24 as part of the choir and the presentation of sacrifices in 15.26 and 16.1, I do not regard these purported additions as evidence for a secondary pro-priestly redaction of Chronicles which added 1 Chron. 23.13b-14, 25-32 and 24.1-31.

Generally speaking, the organization of the musicians followed this pattern. First, David decreed in 1 Chron. 23.3-5 that four thousand singers were to offer praise to the LORD at the new temple. Then he defined their duties more precisely in 23.30-31, lest their ministry within the temple lead to demarcation disputes with the priests over their monopoly of the sacrificial system there. David therefore carefully delineated the position, rank and responsibility of the singers within the temple.

Their task is defined as follows within its context:

v. 25   For David said, 'YHWH, the God of Israel, has given rest to his people and has taken permanent residence in Jerusalem.

v. 26   Thus the Levites need no longer carry the tabernacle and all the equipment used in its service...

v. 28a   Rather their place is beside the sons of Aaron...

v. 30-31 to stand[1] to thank and praise YHWH regularly in his presence, every morning and evening and whenever the burnt offerings are presented on the sabbaths, the new moons and the appointed times, according to the number set by ritual statute for them.'

In this job description David dealt with four matters. First, he delineated the rank and status of the musicians within the temple. In their performance of sacred song they were subordinate to the priests. Secondly, he defined their position in the temple. They were to stand before the LORD as they performed their music for him. From the context it must have been somewhere in front of the altar, since their performance of music coincided with the presentation of burnt offerings. Thirdly, he fixed the times for their performance. They were to perform their ministry whenever the public burnt offerings were presented. Fourthly, the purpose of their ministry was to thank and praise the LORD. After this specification of their duties, David organized the musicians themselves for their ministry at the temple in 1 Chronicles 25. This chapter clearly falls in two parts, linked by the catchword *mispār* in 25.1 and 7. The first, 25.1-6, describes the separation of 24 leaders from the three guilds as heads of their corresponding watches, while the second, 25.7-31, describes the allotment of individuals into their watches and of watches into their rostered order of service.

The system for the organization of the musicians is distinguished by

---

1.   There is a verbal link between *ma'ªmādām* in 23.28 and *la'ªmōd* here. The musicians were to 'stand' in their appointed place where they performed their task at the times for sacrifice.

two features. First, the manner of their organization departs from the general pattern found in these chapters. This is signalled by the use of the verb *hibdîl* rather than *he'emîd* or *hālaq* to describe their appointment in 25.1. In contrast to 1 Chron. 15.16, where David delegated the responsibility for the selection of musicians to the eight chief priests and Levites, here he himself was involved with his military officials[1] in the appointment of the 24 leaders for the watches and the 288 master musicians (25.1-7). The candidates came from the three guilds, with their bank of 4000 potential performers. Some kind of examination was probably necessary for the process of selection, since musical ability is not always inherited. But once the 288 master musicians and 24 heads of watches had been chosen, the rest of the organization was undertaken by the casting of lots.

Since the sense of 25.8, which describes this process, has been the matter of some debate, it is necessary to examine it more closely. It contains two main problems. First, the subject of the verb is uncertain. It could be the three heads of guilds mentioned in v. 6b, or, more likely, the 288 master musicians mentioned in v. 7.[2] While the reference to 288 musicians in vv. 9-31 could favour the latter solution, this is contradicted by the inclusion of students in v. 8b. I therefore take *kaqqāṭōn kaggādōl mēbîn 'im-talmîd*[3] as the subject, for just as the ordinary Levites were involved with the heads of their courses in the casting of lots for their positions in 24.31, so this passage describes the involvement of inferiors with superiors, of students with their teachers, in the preparation of the roster for service.

---

1. The argument of Curtis and Madsen (*1910: 279), that *śārê haṣṣābā'* does not refer to the commanders of the army but to the leaders of the clergy, is contradicted by the Chronicler's stress on the involvement of the army in the royal arrangements for worship in Jerusalem in 1 Chron. 13.1; 15.25; 28.1, 21; 29.6; and 2 Chron. 1.2.

2. The LXX takes the three heads of guilds as the subject, reads *gôrelôt* instead of *gôrālôt*, and so translates: 'they also cast the lots of the daily courses for the small person as well as the great person of the masters and learners'.

3. If, as Rudolph (*1955: 166) maintains, the second pair of terms is a mistaken gloss on the first pair, it would surely have been formulated similarly. The change in formulation, however, shows that the second pair adds something new. While the first deals with the ranking of master-musicians against each other with the three heads of guilds on top, the latter distinguishes the master musicians from their students. Hoenig (1979–80) proposes that we read *'ummat-limmûd* rather than *'im-talmîd*, and translate it as 'the teacher alongside the pupil'.

The second problem is the function and sense of *le'ummat*. Normally it functions as a preposition in construct form before an absolute noun. But here its construct form is not followed by an absolute noun. Its present function may be construed in one of three ways. First, it could function together with the following prepositional prefixes.[1] We could then translate: 'They cast lots... the lesser like the greater'. Secondly, it could be construed as a conjunction before a predicative clause.[2] We could then translate: 'They cast·lots, each watch in correspondence with the principle that the lesser is as the greater'. Thirdly, and most likely, it could be taken as a truncated form of the stock expression *mišmār le'ummat mišmār*, which is to be found in 1 Chron. 26.16 and Neh. 12.24.[3] Whatever the case, the sense is roughly the same. In each watch the lots were cast in the same way, whether for leaders and master musicians or for ordinary members and students. They determined the order of each watch on the roster as well as the membership of each watch. Each watch therefore consisted of both master musicians and students.

The system by which the leaders of the 24 watches were chosen with their 12 members is shown by the difference in the sequence of names in 1 Chron. 25.2-4 and 9-31.[4] At each casting of the lots a choice was made between two given candidates for two positions as

---

1. See Kropat 1909: 56.

2. See Keil *1870: 201-202; BDB, 769.

3. See Rothstein and Hänel (*1927: 452). The Targum repeats the noun. My guess is that we have here a rather awkward combination of three sets of technical idioms for the organization of personnel at the second temple.

a.	*wayyappîlû gôrālôt* N. *le'ummat* N.
	See 1 Chron. 24.31; 25.8; cf. 26.12-13
b.	*kaqqātōn kaggādôl*
	See 1 Chron. 25.8; 26.13; 2 Chron. 31.15
c.	*mišmār (mišmeret) le'ummat mišmār (mišmeret)*
	See 1 Chron. 26.16; Neh. 12.24

4. In a largely ignored article, Hummelauer (1904) argues that the confusing changes in the order of names from vv. 2-4 to 9-31 can be accounted for by the practice of allotment according to a set pattern. While he notes many of the features outlined here, he fails to make complete sense of his data, because he gives undue weight to the placement of Shime-i, Jerimoth and Hananiah in the same relative positions in both lists, so assuming that, from the three extant guilds of four Asaphite, six Jeduthunite and fourteen Hemanite choirs, David created three new mixed guilds: the first of nine choirs, the second of six choirs and the third of nine choirs.

predetermined by an agreed pattern. With the first eight positions, the odd positions from one to seven were assigned to Asaph as the chief guild (25.9), while the even numbers two and four went to Jeduthun, and six and eight were shared between both Jeduthun and Heman. With the second eight positions, the odd numbers nine to fifteen were given to Heman, while the even numbers ten and twelve went to Jeduthun, and fourteen and sixteen were again contested by Jeduthun and Heman. All the last eight positions went to the numerically larger guild of Heman, in which the first four on the list were coupled with the last four.

The results of the allotment can be tabulated as follows:

Cast	Candidates from Guilds	Positions	Result of Allotment
1 (A1, A2)	Zakkur—Joseph	1, 3	Joseph 1: Zakkur 3
1 (A3, A4)	Nethaniah—Asharelah	5, 7	Nethaniah 5: Asharelah 7
3 (J1, J2)	Gedaliah—Zeri	2, 4	Gedaliah 2: Zeri 4
4 (J3, H1)	Jeshaiah—Bukkiah	6, 8	Bukkiah 6: Jeshaiah 8
5 (H2, H3)	Mattaniah—Uzziel	9, 11	Mattaniah 9: Uzziel 11
6 (H4, H5)	Shebuel—Jerimoth	13, 15	Shebuel 13: Jerimoth 15
7 (J4, J5)	Shimei—Hashabiah	10, 12	Shimei 10: Hashabiah 12
8 (J6, H6)	Mattithiah—Hananiah	14, 16	Mattithiah 14: Hananiah 16
9 (H7, H11)	Hanai—Joshbekashah	17, 18	Joshbekashah 17: Hanani 18
10 (H8, H12)	Eliathah—Mallothi	19, 20	Mallothi 19: Eliathah 20
11 (H9, H13)	Gidalti—Hothir	21, 22	Hothir 21: Giddalti 22
12 (H10, H14)	Romamti-ezer—Mahazi-oth	23, 24	Mahazi-oth 23: Romamti-ezer 24

It is clear from this table that those who organized the musicians decided the sequence for the casting of lots according to a pattern determined by the precedence of Asaph, the size of each guild and the number of required watches, but that the final choice of leader for each watch was made by the LORD himself through the fall of the lots.

The second feature of David's organization of the musicians is the hierarchy which he established. David was not only directly involved in the selection and organization of the musicians but also brought them under his direct control (1 Chron. 25.6). The three heads of guilds were accountable to him, while Asaph was specifically designated as his prophet (1 Chron. 25.2). The 24 heads of watches were in turn accountable to the head of their particular guild (1 Chron. 25.2, 3, 6).

Finally, it seems that the 288 master musicians were responsible for
the training of the remaining students. The musicians were thus much
more directly under the control of the king than the rest of the clergy.
They represented him in their performance of the choral service.

By his portrayal of the third and fourth stages of David's organization of the choral rite the Chronicler shows how David established
precedents for its subsequent arrangement. David is said to have fixed
the number of musicians, assigned them their duties as assistants to the
priests in the performance of the sacrificial ritual, divided them into
three guilds and 24 watches, and established a chain of command
under his control. All this was done in preparation for the temple
which Solomon was to build in Jerusalem.

The Implementation and Development of Sacred Song

The Implementation of Sacred Song by Solomon

As Braun (1973: 510-11) has noted, 2 Chron. 8.12-16 is the Chronicler's
conclusion to his reshaped account of the temple's construction which
began at 2 Chron. 1.18. In it he completely reworks the data from
1 Kgs 9.25 about Solomon's sacrifices at the three great festivals in
order to summarize the essential features of worship at Jerusalem. For
the Chronicler the building of the temple culminated in the inauguration of the regular sacrificial worship with choral music as an important part of it, after the three orders of clergy had been appointed.
The performance of regular worship at the temple by the clergy was
the goal of the work of David and Solomon as described in Chronicles.

The structure of this section is as follows:

    A.   Solomon's Fulfilment of the Mosaic Commandment
          is accomplished by the presentation of burnt offerings (vv. 12-13)
          1.   at the prescribed place,
          2.   in the prescribed number and manner,
          3.   at the prescribed times.
    B.   Solomon's Fulfilment of the Davidic Ordinance
          is accomplished
          1.   by the appointment of the clergy (v. 14):
              a.   the priests in their divisions,
              b.   the Levites in their watches,
              c.   the gatekeepers in their divisions,
          2.   and their fulfilment of the King's command (v. 15).
    C.   The Temple of Solomon is Completed (v. 16).

Thus the temple was only complete when the priests, Levites and gate-keepers began to work together in presenting the burnt offerings as prescribed by both Moses and David.

Within this careful composition, 8.14 stands out as a finely crafted sentence with a simple chiastic structure which may be represented thus:

A   According to the *ritual statute of David* his father, he appointed
B   the *divisions* of the priests for their service
C   and the Levites in their watches to offer praise and minister before the priests according to the daily requirements,
B′   and the gatekeepers in their *divisions* for each gate,
A′   for that was the *commandment of David*, the man of God.

Thus the verse focuses on two things: the exact fulfilment of David's command, and the appointment of the Levites. They were appointed to their watches for two purposes: some as musicians to offer praise, and others as assistants to the priests to perform the sacrificial ritual at the temple.

Thus the Chronicler held that Solomon implemented David's plans for sacred song as given in 1 Chronicles 23 and 25. In fact, so closely was he eventually identified with sacred song that, by the time Neh. 12.45 was written, the organization of the musicians was ascribed both to him and to his father.

The Maintenance and Development of Sacred Song by Solomon's Successors

From the time of Solomon, liturgical music was regarded by Chronicles as an essential part of properly constituted worship at the temple in Jerusalem. This is shown by the reference to its restoration by Jehoiada in 2 Chron. 23.18 after a period of liturgical disorder under Ahaziah and Athaliah, and by his characterization of the reform by Josiah in 2 Chron. 35.15 after the period of apostasy under Manasseh. Since choral music was part and parcel of orthodox worship, its maintenance and restoration was a mark of faithfulness to the LORD.

The most notable instance of its cultivation comes in the account of Hezekiah's reformation after the corruption of the sacrificial ritual under Ahaz. The Chronicler maintains that Hezekiah not only restored the choral rite to its proper condition (2 Chron. 29.25-29; cf. 31.2), but also authorized the use of psalms by David and Asaph for the praise of the LORD (29.30).

This regulation of psalmody represented a significant, far reaching innovation, even if it initially merely confirmed current practice. The importance of this measure is shown by the deliberate echoing of 1 Chron. 15.16 in 2 Chron. 29.30. Just as the decree of David had inaugurated the creation of the choral rite, so the decree of Hezekiah inaugurated the canonization of its contents. The Levites were to collect the psalms of David and Asaph and to use them as a kind of anthem book for the praise of the LORD. It is uncertain whether this measure was meant to exclude contemporary compositions or merely to provide a yardstick for their assessment. But the author of Chronicles almost certainly traced the compilation of the psalter that he knew back to this decree. As a result of this decree, some psalms were selected for use in divine worship. They were thus given canonical status and authority as 'the song of the LORD' (29.27) by virtue of their reputed origin and liturgical use. With that the institutionalization of choral music was considered to be complete by the Chronicler.

The Chronicler shows that the successors of David implemented what he had planned. The choral rite, which began at the temple with Solomon, was maintained only by some of his successors. Most distinguished among these was Hezekiah, who authorized the psalms of David and Asaph for divine praise and so confirmed their canonical status.

Conclusion

The Chronicler maintains that David did not institute choral music at Jerusalem by his own royal authority but at the command of the LORD through his prophets Nathan and Gad. Since the choral rite was divinely ordained, it was an effectual agency for the ritual interaction between the LORD and his people at the temple in Jerusalem. The introduction of sacred song did not constitute a disruptive innovation ritually, but served to fulfil the LORD's instructions through Moses, that the priests should proclaim him by the blowing of trumpets over the burnt offerings, that the Levites should minister to him in his name, and that the people should rejoice in him as they presented their sacrifices to him. Thus the decrees of David, by which he created and organized the temple choir and the choral rite, are shown by Chronicles to fulfil the law of Moses for divine worship.

Since David had received divine authorization for his project, he proceeded to organize the musicians and their music as an integral part of the sacrificial ritual. His organization was carried out in three stages. First, he arranged for the creation of an orchestra to accompany the ark in procession to Jerusalem. Secondly, after the ark had been deposited there, he organized the simultaneous performance of daily praise before both the ark in Jerusalem and the altar at Gibeon. This choral performance in two parts coincided with the presentation of the burnt offering at Gibeon. Finally, he organized the musicians for choral music at the temple by fixing the number of singers, by defining the function of music within the sacrificial service, and by providing the singers with an efficient system of management.

These plans were duly enacted by Solomon. While some of his successors neglected the sacrificial ritual with its associated choral music, Hezekiah and Josiah are singled out by Chronicles for special mention, because they restored the choral rite as established by David. Hezekiah went even further than that by arranging for the collection of psalms by David and Asaph for the performance of divine praise. Thus the account by Chronicles of the development of choral music begins and ends with David, its ritual founder and patron.

Chapter 3

THE RITUAL COMPONENTS OF THE LORD'S SONG

If, as I maintain, the performance of sacred song was an integral part of the total sacrificial ritual at the temple in Chronicles, its various components should then combine to produce a congruent ritual performance consistent with its larger ritual context. While these components could theoretically be distinguishable from each other, they would nevertheless together constitute a single ritual performance and each contribute in some measure to its total impact.

In this chapter I shall therefore investigate the various ritual components of the choral music to show how they were integrated practically and symbolically into the general ritual pattern of worship at the temple. Liturgical song will be treated as a ritual enactment with sacred words that were sung at a sacred place at sacred times with the help of sacred instruments by sacred people. Each of these components will be covered separately to show how they interacted with each other and their environment during the choral performance.

The Words

The Ritual Proclamation of the Holy Name
Ritually speaking, the most important element of sacred song was the proclamation of the holy name. The ramifications of this can only be fully appreciated if it is considered together with the discussion on the relationship between the divine name and divine presence in Chronicles.[1] As Solomon himself admitted, the temple could not contain the LORD as the heathen temples contained the idols of their gods (2 Chron. 2.6; 6.18). He therefore built the temple for the name of the LORD (1 Chron. 22.7, 8, 10, 19; 28.3; 29.16; 2 Chron. 1.18; 2.4; 6.7,

---

1. See Japhet 1989: 65-71 for an analysis of the relationship in Chronicles between God's name and his presence.

8, 9, 10, 34, 38; 20.8), which took the place of the idol in the pagan temple (2 Chron. 33.7). This temple was understood functionally as the place for performing the sacrificial ritual before him (2 Chron. 2.4, 6). The Lord had revealed this name to Moses, when he had shown him his glory and goodness on Mt Sinai by proclaiming it to him (Exod. 33.18–34.7). By filling the temple with his glory (2 Chron. 5.13-14; 7.1-3) and accepting it as a place of sacrifice and prayer to him (2 Chron. 7.12-16), the LORD set his name there (2 Chron. 6.20; 12.13; 33.7), so that it would be there for them (2 Chron. 6.5, 6; 7.16; 20.9; 33.4). Through his name the LORD was therefore accessible to his people and present with them at his temple. Since God's name was in the temple, the people who invoked him there stood in his presence (2 Chron. 20.8-9).

The nature of the LORD's presence is explained in 2 Chron. 7.15-16, most of which is not found in Kings. Where the LORD's name was placed, there his ears, eyes and heart were present (cf. 2 Chron. 6.20, 40). This remarkable anthropomorphic imagery from 1 Kgs 8.29, 52 and 9.3 is interpreted by the Chronicler as God's pledge that those who acknowledged his name at the temple (2 Chron. 6.24, 26) would be admitted to his heavenly presence, even here on earth, and so have access to him personally in their prayers; he would hear the prayers offered to him at the temple with the appointed sacrifices, and grant their petitions as Solomon had requested in 2 Chron. 6.20 and 40. His presence was therefore given to his people through the pronouncement of his name during the performance of the sacrificial ritual.

The choir was instituted as an agency for the ritual pronouncement of the holy name on behalf of the King and the congregation of Israel. Through their song the singers remembered YHWH (1 Chron. 16.4) by proclaiming (1 Chron. 16.8),[1] thanking (1 Chron. 16.35) and glorying in his holy name (1 Chron. 16.10). In their thanksgiving and praise they mentioned him by name as their God (1 Chron. 16.14a); their songs were all about him and his achievements.[2] Thus the words of these songs were not addressed to him in the second person; they

---

1. Just as the LORD showed himself to Moses by 'proclaiming' his name (Exod. 33.19; 34.5-7), so the singers 'proclaimed' his name in their song. This idiom has been analysed by Niles (1974). He notes that it means 'invoke' in a petition and 'proclaim' in a thanksgiving (75-95).

2. See the use of *leYHWH* in 1 Chron. 16.4, 7, 41; 23.5, 30; 25.3; 2 Chron. 5.13; 7.3, 6; 20.19, 21; 29.30; 30.21.

were addressed to the people and so spoke about him rather than to
him.[1] On the one hand, the singers announced the LORD to the people,
as they proclaimed his name to them. On the other hand, they
addressed the congregation in their song, as they invited them to join
them in their praise of his name. The song which was sung was therefore called 'the song of YHWH' (2 Chron. 7.6; 29.27) or the 'song
about YHWH' (1 Chron. 25.7), because it involved the ritual proclamation of his holy name.

Whenever that name was spoken at the altar during the presentation
of the sacrifices, the LORD himself came to his people and blessed
them, as he had promised in Exod. 20.24. The choral rite was thus not
offered for the LORD's benefit but for the benefit of the congregation.
It was the means by which the LORD's people were granted an
audience with their heavenly King.

The Contents

According to Chronicles, David decreed that the holy name, which
had been instituted for Israel's worship by the LORD himself through
Moses at Mt Sinai, should be proclaimed in thanksgiving and praise
(1 Chron. 16.4).[2] By these two verbs he determined the basic shape
and content of the sacred song.

While *hillēl* and *hôdâ* are indeed used by the Chronicler for a non-
musical expression of praise, as mentioned in David's prayer in
1 Chron. 29.13 and performed by the congregation in 1 Chron.
29.20, the two words usually refer to the performance of sacred song.
They are, in fact, virtually synonymous in Chronicles, and are often
used interchangeably without any appreciable difference in meaning.
Thus the thanksgiving refrain is used not only to 'thank' the LORD
(1 Chron. 16.34, 41; 7.3, 6) but also to praise him (2 Chron. 5.13;
7.6; 20.21). Nor do they refer to two different ritual practices, such as
praise during the presentation of the burnt offering and thanksgiving
during the presentation of thank-offerings, since the singing during
the burnt offering is described as 'praising' (2 Chron. 8.14; 29.30),
'thanking' (1 Chron. 16.41), and 'thanking and praising' (1 Chron.
23.30), while singing during the thank-offering is described as

1.   See 1 Chron. 16.8-34, 41; 2 Chron. 5.13; 7.3; 20.21; cf. Gunkel 1933: 47.
2.   The discussion by German scholars on whether the basic sense of *hôdâ* is
'confess' or 'thank' is well summarized by Crüsemann (1969: 279-82). He concludes that it is best translated by 'thank'.

'thanking' and 'praising' (2 Chron. 7.6) as well as 'praising' (2 Chron. 30.20). Taken together, they describe the verbal content of sacred song.

Chronicles records the contents of one such hymn of praise in 1 Chron. 16.8-34. This song consists of portions from Psalms 105, 96 and 106, which were reworked and recombined to produce this remarkable liturgical text. The song itself begins and ends with a call to thanksgiving. A concluding petition and doxology are appended in 16.35-36. We thus have in 1 Chron. 16.8-34 a carefully crafted composition which has been placed here to demonstrate the basic pattern of thanksgiving which David instituted for performance by the singers in Jerusalem.

The psalm as a whole deals with two aspects of praise which are relevant to our present discussion. First, the contents of the psalm show the full extent of the LORD's praise. The singers who actually performed the ritual of thanksgiving widened the circle of praise by calling on God's people (vv. 8-22), the earth and all its peoples (23-30), and even the universe itself (31-33) to join with them in their song of thanksgiving.[1] So the words of thanksgiving were to reach out first to a national audience and then to an international, cosmic audience. The words of praise were thus universal in scope, even though they were performed in the LORD's presence at Jerusalem. By praising the LORD, the speech of each nation somehow transcended all human languages, so that what was said and sung harmonized with the inarticulate praise of the whole created cosmos.

Secondly, while the LORD alone was the subject of all thanksgiving, the reason and content of thanksgiving varied with his varied blessings to various recipients. The Israelites were to thank the LORD for his covenant with them, by which he had granted them his land and his protection (16.12-22); the earth and its peoples were to praise him as the creator of the heavenly powers and the earth with its stability (23-30); the universe itself was to praise him as its King in anticipation of his universal epiphany in judgment (31-33). The common theme for all their thanksgiving was the LORD's goodness and generosity as it had been manifested to all of them (16.34).

In 1 Chron. 16.8-34 we have an epitome of thanksgiving. Its contents derive from David's institution of thanksgiving by the Levitical choir.

---

1.   So Becker (*1986: 72). Becker observes that Ps. 96.10a has been relocated after 11a in 1 Chron. 16.31 to highlight this threefold distinction; cf. Hausmann 1986: 86-87.

While the words varied with the focus of thanksgiving, its subject, extent and reason remained the same.

The Authorization of Psalms

When Hezekiah reconstituted the daily sacrificial ritual at the temple in Jerusalem, he also re-established the choral rite according to its institution by David (2 Chron. 29.25-29). In addition to this, he and his princes, who together represented the nation, directed the Levites to offer praise to the LORD 'with the words of David and the seer Asaph' (v. 30).

Now while this directive could conceivably have been intended only for that occasion, it seems more likely that it was meant to set a precedent for all subsequent worship. Whereas Hezekiah alone gave the command for the other temporary measures for this occasion in 29.5, 21b, 24b, 27 and 31, he issued the command together with his princes in 29.30, the only one of these passages that mentions his royal authority. The directive could refer to one of three things. First, it could have institutionalized the measures taken in 29.25. Henceforth the Levites were to praise the LORD according to the instructions given by David and Asaph.[1] But if that were the case, reference should be made to Gad and Nathan rather than to Asaph. Secondly, it could have prescribed that the LORD's song be performed in the manner of David and Asaph.[2] Such a use of *b^edibrê* is, however, unattested elsewhere. Lastly (and this is most likely), the directive authorizes the use of certain psalms for performance during worship.[3] If there was no collection of psalms attributed to David and Asaph, this decree would have authorized the preparation of such an edition.[4] These were thereafter to be used to praise the LORD as the public burnt offering was presented at the temple.

1.   Kropat (1909: 39) argues that *b^edibrê* may have the same sense here in 2 Chron. 29.30 as in 1 Chron. 25.5 and 2 Chron. 29.15.

2.   See Köberle 1899: 94.

3.   So Curtis and Madsen *1910: 468.

4.   Zalewski (1968: 298-303) holds that in 1 Chron. 25.5 we have a reference to the performance of certain psalms in the choral service. While all three heads of guilds are considered prophets in 25.1, only Asaph (25.2) and Jeduthun (25.3) are commissioned to prophesy in the body of the text. Heman, however, is described as the King's seer 'in the words of God' (25.5). By virtue of the parallel with 2 Chron. 29.30, Zalewski argues that Heman was to sing the lyrics of certain canonized psalms.

So then, the first and most important component of choral music for Chronicles was the words which were sung to musical accompaniment by the choir. Initially only two things were prescribed for its verbal performance: the use of the holy name to announce the LORD's presence, and the basic pattern of proclamation by thanksgiving and praise. Within these parameters the singers composed the words of their songs to suit the occasion. Eventually Hezekiah authorized the collected psalms of David and Asaph for the performance of praise during the presentation of the burnt offering. The words of these songs therefore became an integral part of the whole sacrificial ritual and so achieved their authoritative status from their use within that context.

The Place

The Location of the Musicians

The author of Chronicles held that the design and construction of the temple in Jerusalem fulfilled the law of Moses for the tabernacle of the LORD. He therefore took great care to trace the continuity of Solomon's temple in Jerusalem with the tabernacle at Gibeon.[1] The temple was its legitimate successor in every possible way.[2] First, the temple in Jerusalem housed the ark of the covenant (2 Chron. 5.7-10). Secondly, it became the final residence for the tent of meeting and its vessels (2 Chron. 5.5; cf. 1.3). Thirdly, since the site of its altar went back to Abraham (2 Chron. 3.1), was designated by an angelic theophany (1 Chron. 21.14-18; cf. 2 Chron. 3.1), and was confirmed by fire from heaven (1 Chron. 21.26–22.1), it replaced the altar at Gibeon as the place for the performance of the sacrificial ritual as prescribed by Moses (2 Chron. 8.12-13). Lastly, as the legitimate successors of those appointed by Moses, its priests performed the duties prescribed by the LORD through Moses and Aaron (1 Chron. 6.49-53; cf. 24.19).

The identification of the two was so complete that the temple was called 'the tabernacle of the LORD' (2 Chron. 29.6) and 'the tabernacle of God's house' (1 Chron. 6.33) as well as 'the tent' (1 Chron. 9.19)

---

1.   Note the links established in 1 Chron. 6.32, 48; 9.19, 23; 16.39; 21.29–22.1; 23.32; 2 Chron. 1.3, 6, 13; 5.5; 29.6.

2.   Drawing together the observations of previous scholars, Mosis (1973: 136-47) has shown how the description of the temple's construction in Chronicles reflects the account of the tabernacle's construction in Exodus.

and 'the house of the tent' (1 Chron. 9.23). The inner gates of the temple were even called 'the gates of the LORD's camp' (2 Chron. 31.2; cf. 1 Chron. 9.19). While this may be historically confusing, it is essential to the theology of Chronicles. Its symbolism provides us with the basic framework necessary to understand the sacrificial ritual at the temple.

In this way of thinking which was derived from the priestly tradition in the Pentateuch, the arrangement of ritual space was especially significant, for it not only clearly illustrated the basic categories of the sacred and the profane, the clean and the unclean, but also carefully distinguished them from each other.[1] Within this system of sacred architecture and geography, the location of a ritual and its celebrants was especially significant. So, for instance, the priests were distinguished from the Levites by defining their respective areas of responsibility within the sacred precincts in Num. 18.3-7, which in turn expressed the distinction between holiness and purity.

The concept of location in ritual space lies behind the use of the terms 'stand' and 'station', which were examined in the previous chapter. Each group has its proper place within the temple, whether priests (2 Chron. 35.10; cf. 7.6a), Levites (2 Chron. 30.16; 35.5), singers and gatekeepers (2 Chron. 35.15), the king (2 Chron. 34: 31; cf. 6.12-13; 20.5)[2] or the people (2 Chron. 20.9; cf. 6.3; 7.6b). The ritual function and status of a person is thus evident from his location. Hence the place of the singers in the temple tells us much about the ritual function and significance of their choral performance.

In his organization of the two-part choral performance at Jerusalem and Gibeon, David first defined the position of the singers ritually in terms of their relationship with the three most important holy objects. While the guild of Asaph was to minister before the ark of the LORD at David's palace in Jerusalem (1 Chron. 16.4, 37; 2 Chron. 8.11), the other two guilds were to cooperate with the priests as they performed the sacrificial ritual at the altar before the *tent of meeting* in Gibeon (1 Chron. 16.39-41). Their location before these three objects was ritually significant. Their location before the ark, which represented the LORD's presence as the footstool of his throne (1 Chron. 28.2; cf.

---

1. For a discussion of these concepts, see Wenham 1979: 18-25 and Jenson 1992: 39-55.

2. See Poulssen 1967: 159-66 for a discussion of the king's position in the temple as an indication of his status and relationship to the priests.

28.18), placed them in an intermediate position between him and his people; their location before the altar, the place for atonement and the reception of divine help (1 Chron. 21.26–22.1), stationed them on the threshold between the sacred and clean domains; by their location before the tent of meeting they participated in the meeting between the LORD and his people. In each case, then, their allocated place involved them with the priests in their responsibility for the administration of the holy things (1 Chron. 16.39-41) and with the gatekeepers in their duty to protect the holy things from defilement (1 Chron. 16.4-6, 37-38, 41-42). Thus both their function and their status is evident from their physical location vis-à-vis these holy objects (see diagram, p. 98).

When David redefined the 'station' (1 Chron. 23.28) of the Levites in preparation for their service at the temple, he also clearly defined the position of the singers there (1 Chron. 23.30-31). They were to stand 'in the presence of the LORD' to perform their ministry of sacred song. This term suggests two things. First, and most immediately in this context, the synchronization of their singing with the presentation of the burnt offerings 'before the LORD' indicated that they stood before the altar of burnt offering (cf. 2 Chron. 1.6). Secondly, since the temple was envisaged as the palace of the heavenly king (1 Chron. 29.1, 19), they worked within his house, like the courtiers of a king in his palace, and so had access to his presence. By standing before the altar, they 'stood in his presence' and helped to administer his affairs (1 Chron. 23.30; cf. 2 Chron. 29.11).[1]

The Position of the Musicians at the Altar
The exact location for the performance of the sacred song is given in 2 Chron. 5.12 (cf. Sir. 47.9). The singers stood at their post east of the altar. This placed them either within the inner court, in the area between the inner gate and the altar, or else on top of the steps that led into the inner court.

It seems to me that the second of these is the most probable, for six reasons. First, these steps are called 'the stairs of the Levites' in Neh. 9.4. Secondly, in 2 Chron. 31.2 the Levites were appointed to minister with thanksgiving and praise 'within the gates of the LORD's camp'. While the phrase could refer to the 'bounds' of the temple, as $b^e \check{s}a^{'a}r\hat{e}$ refers to the 'bounds' of the cities in Deuteronomy, it could also

---

1. 2 Chron. 20.9 shows how Chronicles equates location at the temple with proximity to the LORD's presence.

72   *The LORD's Song*

indicate that they stood within the gates of the sanctuary.[1] Thirdly, the
location of the singers in these gates would explain why they were so
often connected with the gatekeepers and even partially identified with
them. If both were stationed at that place, there could have been some
overlap in their respective responsibilities. Furthermore, if this inner
gate corresponded with the former guard-post in front of the ark
(1 Chron. 15.23b, 24b), it would also account for the inclusion of Obed-
edom and his associates among the singers in 1 Chron. 15.18, 16.5 and
16.38. Fourthly, in Ezek. 40.44 we read of a chamber for singers close
to the inner gate. Now even if the text here is corrupt as most commentators maintain on the basis of the LXX,[2] the reference does show
that the editors of Ezekiel were influenced by current circumstances in
identifying this gate and its chambers with the singers.[3] These were
most likely the chambers mentioned in 1 Chron. 9.33. Fifthly, since
the singers performed their songs for the people and called on them to
join in with their praise, they would best be stationed on the steps,
where they could be readily heard by the congregation in the outer
court. Lastly, according to later tradition codified in the Mishnah,
they stood on a special platform on top of the stairs within the Court
of the Israelites.[4]

The singers then stood at the summit of the steps leading to the altar
and the inner court beyond it. There they stood 'opposite' the priests
who sounded the trumpets (2 Chron. 7.6). The most likely interpretation of this is that the singers faced the altar, while the trumpeters stood

1.   Already the LXX had difficulty in making sense of the reference to thanksgiving and praise 'in the gates of the LORD's camp'. It dealt with the problem in two
ways. First, it took the phrase as a figure of speech for 'the gates and the courts of
the LORD's house'. Secondly, it supposed that the phrase was misplaced and should
follow *lešārēt*. It therefore described the place for the ministry of the gatekeepers
rather than the musicians. Its lead in transposing the phrase is followed by Curtis and
Madsen (*1910: 478), Goettsberger (*1939: 352), Rudolph (*1955: 304) and the
RSV. Yet the MT makes good sense, if we suppose that the gates mentioned here led
from the outer court to the altar in the inner court of the temple.
2.   E.g. Zimmerli 1969: 1021-22.
3.   Köberle (1899: 18-19) argues that *lišekôt šārîm* was not a later misreading for
lišekôt štayīm but rather a case of haplography. Thus we should read *welišekôt
štayīm* after *lišekôt šārîm*. Furthermore, he argues that it could hardly have been a
later gloss, since the singers were called *mešōrerîm* in the postexilic period. Cf.
Hurvitz 1986.
4.   See *m. Mid.* 2.5, 6 and *m. 'Arak.* 2.6; cf. Seidel 1989: 84.

between them and the altar facing the congregation. Thus as the singers performed their ministry they stood before the altar and faced it.

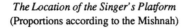

The Location of the Singer's Platform
(Proportions according to the Mishnah)

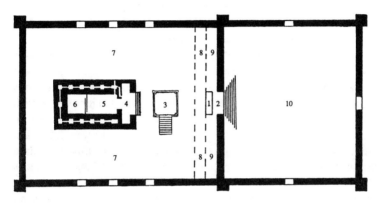

1.	Singers' Platform	6.	The Holy of Holies
2.	Steps into the Sanctuary	7.	The Temple Court (Azarah)
3.	Altar for Burnt Offering	8.	The Court of the Priests
4.	The Porch of the Temple	9.	The Court of the Israelites
5.	The Holy Place	10.	The Court of Women

3. *The Importance of this Location*

The place assigned to the singers was so important that it was defined by a ritual statute of David (1 Chron. 6.32; 2 Chron. 29.25; 35.15). It had, in fact, been given by the LORD through his prophets Gad and Nathan. This divine legislation prevented any demarcation disputes between the priests and the singers. By assigning them this intermediate position, David also defined their ritual function and status relative to the priests. Since they stood between the people in the outer court and the presence of the LORD at the altar in the inner court, they acted as intermediaries between him and his people. They ministered there for the people by praying for them; they ministered to the LORD by announcing his royal presence and favourable attitude to them. Yet in all this their focus was on the altar, for their ministry was subordinate to the priestly ritual which was enacted there.

The position for the performance of liturgical song then revealed its mediatorial function. According to divine legislation, the singers were

stationed before the altar in the temple. There they stood at the point
of transition from the ritually clean profane domain to holy ground.
There they occupied an intermediate position between those two
domains and so mediated between those who occupied them.

The Times

The Occasions for Sacred Song

Together with the notion of sacred space, the author of Chronicles
took over the notion of sacred time from the ritual legislation of the
Pentateuch. There these two systems of symbolism were integrated
ritually by the regular presentation of the burnt offerings at the altar
and conceptually by the term *mô'ēd*. This was the word for an
'appointed place' of meeting as well as its 'appointed time'. Through
the performance of the sacrificial ritual at its proper time and place
the LORD 'met' with his people in time and space (Exod. 29.38-46).
For this meeting to occur it was thus essential that the burnt offering
be presented at the right times, for that was why the LORD himself
had instituted these times for Israel (2 Chron. 31.3), and that in
perpetuity (2 Chron. 2.3).

Generally speaking, the appointed times were set at the important
points of transition in the temporal cycle. First, there were the daily
points of transition at mid-morning and at mid-afternoon. Then there
was the weekly transition on the sabbath as well as the monthly transition at the new moon. Finally, there were the annual points of transition from season to season at the Feast of Passover, the Feast of Weeks,
and the Feast of Tabernacles with its associated times of preparation
on New Year's Day and the Day of Atonement. These were all ritually
significant for Chronicles, because on them the priests presented the
burnt offerings for the people (1 Chron. 23.30-31; 2 Chron. 2.4;
8.12-13; 13.11; 31.3).

According to Chronicles, David fixed the times for the choral performance, so that they coincided with presentation of the public burnt
offering. The liturgical calendar with its times and seasons therefore
served to clarify its ritual function and significance. Hence the times
for the performance of the LORD's song at Jerusalem and Gibeon
were synchronized with the times for the presentation of the burnt
offering in the morning and at the evening in Gibeon (1 Chron.
16.40). This is indicated by the use of the term *tāmîd* in 16.37 and 40.

Besides that, the phrase *lidᵉbar-yôm bᵉyômô* in 1 Chron. 16.37, borrowed as it is from the liturgical calendar in Lev. 23.37, suggests that, just as the daily burnt offering was augmented on other sacred occasions, so additional anthems were to be sung during their presentation on these occasions.

What is hinted at in 1 Chron. 16.37 and 41 is stated explicitly by the regulations of David for the choral service in Solomon's temple in 1 Chron. 23.30-31. The singers were to perform the song each morning and evening as the burnt offering was presented. Included in this decree is a rather comprehensive list of sacred times which agrees with the lists in 2 Chron. 2.4, 8.13 and 31.3.[1] Three categories of sacred times are listed besides the times for the daily sacrifices. First, there are the weekly sabbaths. Secondly, there are the new moon days. Thirdly, there are the *môʿᵃdîm* which are defined in 2 Chron. 8.13b as the three great festivals for pilgrimage, when attendance at the temple was obligatory for the people. Thus the times for sacred song were deliberately synchronized with the times for the presentation of the public burnt offerings at the altar in Jerusalem.

The Synchronization of Sacrifice and Song
Since the times for song were the occasions for sacrifice and prayer, they were also times for the reception of divine blessings as well as for response to their reception in rejoicing and festivity. This was especially so for the three great festivals for pilgrimage which figure so prominently in the books of Chronicles after the construction of the temple.[2] On them the whole congregation of Israel assembled at the temple and rejoiced in his presence.

---

1.   These lists differ from Num. 28.9–29.38 and Lev. 23 by their omission of the Day of Trumpets and the Day of Atonement and from Lev. 23 by their inclusion of the new moon days. For an analysis of the Chronicler's use of the term *môʿēd* and its divergence from the Pentateuch, see Shaver 1984: 137-39.

2.   Cancik (1970) has devoted a study to the significance of feasts for the Chronicler. He claims that for the Chronicler, the history of Israel culminates in these festivals (339). Once the temple had been constructed, they came into their own (2 Chron. 8.13). All three festivals are mentioned at the conclusion of decisive episodes in the history of the cult—the Feast of Tabernacles after the completion of the temple (2 Chron. 5–7), the Feast of Weeks after the removal of idols from the land by Asa (2 Chron. 15.10-15) and the Feast of Passover after the purification of the temple by Hezekiah (2 Chron. 30) and the reformation of Josiah (2 Chron. 35.1-19).

This connection is explored in the account of the celebration of the passover by Hezekiah in 2 Chron. 30.21-22:

> v. 21   A   Then the Israelites present at Jerusalem celebrated the Feast of Unleavened Bread for seven days with great rejoicing;
>
>   B   the priests and Levites were praising YHWH day by day with the powerful instruments of YHWH.
>
> v. 22   B′   Hezekiah commended all the Levites who had shown good understanding of YHWH.[1]
>
>   A′   They ate[2] the appointed meal for seven days, sacrificing peace offerings and giving thanks[3] to YHWH, the God of their fathers.

With its chiastic structure this passage highlights the link between the rejoicing of the people during the week of the festival and the daily praise sung by the temple choir.

The connection between the time for the rejoicing of the people and the time for the performance of sacred song is explained in two ways by this passage. First, as indicated by the structure of the passage, the great joy of the people came from 'the good understanding of the LORD' which the Levites had shown in their praise of him. The use of the participle *hammaśkîlîm* with its cognate accusative *śēkel ṭôb* is probably deliberately ambiguous. On the one hand, the skill of the musicians in their performance of the sacred song showed the depth of their insight into the LORD. On the other hand, by the skilful rendition of their anthems, they communicated their insight to the people and so taught them, affectively as well as cognitively, about the LORD and his goodness through their musical performance of praise. Thus the understanding of the Levites is an understanding of the LORD's goodness. That understanding motivated their praise which in turn stimulated the rejoicing of the people.

---

1.   The phrase *śēkel ṭôb* can mean 'insight into goodness' as well as 'good insight'.

2.   While the nearest plural antecedent is 'all the Levites', the subject of this verb is obviously the Israelites mentioned in v. 21.

3.   *yādâ* in the *hithpael* is found only here in Chronicles. It is used elsewhere for the confession of sins, but without the qualification *lᵉYHWH* (e.g. Lev. 5.5; 16.21; 26.40). While some combination of praise with the confession of sins could be intended here, as in Neh. 9.6-37, that seems rather unlikely in view of its association with liturgical song and peace offerings, as well as the general emphasis on rejoicing in 30.21, 23, 25, 26. Even though BDB (392) proposes that it means to give thanks here, Bertheau (*1854: 394) is probably right in taking it to describe the presentation of thank-offerings with songs of thanksgiving.

Secondly, there is the odd expression in 30.22: *wayy'ōkᵉlû 'et-hammô'ēd*.[1] By this startling phrase the author of Chronicles describes the people's appointed 'enjoyment' of their sacrificial banquets and connects it with the performance of sacred song at the appointed times for the presentation of the sacrifices. Thus the festive times for praise which celebrated the LORD's goodness became times to enjoy the meeting of the LORD with his faithful people.

In sum, the performance of the sacred song was quite deliberately synchronized with the holy times set for the presentation of the public burnt offering at the temple. As shown in 1 Chronicles 16, the efficacy of sacred song did not depend as much on its performance at the *place* of sacrifice as at the *times* for sacrifice. The time for praise and its performance at the holy times was thus more important than the place for praise and its performance there. Sacred song derived its ritual function and significance in part from this temporal context; it also in turn contributed much to the proper celebration of the festivals as times for rejoicing in the LORD.

The Instruments

Musical Instruments as Temple Vessels

Like the vessels of the tabernacle in the Pentateuch, various ritual objects were essential for the performance of the sacrificial ritual at the temple.[2] They were divided into two groups—those which were

---

1. Fishbane (1985: 158 n. 38) follows Kimḥi in taking it as an ellipsis for 'they ate the sacrificial meat of the festival'. The LXX sidesteps the problem by reading *wayᵉkallû*.

2. The credit for demonstrating the significance of the temple vessels in the theology of Chronicles goes to Ackroyd (1972). The treatment of them by the Kings of Judah served as the touchstone for their piety with its consequent prosperity, as well as for their impiety with its consequent disasters. Thus, while the temple vessels were cared for and made by David and Solomon (1 Chron. 18.8-11; 22.19; 28.13e-18; 2 Chron. 4.19–5.1), added to by Asa (2 Chron. 15.18), restored by Jehoiada and Joash (2 Chron. 24.14), and reconsecrated by Hezekiah (2 Chron. 29.18-19), they were also confiscated for their idolatrous abuse under Amaziah (2 Chron. 25.24), destroyed by the apostate Ahaz (2 Chron. 28.24), and plundered by the pagan Babylonians for their defilement under Jehoiakim (2 Chron. 36.7), Jehoiachin (36.10) and Zedekiah (36.18). Chronicles contrasts their placement in the temple by David and Solomon (1 Chron. 22.19) with their removal by the Babylonians (2 Chron. 36.7, 10, 18). Since the vessels were the instruments by which the LORD came into contact with his people, special provision was made for their protection

handled by the priests, because they were used in the regular sacrificial ritual, and those which were handled by the Levites, because they were used in secondary aspects of the ritual. In Chronicles the former are called 'holy vessels',[1] while the latter are 'vessels of service'.[2]

Chronicles includes the musical instruments among these vessels, since they too were used in the ritual at the temple. While the trumpets which were played by the priests were probably regarded as 'holy vessels' (cf. Num. 31.6), the other instruments, which were regarded as 'vessels of service', were called 'vessels of song'.[3] Because of their ritual significance they were stored with the trumpets before the altar (1 Chron. 16.42a). The place for their storage at the temple was most likely the chambers mentioned in 1 Chron. 9.33 (cf. *m. Mid.* 2.6). They remained there, because they belonged to the LORD (2 Chron. 30.21).

Just as David had instituted the words, place and times for the choral performance, so he is said to have 'made' the musical instruments for praise (1 Chron. 23.5; 2 Chron. 7.6). They are therefore called 'the instruments of David' (2 Chron. 29.26, 27). He also determined the particular combination of instruments which was used in worship. To the trumpets which the LORD had ordained through Moses, he added the cymbals, lyres and harps (1 Chron. 15.16; 16.5-6). The importance of this combination is emphasized by the insistence in 2 Chron. 29.25 that the instruments for sacred song, like the place of the musicians in the temple, had been instituted at the LORD's command. It was this divine command which gave them their significance and power.

The Ritual Function and Purpose of the Instruments
Over the last hundred years many musicologists have investigated the development of musical instruments in the ancient world and have contributed much to our understanding of their construction, nature and use.[4] Many Old Testament scholars have combined musicological findings with the data from the Old Testament to determine the identity,

and maintenance by the Levites (1 Chron. 9.28-29; 23.28).
   1. *kᵉlê haqqōdeš*. See 1 Chron. 9.29; 22.19; 2 Chron. 5.5.
   2. *kᵉlê hāʿabôdâ*. See 1 Chron. 9.28; 23.26; 28.13b; cf. *kᵉlê šārēt* in 2 Chron. 24.14.
   3. See *kᵉlê šîr* in 1 Chron. 15.16; 16.42; 2 Chron. 7.6; 34.12; and *kᵉlê haššîr* in 2 Chron. 5.13; 23.13.
   4. The most influential studies have been those by Galpin (1937), Sachs (1940), Stauder (1961) and Hickmann (1970).

nature and use of each instrument.[1] Among these, the historical survey of scholarship by Wohlenberg (1967), the study of the development of music in ancient Israel by Seidel (1989) and the musicological synthesis of Sendrey (1969) are most noteworthy. Since I intend to limit the following discussion to the ritual function and purpose of the instruments mentioned in Chronicles, I shall, however, not deal with these historical questions unless they have some bearing on my argument.

The Trumpets

The trumpets were the only instruments ordained by the LORD in the Pentateuch for use in public worship (Num. 10.10).[2] By the time that Chronicles was written, they seem to have taken over most of the important ritual functions of the more ancient horn.[3] The ritual trumpets were made of beaten silver (Num. 10.2) and were played only by the priests.[4] Their number ranged from two in daily worship (1 Chron. 16.6; cf. Num. 10.2) to seven (1 Chron. 15.24; cf. Neh. 12.33-35a, 41), or even 120 on special occasions (2 Chron. 5.12; cf. *m. 'Arak.* 2.6; *b. 'Arak.* 13b). Since the trumpets had no valves, their range was probably limited to three or four tones which were used in different combinations of intensity and duration.[5]

Practically speaking, the function of the trumpets was not to sound a tune and so to accompany the song, but to give various signals (cf. Num. 10.3-7). They were used to signal the coming as well as the presence of the ark (1 Chron. 13.8; 15.24, 28; 16.6). In worship at the temple they gave the signal for the prostration of the congregation

---

1. See Graetz 1881; Weiss 1895; Gressmann 1903; Finesinger 1926; Maecklenburg 1929; Sellers 1941; Kolari 1947; Wohlenberg 1967; Sendrey 1969; Sendrey 1974; Keel 1978: 335-52; Eaton 1984[a]; Jones 1986; Jones 1987; Seidel 1989.

2. The most comprehensive study of the significance of the trumpet in the Old Testament is by Friedrich (1964).

3. The earliest historical mention of the trumpet is at the coronation of Joash in 2 Kgs 11.14 (2 Chron. 23.13), where it replaced the horn used at the coronation of Solomon in 1 Kgs 1.34, 39, 41 and that of Jehu in 2 Kgs 9.13.

4. The one possible exception was at the coronation of Joash in 2 Chron. 23.13, when the people of the land blew the trumpets. Sendrey (1969: 334) surmises that, as in Egypt, the trumpets used in secular occasions were distinguished from the ritual trumpets by being made of bronze rather than of silver.

5. See Sendrey 1969: 336-41; cf. *b. 'Arak.* 10a.

during the presentation of the burnt offerings and the performance of the choral service (2 Chron. 29.27-28). Since prostration at the temple was associated with prayer through the performance of the choir, they also gave the signal for prayer in the temple or on the battlefield (2 Chron. 13.14; cf. Sir 50.16-19; 1 Macc. 3.50-54; 4.40; 5.31-33; 2 Mac. 15.25-26).

While the trumpets were an essential part of the musical performance at the temple, they differed from the other instruments in their ritual function. This is shown by the description of the arrangement of the temple orchestra. While the Levitical musicians faced the altar, the trumpeters stood facing them in front of the altar (2 Chron. 5.12; 7.6). Their position relative to each other is described even more exactly in 2 Chron. 29.27b:

> At the same time that the burnt offering began, the song of YHWH began with the trumpets[1] which[2] were alongside[3] the instruments of David, the king of Israel.

1.   The *waw* here expresses the notion of concomitance as in 2 Chron. 16.14; cf. GKC §154a n. 1(b). *haḥᵃṣōṣᵉrôt* should not therefore be taken with *šîr* as the subject of the singular verb as is done by Kittel (*1902: 162) and Rudolph (*1955: 296).

2.   The apparently redundant *waw* which is omitted by the LXX functions explicatively. See Curtis and Madsen *1910: 470; cf. GKC 154a n. 1(b).

3.   *'al-yᵉdê* is usually interpreted in one of two ways. First, since the phrase means 'under the direction of' in 1 Chron. 25.2, 3, 6 and 2 Chron. 23.18, trumpets are said to be under the leading of the other instruments, i.e., they fitted in with the instrumental music (BDB, 391; Keil *1870: 340; Rudolph *1955: 298). But this would reverse the relationship between the trumpets and the other instruments as shown in 2 Chron. 5.13. It would also contradict the subordination of the Levitical musicians to the priests. Furthermore, by this interpretation, the trumpets would have sounded for the duration of the song. The trumpets would thereby have forfeited their task of signalling an important event and would have been reduced to ancillary musical instruments without any special ritual function. Secondly, Myers (*1965ᵃ: 167) speaks of the song and the trumpets as accompanied by the other instruments. Yet since the trumpets did not play the tune for the song, they could not have been accompanied by the other instruments. Dillard (*1987: 231) circumvents this difficulty by speaking of both sets of instruments accompanying the song. While this makes sense, it violates the grammar. Since neither of these solutions is satisfactory, I propose that *'al-yᵉdê* here means 'next to', or possibly even 'on both sides of' (See 1 Chron. 7.29; cf. Num. 34.3; Judg. 11.26; Job 1.14, and *'al-yad* in 2 Chron. 17.15, 16, 18; 21.16; cf. Braun *1986: 246-47, on 1 Chron. 25.2, 3, 6). Such an interpretation is consistent with the thought of Chronicles which expresses status and function symbolically in terms of location within the sacred precincts.

The normal arrangement would then have been as was described later in the Mishnah (*Tam.* 7.3). The trumpeters stood flanking the head of the choir as they sounded their trumpets. Ritually speaking, this arrangement highlighted their responsibility to give the signal for congregational prostration, their status relative to the musicians, and their purpose in announcing the LORD's presence with his people.

The ritual significance of blowing the trumpets is expressed most clearly in Num. 10.9-10. They brought the people to the LORD's remembrance; they proclaimed his presence and announced his help to the people. Together with the song of thanksgiving and praise, they proclaimed the LORD's presence at the ark in Jerusalem (1 Chron. 16.4); together with the music of the full Levitical choir, their fanfare announced the entrance the LORD into the temple at its dedication (2 Chron. 5.12-14).

The trumpets, which were used in the cult, in the court and in war in Egypt,[1] seem to have gained royal significance in Israel. In Israel they were used to celebrate the Davidic ruler (2 Kgs 11.14 = 2 Chron. 23.13) as well as his heavenly suzerain (Ps. 98.6). So when the priests sounded the trumpets before the ark as it was being transferred to Jerusalem, they announced the coming of the heavenly King to take up his residence in his earthly city (1 Chron. 15.24, 28); when they sounded them before the ark housed in the tent at Jerusalem, they proclaimed his presence there at the times for daily sacrifice and prayer (1 Chron. 16.6). The trumpets were also used to signal the presence of the heavenly King with his earthly armies as they marched into battle (2 Chron. 13.12, 14).[2] After the battle was won, they announced his return in triumph to his temple in Jerusalem (2 Chron. 20.28). Both in the transferral of the ark and the onset of battle the announcement by the trumpets of the LORD's royal presence was greeted by the vocal acclamation of his people (1 Chron. 15.28; 2 Chron. 13.12, 15). Most importantly, the trumpets announced the prostration of the king and his people before their heavenly monarch during the presentation of the burnt offering at the temple (2 Chron. 29.28-29).

1. For the cultic use of trumpets in Egypt, see Hickmann 1950; cf. Seidel 1989: 108-16 for their possible Davidic origin and royal use in Israel.

2. In 2 Chron. 13.12 the trumpets replaced the ark as the sign of God's presence with his people in holy war. See also 1 Macc. 4.13; 5.31-33; 7.45; 9.12; 2 Macc. 15.25 for their use in the Maccabean wars, as well as the discussion on their place in the martial theology of Qumran by Yadin (1963: 87-113).

The ritual function of the trumpets then far outweighed their musical utility in the performance of sacred song. By virtue of their divine institution through Moses, they served to announce the gracious presence of the LORD with his people in the worship at the temple in Jerusalem. Since they were divinely ordained, they are described in 2 Chron. 29.28 as active agents rather than as mere instruments wielded by the priests.[1] They were so important that only the priests were allowed to play them, which in turn enhanced the status and significance of the trumpets.

The Cymbals

The cymbals, which are rarely mentioned elsewhere, figure prominently in the lists of liturgical instruments in Chronicles.[2] As indicated by the dual form for them, the cymbals were used in pairs. They were made of bronze (1 Chron. 15.19) and probably consisted of two metal plates with reflexed rims about 20–30 cm wide. When these were struck together vertically, they produced a ringing, tinkling sound.

Contrary to common opinion, the cymbals were not used by the precentor to conduct the singing by beating out the rhythm of the song,[3] but rather to announce the beginning of the song or a stanza in the song. Since they were used to introduce the song, they were wielded by the head of choir on ordinary occasions (1 Chron. 16.5b)

---

1.   Even if *haḥ*ᵃ*ṣōṣ*ᵉ*rôt* could conceivably stand for the trumpeters here and in 2 Chron. 23.13, since it is qualified by a masculine plural participle (BDB, 348; Keil *1870: 340; Rudolph *1955: 298; Dillard *1987: 231), this would still not explain why the author chose this puzzling form, rather than just the participle in 2 Chron. 5.13, or the participle with the plural of trumpets, as in 2 Chron. 5.12 and 13.14. It seems to me that this phrase with its even odder antecedent clause: *wᵉhaśśîr mᵉśôrēr* expresses the power of the trumpets in this ritual context.

2.   See *mᵉṣiltayīm* in 1 Chron. 13.8; 15.16, 19, 28; 16.5b, 42; 25.1, 6; 2 Chron. 5.12, 13; 29.25; Ezra 3.10; Neh. 12.27, and *ṣelṣelîm* in 2 Sam. 6.5; Ps. 150.5. Even though the change of name from 2 Sam. 6.5 to 1 Chron. 13.8 could indicate that *ṣelṣelîm* was the old name for the cymbals, *mṣltm* appears already in the Ugaritic texts: CTA 3.A.i.19, and Ugar. V.2.4.

3.   Most earlier scholars maintained that the cymbals were used to conduct the choir (e.g. Keil *1870: 149; Graetz 1881: 248-49; Delitzsch 1894: 24; Curtis and Madsen *1910: 215-16; Wauchope Stewart 1917: 41-42; Maecklenburg 1929: 201). There is, however, no evidence for this in the Old Testament. Sendrey (1969: 376-77) argues that this is based on a misunderstanding of ancient music, which lacked a regular beat and metrical structure.

or by the three heads of the guilds on extraordinary occasions (1 Chron. 15.19).[1]

The cymbals were closely related to the trumpets in their ritual function, even though they differed from them in their status, since they were neither instituted in the Pentateuch nor played by the priests. Consequently, when they were coupled with the trumpets and distinguished from the string instruments, the trumpets were always mentioned first (1 Chron. 15.28; 16.42; 2 Chron. 5.13). While they shared the status of the string instruments by virtue of their institution at the LORD's command for performance by the Levites (2 Chron. 29.25), they were distinguished functionally from the string instruments as is shown by their mention either before (1 Chron. 15.19; 25.6; 2 Chron. 5.12; 29.25) or after the lyre and harp (1 Chron. 15.16; 16.5; 25.1).

The practical function of the cymbals was to call for the attention of the congregation to the performance of sacred song.[2] This is borne out by the use of *hišmîaʿ* to describe their function and significance.[3] Musically speaking, one could translate this by the verb 'sound'. Hence the head of the guild (1 Chron. 16.5) or the three heads of guilds are said to 'sound' the cymbals (1 Chron. 15.19). Since both the trumpets and the cymbals were played together to announce the beginning of the song, the players of both are called 'sounders' in 1 Chron. 16.42.[4] Jones (1986: 108) therefore proposes that 1 Chron. 16.5b should be translated: 'Asaph was calling for attention with cymbals'.

The use of *hišmîaʿ* in connection with the sounding of the cymbals also indicates their ritual significance. When used absolutely, the verb normally means 'to make a proclamation'.[5] The clashing of the cymbals not only summoned the congregation to attend to the performance of

---

1.   However, according to *m.* '*Arak.* 2.5 and *b.* '*Arak.* 13b there was only ever one cymbal.

2.   See Zalewski 1968: 287; cf. Sendrey 1969: 377.

3.   While this *hiphil* is normally transitive, it is used absolutely with musicians or musical instruments as its subject in 1 Chron. 15.16, 19, 28; 16.5b, 42; Neh. 12.42.

4.   Jones (1986: 108, 111) argues that Ps. 150.5 lends support to this cultic interpretation of the verb by distinguishing 'the cymbals of attention' from 'the cymbals of acclamation'. Since 'the cymbals of acclamation' were probably used to call for ritual cries of acclamation from the people, it seems likely that *ṣilṣᵉlê-šāmaʿ* had a similar cultic sense.

5.   BDB, 1034; cf. Amos 3.9; 4.5; Isa. 41.26; 43.12; 62.11; Jer. 4.5, 16; 5.20; 31.7; 46.14; 50.2.

the song, but also announced the LORD's acceptance of their sacrifice.[1] The cymbals also called for the attention of the congregation to the contents of the sacred song. By their connection with the trumpets and the instruments which accompanied the song, they proclaimed the LORD's gracious presence with his people at the temple.

In sum, David instituted the cymbals at the LORD's command as part of the temple orchestra. Wielded as they were by the head of the choir, they served to introduce the sacred song. Since they called for the attention of the congregation to the performance of praise during the presentation of burnt offerings, they announced the LORD's acceptance of them and assisted in proclaiming his gracious presence with his people.

The Lyres and Harps

The third group of musical instruments in Chronicles was the two sets of string instruments. Like the cymbals they were said to have been instituted by David at the LORD's command for the performance of sacred song (2 Chron. 29.25). They were therefore called 'the instruments of song' (2 Chron. 5.13) or 'the instruments of God's song' (1 Chron. 16.42). They were always used together in the choral service.

In the light of the data at our disposal,[2] it seems that the *kinnôr* was the asymmetrical lyre, which consisted of a sound-box with two out-

---

1.   Mowinckel (1924: 18) argues that YHWH is the implied object in these cases. The purpose of sounding the cymbals would then have been to arouse the attention of the LORD to his people. Sendrey (1969: 377) agrees that this was its original purpose. While this reading has been rightly rejected by Rudolph (*1955: 118), it may not be entirely wrong. Even if the LORD was not addressed by the sounding of the cymbals, he could nevertheless have been their object. Crüsemann (1969: 50-55) has argued that the unusual genre of the instruction to praise the LORD in Isa. 48.20 and Jer. 31.7 derives from the genre of an instruction given to herald in Jer. 4.5, 16; 5.20; 46.14; 50.2; cf. Isa. 40.9-10; 58.1. What interests me in this is the occurrence of *hišmîa'* in all these instances. This verb could possibly have been chosen to describe the ritual performance of music in the postexilic period as the heraldic proclamation of the LORD's presence to his people. By their music the instruments would then have proclaimed the LORD.

2.   Roughly speaking, there are three bodies of data. First, there are the references to the lyre in the Old Testament. Secondly, there are the depictions of it in ancient inscriptions. Those discovered in the Syro-Palestinean area have been recently collated by Görg (1984). Thirdly, there are the descriptions of the lyre from the rabbis, Josephus and early Christian writers.

curved arms of uneven length, connected by an oblique crossbar for the strings.[1] It was held out from the body at an angle of 45 to 90 degrees and was played with both hands; one hand wielded a plectrum, while the other either plucked or damped selected strings.[2] It may have had two kinds of strings: the upper, tuned strings for producing a sweet clear sound (cf. Ps. 81.3), and the lower, untuned strings for 'resonance'.[3] In both secular and sacred contexts it was used to accompany song at times of celebration and rejoicing.

The identification of the *nēbel* is far less certain. Two instruments have been proposed. The first and by far most favoured proposal is the vertical, angular harp shown in the Assyrian palace reliefs from the seventh century.[4] Its resonator, which was fixed to the upper arm of the instrument, extended above the player's head, and its strings descended diagonally to a neck jutting out at right angles to the body of the player.[5] According to Josephus (*Ant.* 7.12.3), it had twelve tones (*phthongoi*) and was played with the fingers. The second, less favoured, proposal is to take it as a different kind of lyre with a jar-shaped sounding box and a curved yoke, like that depicted on the Bar Kochba coins.[6] The absence of any portrayals of the angular harp from the Syro-Palestinean area, and the etymology of its name, which suggests some connection with a jar, is used in support of this identification. Whatever the case, the *nēbel* was used mainly by the cultured upper classes in their festivities (Amos 6.5; Isa. 5.12; 14.11; 1 Kgs 10.12). The reference in 1 Chron. 16.5 to 'instruments of harps' implies that several different kinds of harps were used in worship.

Apart from the specialized use of the lyre in prophecy (1 Chron. 25.3), the lyres and harps were always played together at the temple.[7]

---

1.   See the depiction on a seal discussed by Avigad (1978).

2.   See Josephus, *Ant.* 7.12.4. While Josephus maintains that the temple lyre had ten strings and Rabbi Judah (*b. 'Arak.* 13b) claims that it had seven, the number of strings depicted in the inscriptions listed by Görg (1984) varies from three to twelve.

3.   See *higgāyôn* in Ps. 92.4; cf. Wohlenberg 1967: 542; Eaton 1984[a]: 87.

4.   See Kolari 1947; Wohlenberg 1967; Sendrey 1969; Eaton 1984[a]; Foxvog and Kilmer 1986.

5.   According to *m. Kin.* 3.6, its strings were made from the large intestines of a sheep. The discussion in *b. 'Arak.* 13b on the strings for the lyre of the world to come shows that from the mention of a ten-stringed harp in Ps. 33.2 and 144.9 the rabbis deduced that it had ten strings.

6.   So Bayer 1968 and Keel 1978: 346-50.

7.   Sendrey (1969: 282) describes the relationship between the two thus: 'Since

For the transferral of the ark, eight musicians played harps, while six played lyres (1 Chron. 15.20-21). Since the harps probably made a deeper, louder sound than the lyres, they would have dominated the proceedings. Apart from the head of the choir with the cymbals, there were normally either nine (1 Chron. 16.5a) or eleven musicians (1 Chron. 25.9-31).[1] Since the accent in regular worship was on the performance of song rather on the creation of exuberant sound to promote rejoicing, the lyres would have outnumbered the harps, so that the music did not drown out the vocal production of the song.

The purpose of these instruments was to accompany the songs of praise and thanksgiving to the LORD (1 Chron. 23.5; 2 Chron. 5.13; 7.6). The musicians who played them would themselves have sung the song to their own accompaniment as was normally the case in the ancient orient.[2] Hence they were called *mᵉšōrᵉrîm* (1 Chron. 9.33; 15.16, 19, 27; 2 Chron. 5.12, 13; 20.21; 23.13; 35.15a), which shows that they were both singers and instrumentalists. The song of the LORD was thus performed to the accompaniment of the string instruments. In fact, 2 Chron. 29.28 goes so far as to imply that the divinely appointed instruments were themselves active agents in the production of sacred song.[3] Because of its accompaniment by these instruments of song (1 Chron. 16.42; 2 Chron. 5.13), it was as if the song was 'singing' its words rather than being sung.

Thus the lyre and the harp were the instruments for the accompaniment of sacred song at the temple. By virtue of their divine institution, they not only accompanied the song but also helped to produce the affective power of the song both for the singers and the congregation.

---

the *nebel* is supposed to have been the larger, therefore lower sounding instrument, the *kinnor* generally had the lead, which means that the *kinnor* doubled the melody, while the *nebel* had a more subordinate, accompanying function'.

1.   According to later tradition, while the number of harps ranged from a minimum of two to maximum of six (*m. 'Arak.* 2.3), the normal quota of lyres could be increased indefinitely (*m. 'Arak* 2.5). Normally the choir consisted of twelve musicians, as shown in 1 Chron. 25.9-31: nine to play the lyres, two to play the harps, and one to sound the cymbals (*b. 'Arak.* 13b).

2.   Singing is synonymous with the playing of an instrument in Pss. 33.2-3; 57.7-9; 71.22-23; 92.1-4; 108.1-3; 137.1-4; 147.7.

3.   This seems to be the point of the strange clause: *wᵉhaššîr mᵉšōrēr*. An active *polel* participle occurs where a passive participle is expected. While Holladay (Holl, 367) suggests that the song of the LORD resounded, the literal sense is: 'the song of the LORD was singing'.

3. *The Function and Significance of the Combined Instruments*

The three groups of instruments differed in their institution, function and significance. The trumpets, which were instituted by the LORD through Moses, announced the presentation of the burnt offering at the temple and called for the prostration of the people. They served to proclaim the LORD's presence at the temple. The cymbals, which were instituted by the LORD through his prophets, announced the performance of the sacred song by the Levitical choir. They served to announce the LORD's acceptance of the burnt offering. The lyres and harps, which were also instituted by the LORD through his prophets, accompanied the singing of the LORD's song. They served to praise the LORD in the performance of the sacred song.

Despite this diversity, they all combined to fulfil certain common ritual goals in the worship at the temple. These goals are expressed in three ways by Chronicles. The first and most obvious expression of their common purpose is recorded in the description of their combination at the dedication of the temple in 2 Chron. 5.13.

The reference to 'one voice' in this verse is not, as has been traditionally argued, to the performance of music in unison,[1] but rather to a synchronized mass performance, in which the instrumental music combined with the singing to achieve a unified, harmonious effect.[2] All the musicians played their instruments together to present a single performance of thanksgiving to the LORD. Thus the common purpose of all the instruments was to join with the song in thanking and praising the LORD for his goodness.

The second way of expressing their common purpose was by the extension of the functions of the trumpets and the cymbals to all the instruments. Whereas in Num. 10.10 the trumpets had been ordained for Israel's 'remembrance' of and by the LORD, in 1 Chron. 16.4-6 this task was extended to all the instruments. Likewise the duty to 'announce' the LORD's presence, which in 1 Chron. 15.19 and 16.5b was restricted to the cymbals, was extended to the trumpets in 1 Chron. 16.42 and to all the instruments in 1 Chron. 15.16. All these

---

1. So Keil *1870: 242 and Williamson *1982: 215. While Rudolph (*1955: 211) still uses the term unison to describe the effect of the performance, he rightly describes it as the harmonious synchronization of music and song.

2. See Wohlenberg 1967: 580 and Sendrey 1969: 215-16, 537. Both these scholars consider that 'as one' and 'one sound' describe the unity and precision of this mass performance.

together produced the song which 'proclaimed' his gracious presence (2 Chron. 5.13).

The third and most startling expression of their common purpose is found in 2 Chron. 30.21b: 'the priests and Levites were praising the LORD with instruments of power belonging to the LORD'. Here the instruments used by both the priests and the Levites during the celebration of great Passover under Hezekiah are called $k^e l\hat{e}$-'$\bar{o}z$, that is, 'instruments of power'. The singularity of the phrase has led most modern scholars to emend it to $b^e kol$-'$\bar{o}z$, as in 1 Chron. 13.8, with the consequent omission of the second $l^e YHWH$ as dittography.[1] There is, however, no warrant for this in the versions. While the LXX fails to translate '$\bar{o}z$, it does mention the instruments of the LORD.

Apart from this conjectural emendation, the text has been understood in four ways. First, the AV translates the phrase by 'loud instruments' which has not found much favour, since '$\bar{o}z$ is not used elsewhere in this sense. Secondly, K.-M. Beyse (1984: col. 185) takes '$\bar{o}z$ as a synonym for praise by regarding this verse as similar in sense to 1 Chron. 23.5. Thirdly, Keil (*1870: 350) argues that these were instruments for ascribing power to the LORD by praising him. Lastly, Rudolph (*1955: 302), Myers (*1965[a]: 175), and Dillard (*1987: 239) translate it by 'with mighty instruments of Yahweh' without explaining their translation.

It seems to me that the instruments were regarded as powerful, because they belonged to the LORD. And they were powerful in two ways. They were powerful in their effect upon the people. By using them in praise, the musicians proclaimed the LORD's goodness to the people (2 Chron. 30.22) and so motivated them to rejoice with much jubilation (30.21, 23, 25, 26). Like the ark with its power (2 Chron. 6.41), they were also powerful instruments for evoking the LORD's presence and power (cf. Ps. 21.13). There is, as is shown in 1 Chron. 16.8-34, a connection between divine empowerment and the performance of praise. Those who sought the LORD at the ark in Jerusalem could also seek his saving power there (1 Chron. 16.11). Now the proper way for seeking the LORD's presence was by ascribing glory and strength to him through the presentation of offerings and praises (1 Chron. 16.10-11). Both strength and joy come from him and are given to those who acknowledge his sovereignty in their praise

---

1. So Curtis and Madsen *1910: 475-76; Galling *1954: 158; Goettsberger *1939: 350.

(1 Chron. 16.27-28). So, since the musical instruments moved the people to present their offerings to the LORD with thanksgiving (2 Chron. 30.22), they were powerful in conveying his power and joy to them through the performance of sacred song.

The musical instruments were therefore an important component in the ritual performance of praise. By virtue of their divine institution, those instruments which belonged to the LORD were powerful in fulfilling the ritual purpose for which they were instituted. While each set of instruments had its own task to perform, they all combined, each in its own way, to announce the LORD to his people, to proclaim his presence with them, and to praise him for his goodness.

The Performers

Their Divine Authorization

Like the words, place, times and instruments for the sacred song, the agents for its performance were prescribed by royal statute (1 Chron. 6.32; 2 Chron. 8.14; 23.18; 29.25; 35.15a). This was not merely a matter of good order but of ritual necessity, since choral music had to be performed by the right people, if it was to serve the welfare of God's people.

As was the case with the other components of sacred song, the choice in 1 Chronicles 23–25 of its performers was consistent with the pattern of ritual legislation in the Pentateuch. In Chronicles, as in the Pentateuch, the tribe of Levi was responsible for the enactment of the sacrificial ritual on behalf of the nation (1 Chron. 6.1-53; 23–26; 2 Chron. 13.10). This tribe in turn was divided into two parts, each with its own clearly defined area of responsibility and sacral status. On the one hand, the Aaronic priests who were holy to the LORD, handled the holy things needed for the sacrificial service at the holy place (1 Chron. 6.49; 23.13; cf. Num. 18.5, 7). On the other hand, the rest of the Levites, who were subordinate to the priests, represented the people of Israel at the sanctuary by performing their ritual duties for them there, so shielding them from liability for desecration (1 Chron. 6.48; 2 Chron. 30.17; 35.6). According to 1 Chron. 23.32 they had three main areas of responsibility: the maintenance of the temple, the protection of the holy things from defilement, and the assistance of the priests in the performance of the sacrificial ritual.[1]

---

1. Milgrom (1970: 8-16, 60-72) argues that the Levites had two areas of

The personnel chosen by David for the choral service came from these two groups. While the trumpeters were priests, the musicians came from the ranks of the Levites. Thus, since both were drawn from the established clergy, their appointment recognized the given order which indicated their function and status within the clerical hierarchy.

The Priestly Trumpeters

There was no need for David to make any new regulations for the players of the trumpets, since the priests had already been detailed for that task by Moses in Num. 10.8. The only innovation for them by David was their combination with the Levitical choir in the performance of sacred song before the ark in Jerusalem (1 Chron. 16.4-6). They were presumably already involved in the presentation of the burnt offerings at Gibeon where they continued their service together with the singers appointed there (1 Chron. 16.39-42).

Since the priests blew the trumpets, these instruments gained a special ritual status quite apart from their musical function. They were holy instruments. Through the priests the trumpets were also linked ritually with the ark and the altar which, since they were most holy, were out of bounds for the Levites. The priests who blew the trumpets thus connected the performance of song personally and sacrally with the ministry of their fellow priests at the altar and in the holy place. In fact, the power of sacred song to communicate the LORD's presence and help to his people depended in part upon the involvement of the priests with the Levitical musicians in the choir, for wherever the priests were with their holy trumpets, the LORD himself was present with his people (2 Chron. 13.12). They ensured the coordination of praise with sacrifice, so that, by the performance of liturgical song, the benefits of the sacrifice would be proclaimed to the people and received by them. Through them choral music became part of the sacrificial ritual.

---

responsibility in Numbers: guard duty at the tabernacle, and its movement. He maintains (82-83 n. 307) that the second area of responsibility was changed in 1 Chron. 23.32 by a redefinition of *mišmeret qōdeš*, so that it no longer referred to the duty of the Kohathites to protect the sancta in transit but covered the preparation of the show bread and cereal offerings (1 Chron. 23.29) and the protection of the sancta from impurity (1 Chron. 23.28).

The Levitical Musicians

The Chronicler maintains that the most significant innovation of David in his organization of the choral service was the decision to appoint the musicians from the Levites (1 Chron. 15.16; 16.4; 23.5). This, however, was not done under his own authority but at the command of the LORD through Gad and Nathan (2 Chron. 29.25). Hence the three musical guilds were derived from the three Levitical clans. So important was their Levitical status for the Chronicler that he not only traced the Levitical origins of the three heads of guilds in 1 Chron. 6.33-47 but also repeatedly referred to the musicians as Levites (1 Chron. 16.4; 2 Chron. 5.12; 7.6; 8.14; 29.25, 30; 30.21-22; 31.2).[1]

Now while the selection of the musicians from the ranks of the Levites was consistent with the regulation of the clergy in the Pentateuch, it is not immediately apparent why they were chosen for this task rather than the priests. 1 Chronicles 15 suggests that the performance of sacred song was in some way ritually similar, if not equivalent, to the transportation of the ark. Both were 'ministries' to the LORD (1 Chron. 15.2). Hence the musicians were appointed initially to 'minister' both before the ark in Jerusalem (1 Chron. 16.4, 37) and the tent of meeting in Gibeon (1 Chron. 6.32). Later the Levitical musicians 'ministered' at the temple by giving thanks and praise to the LORD (2 Chron. 31.2). The Levites then were chosen as musicians, because their performance of music was to be a 'ministry' akin to their care of the ark.

When Chronicles describes the ritual task of the musicians as 'ministry', it presupposes the various definitions of the ministry by the Levites in Numbers. There the Levites are said to 'minister' to the tabernacle (Num. 1.50) at the tabernacle (Num. 8.26), like courtiers at the headquarters of their king. Since they were subordinate to the priests, they are said to 'minister' to them by attendance to the tabernacle and its precincts (Num. 3.6; 18.2). This ministry, however, was vicarious, since they ministered there for the people of Israel (Num. 16.9). This understanding of the Levites as the ritual representatives of the congregation, which is developed at some length in Num. 3.40-51 and 8.5-26, is assumed by the description of the musicians' duties as ministry in Chronicles. Just as the Levites who acted as ritual

---

1. The participle *mᵉšārᵉtîm* is used secularly in Chronicles for the king's officials, who ranged from personal attendants of royal blood (2 Chron. 22.8), to courtiers (2 Chron. 9.4) and generals (1 Chron. 27.1; 28.1; 2 Chron. 17.19).

substitutes for all the first-born Israelites, helped to make atonement by doing 'service' for the people of Israel at the tabernacle (Num. 8.19), so the Levitical musicians also helped in the sacrificial ritual by performing the 'service' of song for them (1 Chron. 6.32 [6.17]; 25.1, 6; 2 Chron. 30.22). Like their fellow Levites they ministered before the priests at the temple (2 Chron. 8.14).

The vicarious character of sacred song as performed by the Levitical musicians is confirmed by three passages in Chronicles. First, in 1 Chron. 16.7 there is this notice: 'Then on that day David as the leader[1] arranged[2] for thanksgiving to the LORD by means of[3] Asaph and his kinsmen'. The emphasis here is on David's performance of thanksgiving to the LORD through the agency of the Asaphites. Thanksgiving was thus not just given by them but by David through them as his representatives. They represented the king and the people, for David had made this arrangement as the head of the people. David then offered thanksgiving to the LORD on behalf of the nation through his appointed musicians. Through them he commanded Israel and the nations to praise the LORD.

Secondly, in 2 Chron. 7.6 David is said to have offered praise through the performance of the choral service, which is rather odd, since the occasion was the dedication of the temple, and David had long since been dead. Yet, even though Solomon was king, David still

---

1. *bārō'š* is usually translated as 'at first'. It is, however, never used in this sense anywhere else in the Old Testament. As Bagley (1987: 16) notes, the usual word in Chronicles for 'at first' is *bārī'šônâ* (1 Chron. 11.6 *bis*; 15.13; 17.9). He therefore suggests that it should be construed with *dāwîd* and translated by 'as the leader', as in 2 Chron. 13.12 (cf. 2 Chron. 20.27). This would be similar to the use of *bᵉrō'š* in Jer. 31.7, where, as Crüsemann (1969: 52 n. 2) argues, the people are called to proclaim Israel's deliverance 'at the head of the nations' (cf. 2 Chron. 20.27). So through the appointment of singers, David as the leader took the lead in thanking the LORD. The LXX gives another possible solution which has been accepted by Rothstein and Hänel (*1927: 291). It connects *bārō'š* with *lᵉhōdôt*, interprets *rō'š* as beginning, and regards the infinitive as a gerundival object. Hence it translates: 'David arranged for the beginning of thanking the LORD'.

2. *nātan* can be taken in one of two ways. First, it could be construed with *bᵉyad* and translated as 'he commissioned' (Holl, 249 and Bagley 1987: 13-16). The problem is that it needs a personal object which is missing. Secondly, it could be taken in the same sense as in 16.4 and translated as 'he appointed' or 'arranged for'. While it could be argued that these are dissimilar, since *nātan* lacks an object in 16.7, *lᵉ* is often used in Chronicles for a personal accusative (see Polzin 1976: 64-66).

3. *bᵉyādām*; cf. 2 Chron. 7.6.

offered praises 'through their hand', that is, by means of the Levitical choir which he had endowed and the instruments which he had made for this purpose (cf. 1 Chron. 23.5; 2 Chron. 29.26-27). Thus the Levitical musicians were instituted and maintained by the Davidic monarchy to perform praise with the instruments of David for the monarchy and the nation, just as the English kings established the chapel and choir of King's College in Cambridge to offer prayers for the welfare of king and country.

Thirdly, the notion of vicarious praise is also reflected in 1 Chron. 25.6b. If the three heads of guilds were to act *'al y^{e}dê hammelek*, they were not only to perform music under his authority but also as his representatives. Since the performance of the song was under his patronage and direction, it was also given for his benefit. Furthermore, this helps to explain the special position of Asaph in 25.2. If he was singled out to prophesy *'al-y^{e}dê hammelek*, this meant that he did so for the king, as commanded in 1 Chron. 16.7. So then, just as the king offered sacrifices for himself and his people through the priests (2 Chron. 8.12), he also offered praise to the LORD on behalf of himself and his people through the ministry of the Levitical musicians (2 Chron. 7.6).

Despite their Levitical status, the position of the musicians was somewhat ambiguous. On the one hand, Chronicles usually calls them Levites rather than musicians. As such they were embedded in the three Levitical clans (1 Chron. 6.16-48; 15.17; 23.2-32) and subject to their chiefs (1 Chron. 15.4-16; 23.2; 2 Chron. 29.12-13). Like all the Levites, they were subordinate to the priests (1 Chron. 23.28, 32). As musicians they were also closely associated in their ritual duties with some of the gatekeepers. The duties of the singers overlapped with the duties of the keepers at the gate which led into the inner court, since both were located there. Hence the gatekeepers Obed-edom and Jeiel were included among the musicians in 1 Chron. 15.18, 21 and 16.5. The musicians then were Levites, who were connected with some of the lower-ranked gatekeepers in their duties.

On the other hand, they had their own chiefs who functioned on the same level as the other Levitical chiefs (2 Chron. 29.12-14). By virtue of their position before the altar in the temple, they were also set apart ritually from their fellow Levites. Most significantly, like the priests they were vested in linen both at the transferral of the ark to Jerusalem, when all the Levites who carried the ark and even David were similarly vested (1 Chron. 15.27), and at the dedication of the temple (2 Chron. 5.12).[1] They therefore belonged to those Levites who were most like the priests.

Like the priests, all the Levites (and with them the singers) were considered holy in Chronicles (2 Chron. 35.3). On the face of it, this seems to contradict the Pentateuch, which only designates the priests as holy (Num. 16.5-7). Yet this did not necessarily represent any major change in their ritual duties,[2] since the priests retained exclusive access to the altar and the inside of the temple (1 Chron. 6.34; 2 Chron. 13.11); the Levites were also still subordinate to them (1 Chron. 23.28, 32). Their designation as holy may derive from the redefinition of the whole inner court as 'the house of the LORD' (2 Chron. 23.5-6) and its consecration as 'the holy place' (2 Chron. 29.7; 30.19; 35.5)[3] by the sacrifices presented there at the dedication of the temple (2 Chron. 7.7). The Levites who served in the inner court, as the singers did, were therefore subject to the same demands for sanctity as the priests on duty there. Thus, just as the priests were required to sanctify themselves ritually for service (2 Chron. 5.11; 29.34; 30.3, 24b; 31.18), so the Levites who stood in the holy place were also required to sanctify themselves (2 Chron. 35.5-6),[4] and that together with the priests (1 Chron. 15.12, 14; 2 Chron. 29.5, 15, 34; 30.15). Since the singers were involved in the performance of the sacrificial ritual at the temple, they were considered holy and required to sanctify themselves for their ceremonial duties. They were thus not merely assistants to the priests but also ministers of the LORD who helped administer his affairs.

The singers were chosen from the three Levitical clans. Their selection was not just determined by royal decision based on sacral precedent, but also on a divine command through two prophets. As ministers of the congregation whose ministry was an extension of the traditional representative ministry of the Levites, they performed the choral service on behalf of the monarchy and the nation; as ministers

---

1. We do not know whether this was the regular custom in the pre-exilic period or not, unless *leḥadrat qōdeš* in 2 Chron. 20.21 means 'holy attire', as claimed by Keil (*1870: 291) and Curtis and Madsen (*1910: 409). According to Josephus (*Ant.* 20.9.6), the musicians were again allowed to wear vestments under Agrippa II.

2. *Contra* von Rad (1930: 62, 98).

3. See Milgrom 1970: 13-15 n. 47.

4. For a discussion of this refrain, see Koch 1961.

of the LORD they stood in the holy place and were subject to its requirements for sanctity.

The Congregation

The members of the congregation did not remain passive spectators at the performance of the choral service on their behalf by the Levitical choir. The choir addressed them directly and invited them to join in its praise (1 Chron. 16.8-13). The congregation did so by responding with certain stereotyped words and refrains (1 Chron. 16.36b). It thereby became an active partner in praise.

There were probably two modes of response to the address by the choir to the congregation. First of all, there was the call *hall^{e}lû l^{e}YHWH*. The response of the people to this would have been *hall^{e}lû Yâ* (1 Chron. 16.36e). Secondly, there was the call *hôdû l^{e}YHWH*. The congregational response to this was either: *kî ṭôb kî l^e'ôlām ḥasdô* (2 Chron. 7.3) or: *kî l^e'ôlām ḥasdô* (1 Chron. 16.41; 2 Chron. 7.6). This seems to have been the commonest response in the postexilic period, if frequency of mention is any indication (1 Chron. 16.34, 41; 2 Chron. 5.13; 7.3, 6; 20.21; Ezra 3.10).

The congregation was invited by the singers to join them in their praise. The call to respond with *hall^{e}lû Yâ* was probably signalled by a fanfare from the trumpets accompanied by the other instruments which were therefore called instruments of praise (1 Chron. 23.5). Thus the singers are said to give the signal for the cry of praise with their instruments. This cry of acclamation was probably uttered at the end of each stanza, which coincided with the act of prostration as signalled by the trumpets (2 Chron. 29.28; cf. *m. Tam.* 7.3). It is less certain when the congregation responded with the refrain *kî l^e'ôlām ḥasdô*. It may have been at the conclusion of a song which began and ended as 1 Chron. 16.8-34, or after each stanza, or after each half verse as in Ps. 136. Whatever the case, the congregation would have been well versed in responding appropriately at the right places in the performance of the choral service.

The members of the congregation were therefore included in the circle of praise with their ritual responses. The call to praise extended to the whole earth with all its peoples and nations (1 Chron. 16.23-30) and to the universe itself with all parts of the natural world (31-33). As potential partners in praise, they too were included with the congregation in the performance of the choir. Just as the choir offered praise for the congregation, so the congregation with its responses offered praise for all peoples and the whole universe. Nothing which God had created was therefore excluded from the performance of his praise.

In sum, certain people were authorized to perform the choral rite at the temple. Their responsibility for this did not rest merely on a royal decree but on its basis in divine legislation. While the priests had been authorized by the LORD through Moses to blow the trumpets during the presentation of the burnt offering, the Levitical musicians were authorized by him through his prophets for their ministry of song. The effectiveness of their performance therefore derived from their divine commission rather than their musical skill. They in turn performed the LORD's song for king and country. The congregation was called to join them in their praise by uttering the appropriate responses. In this way they too became active partners with the choir in the praise of the LORD on behalf of all humanity and the entire universe.

Conclusion

The basic ritual components of sacred song were all in some way instituted by the LORD. While the use of the holy name and the trumpets had been ordained through Moses for the proclamation of his gracious presence in worship, the place, the instruments and the performers of the sacred song were instituted through the prophets Gad and Nathan. Moreover, by the institution of the trumpets for bringing the people of the LORD to his remembrance during the presentation of the burnt offering, the times for the choral service had also been implicitly ordained. Thus the choral service gained its validity and power from the divine institution of its various components.

Since the performance by the musicians was a vicarious activity on behalf of king and country, they were chosen from the Levites who had been expressly set aside as ministers for the people at the tabernacle. In their ministry of song, they used the holy name to announce the LORD's presence to his people during the presentation of the burnt offerings at the altar. This connection of their ministry with the presentation of the burnt offerings determined the times and place of their performance. Whenever the burnt offerings were presented, the choir stood with their instruments before the altar at the temple and performed their ministry of praise there in an intermediate position between the people present in the outer court and the LORD with his presence in the temple. Each group of instruments had its own special ritual function (see diagram, p. 99). While the trumpets gave the signal for prostration, the cymbals announced the sacred song, which was sung to the accompaniment of the string instruments. Yet they all combined to proclaim the LORD's presence, to announce his acceptance of his people and to praise him for his goodness. As instruments which belonged to the LORD, they moved the people to rejoice in his goodness.

These five ritual components were all essential elements of sacred song. They all blended with each other in their ritual context to produce a performance consistent with the pattern of sacrificial worship at the temple.

	Most Holy Domain	Holy Domain			Clean Domain
Space	Holy of holies	Holy place	Court of priests: area around temple and altar	Court of Israelites: stairs with singers' rooms and area in front of the altar	Great court: gates, open area and rooms
Sacred Objects	1. Ark of covenant 2. Mercy seat	1. Incense altar 2. Lampstand 3. Table for showbread	1. Altar for burnt offering 2. Laver	1. Trumpets 2. Musical instruments	
Personnel	High Priest	Priests	1. Priests 2. Priestly trumpeters 3. Levitical slaughterers?	1. Levitical musicians 2. Priestly trumpeters? 3. Levitical slaughterers? 4. Levitical gatekeepers 5. King	Lay people
Ritual Acts	Annual sprinkling of mercy seat	1. Sprinkling and smearing of blood 2. Burning of incense 3. Lighting of lamps 4. Presentation of showbread	1. Disposal of blood 2. Presentation of burnt and fire offerings 3. Pronouncement of blessing	1. Performance of sacred song 2. Prostration 3. Royal prayer	1. Acclamation 2. Prostration 3. Eating of peace offerings

Table 1. *The System of Graded Holiness in Chronicles*

	Trumpets	Cymbals	Lyres and Harps
Normal number	Two	One	Two harps and nine lyres
Institution	Moses	Nathan and Gad: David	Nathan and Gad: David
Players	Priests	Leader of Levitical choir	Levitical musicians
Class	Sounding instruments	Sounding instruments	Instruments of song
Status	Holy instruments	Instruments of service	Instruments of service
Role	Proclamation (hizkîr)	Announcement (hišmîaʿ)	Thanksgiving and praise (hôdâ/hillēl)
Ritual function	Announcement of burnt offering and of congregational prostration	Announcement of sacred song and call for congregational attention	Accompaniment of sacred song
Ritual significance	Proclamation of divine presence	Proclamation of divine acceptance of the sacrifices	Proclamation of divine goodness and generosity

Table 2. *The Musical Instruments*

Chapter 4

The Ritual Function of Sacred Song

Gunkel (1933: 59) maintains that in ancient Israel hymns were sung during the presentation of sacrifices at the temple.[1] The hymn was an essential part of the LORD's sacrifice. This is seldom mentioned in the psalter but can be deduced from Amos 5.21-23. Just as kings in the ancient world were entertained with music and song in their banquets, so the people in antiquity felt that God could not do without song at his sacrifices (Gunkel 1933: 61). Yet despite the importance of this claim for the understanding of the psalms, Gunkel gives scant attention to this insight, apart from listing a few relevant passages in Chronicles and Maccabees. This is no doubt due to the paucity of references in the book of Psalms to the correlation of sacrifice with song.

My contention is that this correlation of sacrifice and praise, implicit in many of the psalms of praise, is made explicit by Chronicles. One could in fact consider this as the distinctive contribution by Chronicles to the development of a theology of worship in the postexilic period. In this chapter I shall therefore investigate the place of liturgical song in the sacrificial worship at the temple. After an examination of how the Chronicler presents the sacrifices and their corresponding rites sequentially with complementary functions in an integrated ritual system, I shall consider how the performance of the choral service was coordinated with the presentation of the public burnt offerings and the ritual prostration of the whole congregation. Finally, an attempt will be made to discover whether the musicians were involved in the presentation of the private thank-offerings at their proper place in the ceremonial order at the temple. My aim in all this is to find out what the function of sacred song was within the sacrificial ritual.

1. Cf. von Rad 1962: 368. Crüsemann (1967: 82) incorrectly maintains that the imperative hymns of praise are mentioned nowhere in connection with the presentation of sacrifices.

The Sacrificial System in Chronicles

The Order and Sequence of the Sacrifices

In an article on the arrangement of sacrifices in the Old Testament, A.F. Rainey (1970) shows that the order for the presentation of the various sacrifices in procedural texts differed from the order given in didactic and administrative texts.[1] The so-called sin offering came first. It was followed by the burnt offering with its prescribed cereal offerings. After these came the peace offerings. Rainey argues that this procedural order is 'the key to understanding the religious significance of the sacrificial system' (p. 498). Yet neither he nor any other scholar has taken up these suggestions and demonstrated how the various sacrifices combined with each other in an integrated sacrificial system.[2]

The clearest presentation of the procedural order for sacrifice is given, as Rainey himself realizes, in 2 Chron. 29.20-35 in connection with the renewal of temple worship under Hezekiah. This account is remarkable for its unusual attention to the general order of the ritual as well as to significant details in its parts. It seems that the Chronicler wished to use the occasion to describe 'the service of the LORD's house' (2 Chron. 29.35). This description of the pattern of worship for the restoration of the temple is of special importance for this study, since it locates the choral service precisely within the larger ritual order and sequence of sacrifices at the temple.[3]

---

1.   Rainey builds on the earlier work of Levine (1965), who later expressed his agreement with Rainey's findings (1974: 26).

2.   Milgrom (1976b: 70 n. 251), Carpenter (1988: 272) and Jenson (1992: 155) all accept Rainey's proposals without modification. His general scheme, however, needs to be modified and corrected at two points. First, the public sacrifices must be distinguished from the private sacrifices. Secondly, the public burnt offering cannot be separated entirely from the sin offering, since some parts of the ritual for it overlap with the rite for the sin offering, as is evident in 2 Chron. 29.22-24.

3.   The Chronicler probably had two reasons for choosing this occasion to describe the order and sequence of sacrifices. First, he needed some festive occasion, since the burnt offering was normally presented by itself without any preceding sin offerings or subsequent thank-offerings. Secondly, by his account of the restoration of temple worship under Hezekiah, he established a precedent for that kind of worship in his own day which was in accord with the LORD's will and so forestalled the possible pollution of the second temple (cf. 2 Chron. 36.14).

Its order is not as difficult as Welch portrays it (1939: 105-106).[1] A number of clear distinctions are made within the general order of the ritual. The public sacrifices, which were offered first (29.21-30), are clearly distinguished from the individual sacrifices, offered at their completion (29.31-35).[2] Moreover, the Chronicler divides the ritual for the public sacrifices into two stages, each clearly related to the other and each with its own separate ritual function.

The first stage in the ritual for the public sacrifices was the blood rite, which consisted of the ritual slaughter of the animals and the ritual disposal of their blood by the priests. The animals for the burnt offerings were slaughtered first by the representatives of the people. From them the priests received the blood and splashed it against the altar. After the representatives of the nation had laid their hands on the he-goats, the priests slaughtered them as sin offerings for the purification of the monarchy, the sanctuary and the people.[3] Then the priest on duty sprinkled some of the blood seven times in front of the veil in the holy place, smeared some of it on the horns of the altar for incense, and poured out the rest at the base of the altar for burnt offering (cf. Lev. 4.16-18). Through this application of the blood in the prescribed manner, the priests made atonement for all the people of Israel (2 Chron. 29.24). This stage of the sacrificial ritual was thus dominated by the sin offering, which was the main sacrifice for atonement.

The second stage in the public sacrificial ritual was the presentation of the burnt offering (cf. Lev. 1.2–2.16; 6.8-23). After the various parts of the burnt offering had been laid out on the altar, the priest on duty added the cereal offerings consisting of flour mixed with olive oil, incense and salt, and then poured out the libation of wine upon the

1.   Welch argues that, since 29.20-24 largely duplicates the sacrifices in vv. 25-30, it is a later pro-priestly insertion. Von Rad (1930: 104), on the other hand, believes that vv. 25-30 has been added by a Levitical redactor to promote the status of the singers. Against these, Rudolph (*1955: 293) argues for the unity of the passage as an attempt to show the coincidence of sacrifice and song. He believes that the process of sacrifice is described twice, first without the song in vv. 21-24 and then with the song in v. 27 after the account of the preparation of the singers in vv. 25-26. In reaction to this rather forced solution, Petersen (1977: 83) notes that we have here the combination of the blood rite with the presentation of the burnt offering as two parts of the total sacrificial process.

2.   See Rendtorff 1967: 69-70, 129.

3.   For a recent analysis of the nature and function of the sin offering, see Kiuchi 1987.

altar. As all this was burnt upon the altar, the musicians performed
the choral service, and the congregation prostrated itself in the outer
court of the temple (2 Chron. 29.27-29).

The presentation of the burnt offering was the centre of the whole
sacrificial ritual. The rite for atonement by the disposal of blood was
regarded by the Chronicler as an act of preparation for it. While the
rite for the disposal of blood from the sin offerings included the disposal of blood from the burnt offerings, the sin offerings were obviously subordinated to the burnt offering by the priority given to the
slaughter of the animals for the burnt offering in 2 Chron. 29.22.[1] Thus
the rite for atonement is distinguished ritually and theologically from
the central rite for the presentation of the burnt offering. Both it and the
choral rite attached to it presuppose the prior enactment of atonement
but are not in themselves directly involved in the rite for atonement.

The public sacrifices were followed on this festive occasion by the
individual sacrifices of the people (29.31-35). These are classified as
'sacrifices of thanksgiving' in 29.31.[2] And they too were divided into
two groups, each with its own rites. First came the burnt offerings
brought by individuals as freewill offerings. They were given that
title, because they had not been commanded by the LORD, nor had
they been promised as votive offerings (2 Chron. 29.31-32; cf. Lev.
22.18-25). They were followed by the peace offerings, which were
called 'holy things', since they consisted of the firstlings which could
only be eaten at the sanctuary (2 Chron. 29.33-35; cf. Lev. 19.8;
22.12; Num. 18.19). They provided meat for the sacrificial banquets
at the temple. Certain portions from both kinds of private sacrifices
were laid upon the public burnt offering and burnt together with it.
They were therefore dependent on the public burnt offering for their
validity and efficacy.

According to Chronicles there was then a set order and sequence
for the performance of sacrificial worship at the temple.[3] While this

1.   While the bulls, rams and lambs could be included with the he-goats in
2 Chron. 29.21 as sin offerings, they are clearly distinguished in 29.22 from the
he-goats for the sin offering in 29.23-24.
2.   I follow Curtis and Madsen (*1910: 469) and Williamson (*1982: 359) in
taking the *waw* epexegetically.
3.   I therefore disagree with Rendtorff (1967: 72) in his emphatic denial of any
attempt by the Chronicler to present the sacrifices in a unified way according to an
integrated conception of them.

order distinguished the various parts of the service from each other
and related them sequentially to each other, like acts within a drama,
it also served to integrate the other sacrifices into the ritual for the
daily burnt offering.

The Public Sacrifices as an Integrated Ritual System
Of all the books in the Old Testament, Chronicles most evidently
envisages the sacrificial ritual as a unified whole, both in the combination of its main parts and in their common purpose. This notion of
an integrated pattern of ritual is explicated in 1 Chron. 6.49, 23.13b,
2 Chron. 2.4-6 and 13.10-11. The first two of these are general sum-
maries of priestly duties, while the last two are descriptions of the
sacrificial ritual in speeches dealing with particular circumstances. Yet
the recurrence of certain common terms, set in a similar frame of
reference, seems to indicate that they are meant to elucidate each other
in their development of common ritual concerns.

First, we have a general programmatic outline of priestly duties in
1 Chron. 6.49 (6.34):

> And Aaron and his sons were *burning up offerings*[1] upon the altar of
> burnt offering and the altar of incense for all the work of the *most holy
> things*,[2] to make atonement[3] for Israel, in accordance with everything that
> Moses the servant of God had commanded.

Here Chronicles summarizes the whole sacrificial ritual which the
priests were to perform in terms of a common activity with a common

---

1. The basic sense of *hiqṭîr* is to 'make go up in smoke'. In the Pentateuch this
verb is not only used for the burning of incense (Exod. 30.7, 8; 40.27) but also for
all 'the fire offerings' (Exod. 30.20), i.e. the guilt offerings (Lev. 7.5), the sin
offerings (e.g. Exod. 29.13; Lev. 4.10, 19), the peace offerings (e.g. Lev. 3.5, 11,
16), the burnt offerings (e.g. Exod. 29.18; Lev. 1.9, 13) and the cereal offerings
(e.g. Lev. 2.2, 9, 11).

2. This phrase can be taken to refer to three sets of things. First, it can refer to
'the most holy place' (2 Chron. 3.8; 4.22; 5.7). Secondly, it can refer to the tent of
meeting with its furniture and the utensils used in the performance of the sacrificial
ritual by the priests (cf. Exod. 30.26-29). Thirdly, it can refer to the substances used
in the sacrificial ritual such as the incense (Exod. 30.36), the showbread (Lev. 24.9),
the left over cerial offerings (Lev. 2.3, 10) and the meat from the sin and guilt offerings (Lev. 6.10, 18, 22; 7.6). By this term the Chronicler then covers the proper care
and use of all these by the priests in their performance of the sacrificial ritual.

3. The infinitive construct with the *waw* is best taken as a continuation of
maqṭîrîm to express its purpose. See GKC §114 p.

purpose. The activity of the priests is described as 'burning up': *maqṭîrîm*.[1] By this single term the Chronicler combines the rite for the burning of incense on the altar in the holy place[2] with the presentation of the burnt offerings on the altar before the temple. Through the enactment of these two parts of the daily ritual, the priests attended to the holy of holies and the most holy things. These were sanctified and kept holy by the daily ritual. The most holy things in turn mediated the LORD's holiness to those who handled them, so that they could stand in his presence and serve him. One purpose of the daily ritual, therefore, was to make atonement for the Israelites. Since this represents no innovation from the Pentateuch, the Chronicler sees no need to explain what it meant.

These embryonic ideas are elaborated in 1 Chron. 23.13b, where the following summary is to be found:

> And Aaron was set apart with his sons to consecrate[3] the *most holy things* by *burning up offerings*[4] in perpetuity before YWHH in ministry to him[5] and to bless in his name in perpetuity.

1. As in 1 Chron. 23.13b, 2 Chron. 2.6 (2.5), 26.18 and 29.11, this verb is used absolutely here for the sacrificial ritual rather than the offering of a specific sacrifice; cf. Edelman 1985.

2. See Haran 1978: 205-29 for an analysis of the ritual complex performed within the holy place.

3. Since the 3ms suffix cannot be construed as the object of the verb, given that the priests were not held to be most holy, it must be taken as the subject of the infinitive. Even though the expression is without parallel, it matches Exod. 29.43-44 in its sense.

4. Without warrant the RSV translates *haqṭîr* here by 'burn incense', as in 2 Chron. 2.6 (2.5); 28.3; 29.11; 32.12; 34.25 (K). While Rudolph (*1955: 156) considers that *lᵉhaqṭîr* and *lᵉbārēk* are governed by *lᵉhaqdîšô*, which is grammatically possible, I would argue that the priests were set aside for the twofold purpose of consecrating the most holy things and of blessing the people. *lᵉhaqṭîr* is then best construed as a gerund to describe how they consecrated the most holy things, as further elaborated in 2 Chron. 2.4 (2.3).

5. It is hard to make sense of this infinitive in relation to the other three infinitives in the sentence. The LXX treats it as a final clause which gives the purpose of the consecration of the most holy things. Yet that makes little sense, unless ministering to the LORD is taken as synonymous with blessing in his name. But, as Rothstein and Hänel argue (*1927: 416), *šrt* is a general term for all the work which the priests performed for the LORD and should therefore be construed here as a gerund.

The LORD's Song

This passage picks up the two key phrases 'most holy things' and 'burning offerings' from 1 Chron. 6.49 (6.34) and explains how they are connected with each other ritually. The most holy things, which were the substances sacrificed to the LORD, were consecrated by the performance of the total sacrificial ritual. In this description of the priests' ministry there is, however, no mention of atonement. Instead it focuses on two other goals. First, by the performance of the sacrificial ritual, the most holy things were made and kept holy, so that the LORD could meet with his people at the sanctuary (cf. Exod. 29.43-44). Secondly, during its performance the LORD's blessing was communicated to the people through the benediction given by the priests. Thus the consecration of the most holy things and the blessing of the people were the two main results of the sacrificial ritual performed by the priests.

In the statement of his intention to build the temple in 2 Chron. 2.4 (2.3) Solomon gives a list of the most holy things and tells how they were to be consecrated:

> I herewith intend to build a temple for the name of YHWH my God to *consecrate*[1] to him sweet incense, the regular layered bread and the burnt offerings, by *burning them up* before him morning and evening as well as on the sabbaths and new moons and the appointed feasts of YHWH our God.

In taking up the terms 'consecrate' and 'burning up' from the previous summary, the Chronicler explains what was consecrated as most holy and how. The process by which the offerings were 'burnt up' is divided into three parts: the burning of incense, the setting out of the showbread and the presentation of the burnt offerings. All these substances were most holy, and all were 'burnt up' to the LORD on the

---

1. The LXX, followed by most commentators and translators, assumes that the temple is the implied object of *leˠhaqdîš*. Yet this is at odds with the use of *qdš* in Chronicles. Solomon did not consecrate the temple to the LORD. While he did 'dedicate' (*piel* of *qdš*) its court (2 Chron. 7.7), he 'inaugurated' (*hiphil* of *ḥnk*) the temple (2 Chron. 7.5; cf. 7.9). The Lord however 'consecrated' (*hiphil* of *qdš*) the temple (2 Chron. 7.16, 20; 30.8; 36.14). I therefore propose that we should take this verse as an explication of 1 Chron. 23.13b and construe the incense, showbread and burnt offerings as the objects of *leˠhaqdîš*. This has the added advantage that there is then no need to assume that the phrases after *qeˠṭōret-sammîm* are truncated clauses connected to it by zeugma without their corresponding verbs, as Keil (*1870: 230) and Curtis and Madsen (*1910: 323) do.

prescribed occasions, even if this happened only to the incense of the showbread rather than the showbread itself (Lev. 24.7). Thus in the performance of the sacrificial ritual, the incense, showbread and burnt offerings were consecrated to the LORD at the temple.

In 2 Chron. 13.10-11 Abijah added a fourth element to the three parts of the sacrificial ritual listed in 2 Chron. 2.4 (2.3) by including the lamps as an object of 'burning up'.[1] This may have happened because olive oil was burnt in the lamps in the holy place and so could possibly qualify as a kind of sacrifice. In any case, the trimming and maintenance of the lamps was regarded in Exod. 30.7 as a part of the daily rite for the burning of incense. Thus the presentation of the burnt offerings, the burning of the incense, the arrangement of bread on the table and the maintenance of the lamps were all involved in the common unified ritual process of 'burning up' offerings to the LORD by the priests with the Levites as their assistants. This basic unity is emphasized still further by calling the whole activity the *mišmeret* of the LORD (2 Chron. 13.11). By their performance of this ritual, God's people guarded his presence from contact with impurity, like royal guards at the palace of a king, and attended to his affairs, like the courtiers of a king. Consequently, the LORD was with his people (2 Chron. 13.12) and used their kings to administer his rule (2 Chron. 13.8).

While the Chronicler uses *hiqṭîr* in these four passages to couple the rite at the altar of burnt offering with the rite for the burning of incense in the holy place, he describes the rite at the altar elsewhere as a unified whole by means of the verb *heʿelâ*. Whereas the verb is used most commonly as the term for the presentation of burnt offerings (1 Chron. 16.40; 23.31; 2 Chron. 1.6; 8.12-13; 23.18; 24.14; 29.7, 27, 29; 35.14, 16), it is also employed for their combination with libations and the fatty parts of the sin offerings and peace offerings (1 Chron. 16.2; 21.26; 29.21; 2 Chron. 29.21). Thus the author shows how all the sacrifices were interrelated with each other by their inclusion in the central rite for the presentation of burnt offerings upon the altar.

Summary

According to Chronicles, the sacrifices offered at the temple followed a fixed sequence within the general order of service. The public

---

1. While the LXX takes the incense and the showbread together with the burnt offerings as the objects of *maqṭîrîm*, it treats the last phrase as a nominal clause, since it probably could not conceive of the burning of the lamps as a sacrifice.

sacrifices came before the individual sacrifices, and both these had their own set sequence and pattern. All the other sacrifices and the supplementary rites were incorporated into the central rite for the presentation of the burnt offerings which was enacted twice every day. It was extended to include all the extra festive burnt offerings (2 Chron. 31.3) as well as all the other sacrifices (2 Chron. 29.20-35). Thus both the preceding public rite of atonement and the subsequent ceremonies for the individual sacrifices were related to this central rite and integrated with it.

The unity which resulted from this arrangement is expressed in Chronicles by his use of the verbs *he'ĕlâ* and *hiqṭîr* for the activity of the priests in presiding over the total performance. While the former verb shows how all the animal and cereal sacrifices at the temple were connected with the burnt offerings by having some of their parts burnt with them upon the altar, the latter verb links the burning of incense and its associated activities in the holy place with the presentation of the sacrifices on the altar of burnt offering.

This integrated system of sacrificial worship had two main goals. On the one hand, by the ritual disposal of the blood from the sacrifices, atonement was made for Israel. On the other hand, the presentation of the public burnt offering, which came after the rite of atonement and in consequence of it, served to consecrate the most holy things, so that the LORD could be present with his people and bless them. Thus the rite of atonement prepared for the meeting of the LORD with his people through the presentation of the burnt offering.

The Ritual Setting of Sacred Song

The Public Burnt Offering and Sacred Song
The most remarkable feature in the institution by David of sacred song was its deliberate synchronization with the presentation of the public burnt offering upon the altar. This ritual synchronization by David is mentioned in three places in Chronicles. First, in 1 Chron. 16.39-41 David is said to have arranged for the regular performance of thanksgiving by the guilds of Heman and Jeduthun during the presentation of burnt offerings by the priests upon the altar at Gibeon. Secondly, the ministry of music by the guild of Asaph before the ark in Jerusalem was designed in 1 Chron. 16.37 to coincide with the regular morning and evening sacrifices at Gibeon. Lastly, as part of

his reorganization of the Levites for their new duties at the temple, David decreed in 1 Chron. 23.30-31 that the Levitical musicians were to offer thanks and praise whenever the public burnt offerings were offered there.

Now this coupling of praise with the presentation of the burnt offering is even more remarkable, since, as Rendtorff (1967: 235) rightly maintains, the act of burning constituted the chief part of the ritual for that sacrifice. Because this arrangement resulted from deliberate regulation rather than by accident, it would seem that, for Chronicles, the performance of praise somehow complemented the presentation of the burnt offerings.[1] It was thus not a peripheral undertaking, conducted, as it were, at the fringes of the sacrificial system, but it was attached to the very centre, around which everything else revolved.

The Synchronization of Sacred Song with the Burnt Offering. In Chronicles the order for the performance of public sacrificial worship was, as has already been established, divided into two parts. The first part revolved around the sprinkling of blood from the animals for the burnt offering and from the animals for the occasional sin offerings in the rite of atonement. The second part had to do with the presentation of the burnt offering upon the main altar before the entrance of the temple.

Whereas earlier in the book of Chronicles (1 Chron. 16.40-41, 23.30-31, 2 Chron. 8.12-14 and 23.18) sacred song had been associated rather generally with the presentation of the burnt offerings, in 2 Chron. 29.27-28 it was coordinated quite precisely with the second stage of the ritual for the public sacrifices. The narrative, which otherwise highlights only some significant features of the ceremony for the restoration of public worship at the temple, states that the song of the LORD began when the burnt offerings began, and ended when they ended. These two activities were then synchronized exactly with each other. Both also occurred in close proximity to each other, for the musicians stood in front of the altar as the burnt offering was presented upon it.

The care which the Chronicler takes in defining the exact relationship between the two shows that this was a matter of some significance

---

1.   Apart from Chronicles, sacrifice is associated explicitly with song only in Amos 5.21-24. It is also alluded to in passing in Pss. 27.6; 50.14, 23; 61.8; 66.1-15; 96.8; 107.22; Isa. 51.3; 62.9; Jer. 33.11.

for him in his theology of worship. It is, of course, also significant for his understanding of the choral service which, however, despite its prominence, is not his main concern in ch. 29. The placement of this account of the choral rite by the author within his detailed delineation of the order and sequence of the sacrifices at the temple suggests that the coordination of sacred song with the presentation of the burnt offerings has something to say about their significance within the whole sacrificial system. Since only the burnt offering is singled out for accompaniment by song, both these must in some way have qualified each other as two complementary activities.

The Significance of this Synchronization. The only scholar who has considered why praise took such a prominent place in the performance of public sacrifices in Chronicles is J. Hausmann (1987: 89-90). She holds that the coordination of sacrifice with praise is an innovation of the Chronicler, and she gives two reasons for it. First, she notes that the performance of praise is mentioned in the accounts of the following main events in the history of worship at Jerusalem: the transferral of the ark there (1 Chron. 15–16), the completion of David's preparations for building the temple (1 Chron. 29.10-19), the dedication of the temple (2 Chron. 5.11-13; 7.1-6), and the temple's rededication by Hezekiah (2 Chron. 29.25-30) with the consequent Feast of Unleavened Bread (2 Chron. 30.21-22). The first function of sacred song was therefore to make thanksgiving for the LORD's actions in establishing and maintaining Israel's worship at its proper place in Jerusalem. Indeed, the whole system of sacrificial worship was regarded as the LORD's great gift to his people. Secondly, she maintains that the singers praised the LORD for his work of atonement in the sacrifices. But she does not back up this point exegetically, nor does she comment any further on its significance.

If the casual reference in Amos 5.21-24 is any indication of the popular theology of worship in Israel, then the Israelites would have presented their sacrifices to the accompaniment of music and song, so that the LORD would thereby be moved to listen to them and accept their sacrifices. They sang their songs in order to induce him to favour them in some way. There are, however, no traces of this popular theology in Chronicles, with its emphasis on the divine institution of the sacrifices; their validity and efficacy depended on their performance according to their divine institution rather than on divine whim. The Chronicler seems rather to have quite deliberately dissociated the LORD's song in 2 Chron. 29.21-29 from the rite of atonement in order to counteract this popular theology, for he associates sacred song quite unequivocally with the presentation of the public burnt offering.

In 2 Chron. 29.21-29 the Chronicler clearly distinguishes the blood rite from the presentation of the burnt offering. The blood rite served to make atonement for all Israel (29.24), but nothing is said in the following verses about the purpose of the rite for the presentation of the burnt offering. This can, however, be established from the context. Hezekiah maintains that, just as the LORD brought his wrath upon his people for turning their faces from him by closing down his dwelling place and ceasing to present the daily burnt offerings in the holy place (2 Chron. 29.6-10), so he would also avert his wrath and show a gracious face to those who participated in the sacrificial worship at the sanctuary (2 Chron. 30.6-9; cf. 29.10). Since the Chronicler conceived of the temple as the LORD's palace (1 Chron. 29.1, 19; cf. 17.14), he seems to have envisaged the sacrificial ritual as the daily audience of the heavenly King with his courtiers and subjects. Thus the LORD, who had demonstrated his acceptance of Solomon's prayer by sending down fire upon the altar of burnt offering, and had sanctified the temple by filling and covering it with his glory (2 Chron. 7.1-3), also assured him that he would continue to receive his people and answer their petitions whenever they offered their sacrifices there to him (2 Chron. 7.12-16; cf. 20.9). The same point is made by the Chronicler at the end of his account of the Passover which celebrated the restoration of the sacrificial ritual under Hezekiah. He notes in 2 Chron. 30.27 that the LORD answered the prayers of his people and conveyed his blessing to them through the benediction spoken by the priests at the festival. So, then, by means of the daily burnt offering, the LORD held his daily audience with his priests and his people, like an emperor at his palace.

As has already been established, the rite of atonement was performed within the first part of the order for the public sacrifices at the temple. It involved the priests disposing in the prescribed way the blood from the sacrificial victims. By the ritual application of the blood which the LORD had given for the purpose of atonement (Lev. 17.11), the LORD himself acted for the benefit of his people.[1] He cleansed them of their impurity and forgave them their unwitting trespasses, so that he could admit them in his presence as recipients of his blessing.

Now it is significant that in both places where the Chronicler mentions the rite of atonement, 1 Chron. 6.49 and 2 Chron. 29.24, he connects it with the musical ministry of the Levites. 1 Chron. 6.49 is part of the programmatic summary of ritual duties at the centre of the genealogies in 1 Chronicles 1–8. There in 6.31-53 the ministry of the singers (6.31-32) is distinguished from the duties of their fellow Levites (6.48) and the priests (6.49). Even though the relationship between these three sections is obscured by the genealogical material inserted in 6.33-47, the two disjunctive participial clauses in 6.48-49 (6.33-34) are obviously built grammatically and syntactically upon 6.31-32 (6.16-17). Thus we have the ministry of song juxtaposed with, and yet distinguished from, the work of the Levites at the tabernacle and the performance of sacrificial atonement by the priests. Yet, while this narrative fragment links the ministry of song with the rite of atonement, it does not show how they were related to each other and why.

That relation is spelled out in 2 Chron. 29.21-30 in the account of the reconsecration of the temple under Hezekiah. The essential feature in the process of its reconsecration was the rite of atonement, by which all impurity was eliminated from the sanctuary, monarchy and nation, so that the LORD's wrath would cease and his presence would once again be restored.[2] Since this occasion had to do with the purification of the temple and the restoration of public worship, it also served the Chronicler as a suitable case for defining the exact relationship between the rite of atonement and the performance of sacred song.

The order is quite unambiguous. First came the rite of atonement (2 Chron. 29.21-24). During its enactment no songs were sung. The rite of atonement was preparatory in character. It cleared away the obstacles in the way of the LORD's acceptance of his people; it created the state of ritual purity which was the necessary condition for his presence; it ensured that the LORD would manifest himself in blessing rather than in wrath to the assembled congregation. Once that had been

---

1. In this I follow the interpretation of Lev. 17.11 given by Kiuchi (1987: 101-109), who argues that this refers to the blood from all kinds of sacrifices.

2. Johnstone (1986: 119) has shown that 2 Chron. 29 serves as a paradigm for the Chronicler's understanding of sacrilege (*ma'al*) and his view of the institutions ordained to deal with its consequences.

completed, the burnt offering was presented upon the altar. Through it the LORD signalled his acceptance of the people and made himself available to them. It was the institutionalized form of the LORD's theophany, which had been foreshadowed by the LORD's response to David in 1 Chron. 21.26 and granted to Solomon in 2 Chron. 7.1-3.[1]

The response of the people to the presentation of the burnt offering in 2 Chron. 29.25-29 mirrored the response of the congregation to the LORD's appearance at the dedication of the temple in 2 Chron. 7.1-3. As the sacrifices were being burnt upon the altar, the trumpets, which announced the LORD's presence, called for the prostration of the congregation in his presence, and the song of the LORD was sung by the musicians. Thus the choral service came after the rite of atonement had been completed. It did not attempt to secure a favourable response from the LORD but presupposed such a response as something already given. The musicians proclaimed the LORD's name during the presentation of the sacrifices, so that he would come to his people and bless them, as he had promised in Exod. 20.24 and demonstrated in 2 Chron. 7.1-3 (see diagram, p. 132).

Summary. The choral rite thus derived its ritual function and significance from its association with the burnt offering. It presupposed that all the obstacles to the LORD's acceptance of his people had been removed by the rite for atonement. It proclaimed the LORD's presence with his people at the altar, his acceptance of them and his readiness to receive petitions from them. The sacred song was coordinated with the presentation of the burnt offering so that it would announce his advent and celebrate his gracious presence with his people. The songs of thanksgiving and praise, arising from the LORD's meeting with his people at the altar, were thus offered as he came and made himself available to them there. In their songs the musicians praised his generosity and rejoiced in him as their good and gracious God, while the burnt offering was presented to him (1 Chron. 16.39-41). Through its coupling with the choral service, therefore, the burnt offering became

---

1.   In both of these cases the LORD's appearance is significant for the Chronicler. First, it authorized the site for worship and David's provisions for worship at that site. Secondly, it established a precedent for what would subsequently happen there in worship. If his people called upon him during the presentation of their sacrifices there, as David and Solomon had done, he would answer them and signal his presence with them there by the fire on the altar.

the means by which the people celebrated God's goodness and rejoiced in his generosity.

Ritual Prostration and Sacred Song

The choral rite was not only synchronized with the presentation of the burnt offering but also with the ritual prostration of the congregation in the LORD's presence. In this way the congregation participated both in the presentation of the burnt offering and in the performance of sacred song. By their synchronization all three rites qualified each other in their ritual function and significance.

The Nature and Significance of Ritual Prostration. In his extensive study on nonverbal communication in the ancient world, M.I. Gruber (1980: 90-145, 187-201) analyses the social and religious significance of prostration in ancient Israel. He shows that it was by no means unique to Israel but was a common gesture in antiquity. The chief verb for this act in the Old Testament is *hištaḥᵃwâ*.[1] In its primary usage it does not denote a mental attitude but a specific bodily act that can convey a variety of attitudes and purposes depending on the context of its enactment. As O. Keel (1978: 309) has shown from Egyptian iconography, the rite of prostration occurred in three stages—stooping from the waist with outstretched hands, kneeling down with one knee bent forward and the other pushed back, and the placing of the face with the hands on the ground before the object of respect.

In the ancient Orient the act of prostration was used in both secular and sacred contexts. Thus people would prostrate themselves before their superiors on meeting with them. In some cases this was prescribed by custom, while in others it was a spontaneous gesture in acknowledgement of their status. As a stock gesture of homage and subservience it not only acknowledged the superior status of another (Gruber 1980: 187-201) but also functioned as an inarticulate expression of gratitude, or as a dramatic act of supplication (Gruber 1980: 98-105).

As a common mode of communication in that cultural context, its 'speech' was more performative than informative. By the formality of prostration, a person did not merely express submissiveness but actually submitted to another person, and that in the most dramatic fashion at

---

1. For the etymology of this verb, see Emerton 1977; Davies 1979; Kreuzer 1985.

his disposal, given the natural human aversion to expressions of sub-servience. Its symbolic significance as a performative enactment led to its use in ritual contexts that combined customary gestures with set modes of speech in a symbolic transaction. Thus custom and protocol required that people prostrate themselves before a king and in the presence of a deity.

Culturally speaking, the Israelite practice of prostration differed from its pagan environment only in its religious application. Here two things stand out most sharply. First, in the decalogue the Israelites were strictly forbidden to prostrate themselves before any idol (Exod. 20.5; Deut. 5.9). This prohibition was extended to prostration before any Canaanite gods (Exod. 23.24) and any deity except the LORD (Exod. 34.14).[1] Secondly and more remarkably, even though prostra-tion before idols and other gods is proscribed, there is no corres-ponding prescription in the Pentateuch for prostration before the LORD except at the presentation of first fruits in Deut. 26.10, nor is there any definition of the proper place for cultic prostration. It seems to be taken for granted that the Israelites would do so at their various sanctuaries, but no directions are given as to when, where and how this should be done. Thus the evidence from the Pentateuch shows that prostration was largely a customary matter.

Yet for all that, it was common for individuals and the congregation to prostrate themselves before the LORD in worship. It is mentioned together with the presentation of the yearly sacrifices by Elkanah at Shiloh (1 Sam. 1.3; cf. 1.19, 28). After the transferral of the ark to Jerusalem, it was practised there (Ps. 132.7). As part of a programme of liturgical centralisation, Hezekiah destroyed all the altars at other sanctuaries and allowed prostration only at the altar in Jerusalem (2 Kgs 18.22; cf. Isa. 36.7; 2 Chron. 32.12). So, when a lay person entered the temple in Jerusalem on a festival, he would come through the inner gates to prostrate himself before the LORD at the altar (Jer. 7.2; 26.2). Apart from this initial act of homage, the individual Israelite is said to have prostrated himself at the temple on three other occasions—at the presentation of the first fruits (Deut. 26.10), in

---

1. By the prohibition of prostration, the Israelites were prevented from partici-pating in the pagan cults, which seems to indicate that this was the most decisive part of the ritual for the pagan devotee. Thus Deuteronomy always links prostration to alien gods with serving them (see *'ābad* in Deut. 4.19; 8.19; 11.16; 17.3; 29.25; 30.17; cf. 5.9).

supplication for divine help (Ps. 5.7-8), and in thanksgiving for divine help (Ps. 138.2). More importantly, prostration seems to have become part of the ritual for the public worship of the congregation. We find mention of corporate prostration in connection with the presentation of the sacrifices (Lev. 9.24; 2 Kgs 17.36; Ps. 96.9), the performance of liturgical song (Pss. 66.4; 96.1-9), and congregational acclamation (Lev. 9.24; Ps. 95.1-2, 6). As a part of the rite for entry into the LORD's holy presence, it therefore became an act of corporate homage to the heavenly King (Pss. 95.6; 96.9; 99.5, 9).

The performance of ritual prostration by individuals and the congregation is thus mentioned in passing in texts from all periods in the history of worship at the temple in Jerusalem. But apart from the absolute prohibition of prostration before idols and alien deities, not much was made of its ritual function and significance, for the point of it was most likely considered self-evident and its sense was uncontested. In his account of Hezekiah's measures in 2 Chron. 29.25-30, the Chronicler, however, picks up the various threads from elsewhere in the Old Testament to show that the singing of the choir coincided with the prostration of the congregation at the presentation of the burnt offering. As attested in Sir. 50.14-19 and *m. Tam.* 7.3, this was the regular practice in the second temple which lasted until its destruction.

The Coordination of Sacred Song with Congregational Prostration. Just as Chronicles presents the gradual development of choral music at Jerusalem from David to Hezekiah, so it also shows how choral music came to be combined with the practice of ritual prostration over the same period.[1] This development which occurred in three stages, is, however, not portrayed as the result of a divine command but as a gradual process of human innovation which led from ritual precedent to ritual custom.

The first stage in this development is mentioned in 1 Chron. 16.29. As part of the daily thanksgiving sung by the Asaphites for David and the Israelites before the ark in Jerusalem, this verse has programmatic

---

1. The combination of music with prostration and the presentation of gifts to a king is already found in a Middle Assyrian ritual text (*KAR* 136.iii, 1-5) from the reign of Tukulti-Ninurta I. These lines, which describe part of the protocol for a king's coronation, have been translated and analysed by K.F. Müller (1937: 14, 32). After the king's coronation, his courtiers prostrated themselves before him, kissed his feet and presented gifts to him, as music was played.

significance here in Chronicles. The purpose of the choral performance was, among other things, to call all the nations of the earth to
sing to the LORD (1 Chron. 16.13-30), as they acknowledged his kingship voluntarily by offering tribute and prostrating themselves to him
(16.29). Thus the ultimate point of the thanksgiving was to elicit the
willing prostration of all the nations with Israel to the LORD.

According to the Chronicler's account, the second stage of this
development was completed at the dedication of the temple by Solomon.
The record of this is found in 2 Chron. 7.1-3:

v. 1   A   When Solomon had finished praying, *fire came down from the heavens* and devoured the burnt offering and the sacrifices,[1]

       B   as *the glory of YHWH was filling the house.*

v. 2   B′   The priests could not enter the house of YHWH, *since the glory of YHWH was filling the house.*

v. 3   A′   When all the Israelites saw *the descent of the fire* and the glory of YHWH over the house, they stooped down with their faces to the ground on the pavement, prostrated themselves, and gave thanks[2] to YHWH, 'Truly he is good! Truly his generosity is for ever!'[3]

This account does not merely repeat what happened in 2 Chron. 5.13-
14, but reports a further development in the LORD's manifestation of
his glory.[4] This is emphasized by the chiastic pattern of the narrative,

1.   The phrase *hāʿōlâ wᵉhazzᵉbāhîm*, which occurs only here in Chronicles,
seems to be equivalent to *hāʿōlâ wᵉhaššᵉlāmîm* in 1 Chron. 16.2 (cf. 2 Chron. 31.2),
hāʿōlâ wᵉhahᵃlābîm in 2 Chron. 35.14 (cf. 7.7), and *ʿōlôt ûšᵉlāmîm* in 1 Chron.
16.1 and 21.26. The singular form shows that this was the regular, prescribed public
burnt offering (cf. 2 Chron. 29.7, 24, 27, 28).

2.   This is best construed as an infinitive absolute (cf. GKC §75 n) in the place
of a *waw* consecutive imperfect.

3.   *kî* can be construed in two ways in this refrain here and in 1 Chron. 16.34,
41; 2 Chron. 5.13; 20.21. It is usually taken as a causal conjunction to give the
reason for the call to praise. Yet Crüsemann (1967: 32-50) has shown that it originally functioned as an emphatic deictic particle to give the words of praise. While *kî*
ceased to function thus in some late hymnic material, he argues that it still executes
the call to praise in Chronicles (1967: 44).

4.   Welch (1939: 37-41) claims that the two sets of sacrifices in 5.6 and 7.1, as
well as the two appearances of the LORD's glory in 5.14 and 7.1-2, are evidence of
the later addition of 7.1-3 to the original text of Chronicles. His arguments, however,
carry little weight. While 5.6 refers to the slaughter of the animals, 7.1 describes
their presentation upon the altar at the temple. In response to a similar assertion by
Bertheau (*1854: 286) that 7.1-3 contradicted the events in 5.13-14, Keil (*1870:
245-46) had already argued that Chronicles presented a double manifestation of the

which correlates the descent of fire with the appearance of the LORD's glory by treating the former as a consequence of the latter. First, the glory of the LORD, veiled in a cloud, filled the temple. Then that glory, presumably still veiled in a cloud, was made manifest over the temple as fire descended to kindle the sacrifices on the altar. Just as according to P the glory of the LORD is said to have filled the tabernacle (Exod. 40.34-35), before regular worship was inaugurated at its altar by the flash of fire from the LORD's presence (Lev. 9.24), so the temple was first filled with the LORD's glory, before he manifested it outside the temple to the people to signal his acceptance of the temple (2 Chron. 7.5) and its altar (2 Chron. 7.9).

The narrative of this event consists of a dense mass of allusions to demonstrate that with the dedication of the temple, we have the culmination of Israel's worship as instituted by the LORD for his presence with his people.[1] Since the glory of the LORD filled the temple, the priests, like Moses with the tabernacle (Exod. 40.34-35), were unable to enter it. As the fiery cloud, which both veiled and revealed the LORD's glory, was 'over' the tabernacle (Exod. 40.36, 38; cf. Num. 9.15-23), so the people saw the glory of the LORD 'over' the temple. The congregation in Jerusalem prostrated itself at the appearance of the LORD's glory, just as their ancestors used to do whenever the glory cloud appeared at the tent of meeting (Exod. 33.10). As fire fell from heaven in answer to Elijah's prayer in 1 Kgs 18.38 and David's prayer in 1 Chron. 21.26, so fire came down from heaven in answer to Solomon's prayer of dedication. Just as the Israelites 'shouted' (*yārōnnû*) and fell on their faces at the appearance of the LORD's glory with the consumption of sacrifices by fire from the LORD on the altar of the tabernacle in Lev. 9.24, so they prostrated themselves on the temple pavement and gave thanks to the LORD at the manifestation of his glory with the fire from heaven, when the temple was dedicated.

LORD's glory, first by the cloud in the temple which was visible only to the priests, and then by the fire upon the altar which was visible to the whole congregation. Furthermore, Williamson (*1982: 222) points out that, since the order of words in 7.1c marks it out as a disjunctive circumstantial clause, *mālē'* is best construed as a participle. Thus the sacrifices were offered as the LORD's glory was filling the temple. He therefore rightly concludes that 7.1-3 is not a duplicate of 5.13-14.

1. See also Mosis 1973: 147-52.

This last allusion to Lev. 9.24 is the most telling, as it brings together sacrifice, prostration and song, by associating them all with the appearance of the LORD in his glory to his people at the temple. In Lev 9.4, 6 the Israelites were told to inaugurate the presentation of sacrifices at the tabernacle, so that the LORD could 'appear' to them in his glory. Then when the people 'saw' his glory as they were blessed by Moses and Aaron, they responded with shouts and prostration.

Now in his account of the temple's dedication, the Chronicler replaces the shouting of the people with their singing of the refrain for thanksgiving. While he could indeed have understood their shouting as singing already in Leviticus, it seems to me that the point of this allusion is both to establish a precedent and to draw a contrast. The response of the people at the dedication of the temple had its precedent in the inauguration of worship at the tabernacle. But, whereas the amazement of the people at God's gracious presence with them could then only be expressed by unspoken joy and unmusical acclamation, the dedication of the temple and the institution of the temple choir meant that it could now be voiced in songs of thanksgiving. Thus, with the construction and dedication of the temple, the people could respond more fully and appropriately than ever before to their God in prostration and praise.

By its use of allusion, this narrative then highlights the response of the people to the LORD's presence. The same point is also made in another way. Even though it is stated quite explicitly in 2 Chron. 5.13 and 7.6 that the Levitical choir sang the refrain of thanksgiving both before and after the prayer of Solomon, 2 Chron. 7.3 says that the people did so at this critical point without mentioning the role of the choir. Now while this could indicate that it was a sheer spontaneous reaction, which is rather unlikely given the obvious formality of this solemn event, or else that they sang the refrain together with the choir, which is much more likely, it seems to me that the author makes a different point altogether. Whereas previously the choir had sung the thanksgiving by themselves for the king and the congregation, the congregation could now also participate directly in their praise due to the new facilities at the temple. The people therefore became involved in the thanksgiving of the choir and made it their own. Now too for the first time the prostration of the congregation could be combined ritually with the performance of sacred song as the proper response to the LORD's acceptance of their sacrifices and to his epiphany to them at the altar.[1]

The third and final stage in the combination of prostration with sacred song is mentioned in 2 Chron. 29.27-30:

v. 27	A	Then *Hezekiah* commanded them to *offer* the burnt offering on the altar.
	B	At the same time that the *burnt offering* began,
	C	the *song of YHWH* began with the *trumpets* alongside the instruments of David, the king of Israel,
v. 28	D	as[2] the whole assembly was *prostrating itself*,
	C′	and the song was resounding, and the *trumpets* were blowing;
	B′	all this (went on) until the completion of the *burnt offering*.
v. 29	A′/D′	At the completion of the *offering* the king and all those present with him stooped down and *prostrated themselves*.
v. 30		Then Hezekiah and the princes commanded the Levites to praise YHWH with the words of David and Asaph the seer. So they offered praise for rejoicing and fell down and prostrated themselves.

This résumé of the ritual reforms undertaken by Hezekiah exhibits a complex pattern of organization. First, it is divided into two parts, vv. 27-29 and v. 30, by the two commands of Hezekiah. Each of these consists of the command and the record of its fulfilment. Secondly, these two parts are united thematically by the mention of prostration in vv. 28, 29 and 30 as well as their concern for the regulation of the choral service. Thirdly, the material in vv. 27-29 is arranged chiastically. In this chiasm the information about the burnt offering frames the description of the choral service. That in turn includes the mention of congregational prostration at the centre of the chiasm which, however, also recurs at its closure.

While the account in 29.27-29 seems to be mainly concerned with the interrelationship of sacrifice with prostration and sacred song, it is difficult to unravel the exact sequence of events as indicated in its syntactical structure. The main problem is the relation of the three disjunctive participial clauses in v. 28 to each other and to the main verb.[3] Since they are disjunctive circumstantial clauses, the activities

1. See Rudolph *1955: 217.

2. Andersen (1970: 48) demonstrates that a disjunctive participial clause indicates discontinuity of activity.

3. Levine (1965: 314) notes that in the Mishnah the participle is used, with or without *hāyâ*, to describe what is proper procedure in ritual texts. This seems to be

which they describe occurred during the singing of the song. Yet we do not know whether they were performed sequentially or simultaneously, or whether they were related to each other in some unspecified way. While it is clear that the song of the LORD was offered simultaneously with the burnt offering, some scholars claim that the trumpets were sounded and the congregation remained prostrate for the duration of the song. Now if that were the case, there would be no need to mention the sounding of the song in v. 28b and the final act of prostration in 29, for the choir would still be singing, and the people would still be prostrate.[1] It makes better sense to take the three participial clauses as circumstantial clauses, which, as in 2 Chron. 7.6, list the various components of the ritual. These consisted of the song accompanied by the musical instruments, the prostration of the people, and the sounding of the trumpets to signal prostration. The trumpets were mentioned first and last, because they announced the initial and final acts of prostration.

By its syntax, vv. 27b-28 makes three points about the prostration of the congregation. First, it subordinates both it and the sacred song to the presentation of the burnt offering. Secondly, it connects the prostration of the congregation with the performance of praise and the blowing of the trumpets, without, however, defining their exact correlation in terms of simultaneity or sequence. The result is that, while v. 29 and v. 30 mention two definite acts of prostration, the participle in v. 28a speaks generally of prostration in connection with the LORD's song without stating when it occurred. Thirdly, it presents the prostration of the congregation at the centre and conclusion of the rite for the presentation of the burnt offerings to show that this was the intended response to the burnt offering and the song.

2 Chron. 29.27-30 thus depicts three kinds of prostration in association with the choral performance.[2] First, there was the prostration of

the case here as well as in 1 Chron. 6.33-49 (6.18-34) and 2 Chron. 7.6.

1. Gruber (1980: 119-20) circumvents this problem by positing that the act of prostration was performed separately by three different groups—the congregation (v. 28), the king and his entourage (v. 29) and the Levites (v. 30). *hannimṣe'îm* in v. 29 must, however, refer to the congregation, as is shown by its use in 2 Chron. 30.21; 31.1; 34.32, 33; 35.7, 17, 18.

2. See Rudolph *1955: 293-94. Williamson (*1982: 358-59) disagrees with him and argues that 29.28 does not refer to an act of prostration, since when the Chronicler intends a specific act of prostration he adds another verb, as in vv. 29 and 30. Yet it hardly makes sense to take *mištaḥ{}^awîm* in v. 28 as an indication of the

the congregation during its performance. There was obviously no set pattern to this. It may have occurred both at the beginning and during breaks in the service as was the later custom (*m. Tam.* 7.3). Secondly, there was the prostration at the end of the song. By the combination of *kāraʿ* with *hištaḥ^awâ* in v. 29, Chronicles alludes to 2 Chron. 7.3, which is the only other place with this combination. By means of this cross-reference, the Chronicler could perhaps imply that, since the LORD appeared to his people in the presentation of the burnt offerings according to the precedent set by his initial theophany at the dedication of the temple, the people were to respond to the burnt offering as they had done at the visible manifestation of his glory. Lastly, after the final act of praise, the singers themselves, now unencumbered by their instruments, since the song was over, performed their act of prostration. In all these the members of the congregation acknowledged the presence of their Lord with them, as announced to them in the choral rite.

The Chronicler holds that Hezekiah completed what David and Solomon had begun. In his ritual reforms he connected sacred song with the rite of prostration, so that the congregation could thereby participate in the praise of the musicians by paying homage to the one whose presence was celebrated in their song.

Summary. The book of Chronicles traces the gradual association of ritual prostration with the performance of praise. Its author uses the ideology of Psalm 96 and the precedent of the events from the inauguration of sacrificial worship at the tabernacle in Leviticus 9 to explore the reasons for their correlation. By the time of Hezekiah, sacred song and the prostration of the congregation are regarded by the Chronicler as a regular part of the ritual for the presentation of the public burnt offering. When they prostrated themselves, the Israelites acknowledged that their Lord had come to be with them and bless them by accepting their sacrifices, as he had promised in Exod. 20.24. Whereas the choral music proclaimed his presence, the act of prostration greeted him in a complex gesture which combined homage with gratitude, and respect with supplication. Thus sacred song was meant to evoke the proper response of the congregation to the LORD's presence with them as expressed ritually in the act of prostration.

congregation's attitude, when all the other verbs in vv. 27-30 describe concrete ritual actions, and the same verb reappears to describe the act of prostration.

The Thank-Offering and Sacred Song

In Chronicles sacred song is most obviously associated with the presentation of the burnt offering. This in itself is remarkable, as singing is most commonly connected with the thank-offering in the psalms. The ritual connection was, in fact, so close that the term *tôdâ* had come to mean both the thank-offering and the thanksgiving performed at its presentation. In the postexilic period it was also the designation for the Levitical choirs (Neh. 12.31, 38, 40). In this section I therefore intend to investigate what the Chronicler says about the rite for the thank-offering and whether the temple choir was involved in the performance of the concomitant thanksgiving.

Thanksgiving and Thank-Offering. The thank-offerings differed from the public burnt offerings by being occasional, individual sacrifices. They, in turn, were distinguished from the votive offerings and freewill offerings (Lev. 7.11-17). While the votive offering differed from the freewill offering by being paid to fulfil a vow, both could be presented either with or without a song of thanksgiving.[1] Thus both freewill offerings (Ps. 54.8) and votive offerings (Pss. 50.14; 56.13; 116.17-18; Jon. 2.9) were regarded as thank-offerings. Furthermore, not only peace offerings but also burnt offerings were presented as thank-offerings with songs of thanksgiving (2 Chron. 29.31b-34; cf. Ps. 66.13-15).

While most scholars agree that the distinctive feature of this sacrifice was its association with the performance of thanksgiving,[2] the actual details can only be deduced from the form and contents of the psalms for individual thanksgiving. The most likely procedure has been outlined by Crüsemann (1969: 225-51). He argues that the alternation in these psalms between the second person mode of address to the LORD and the third person mode of narrative about him originally arose from the two main parts of the ritual for the thank-offering. On the one hand, the person who brought the offering addressed the LORD directly as he presented his sacrifice to him before the altar and so identified its nature and purpose. On the other hand, he addressed his guests and the congregation in his report of what the LORD had

1.   As far as I can discover, this was first proposed by Ewald (1876: 52-53); cf. Eerdmans 1912: 21-22; Stevenson 1950: 488.
2.   See Gunkel 1933: 266-67; Hermisson 1965: 42; Rowley 1967: 179; Mowinckel 1967: II, 31; Mayer 1986: 437.

done for him. In the case of the presentation of the burnt offering for thanksgiving, this could have occurred during the procession into or out of the inner court; in the case of the presentation of the peace offering for thanksgiving, this could have occurred during the subsequent sacrificial banquet. That, however, must remain a matter of conjecture, as the psalms do not themselves describe the exact circumstances of the song.

The Chronicler first associates the presentation of public peace offerings with the performance of praise at the dedication of the temple in 2 Chron. 7.4-6. There he distinguishes the public peace offerings, endowed by Solomon, from the public burnt offerings which had previously been presented in 2 Chron. 7.1-3. By attaching 7.6 to the material on the peace offerings from 1 Kgs 8.62-63, he reinterprets them as a public thank-offering by the king and the people:

v. 4   Then the king and all the people offered sacrifices before YHWH.

v. 5   King Solomon offered 22,000 cattle and 120,000 sheep as a sacrifice.[1] So the king and all the people dedicated the house of God.

v. 6   As the priests were standing at their watches, and the Levites (were standing) with the instruments for YHWH's song, which King David had made for giving thanks to YHWH, 'Truly his generosity is forever!', whenever David offered praises through them, and the priests were blowing trumpets opposite them, all the Israelites were also standing.

In this account the Chronicler has three things to say about the performance of song during the presentation of the public thank-offerings. First, David had instituted the temple choir with their instruments to perform songs of thanksgiving for himself and the people. Secondly, in contrast to the act of prostration during the performance of praise with the presentation of the burnt offering, all the clergy and the whole congregation stood at attention in their respective places during the song of thanksgiving for the thank-offerings, just as the subjects of King David stood during their audience with him. Thirdly, the priests with their trumpets were involved with the Levitical musicians in the performance of thanksgiving (cf. 2 Chron. 30.21-22). Thus in 2 Chron. 7.4-6 the Chronicler traces the performance of choral music during the presentation of the public thank-offerings back to the institution of

---

1.   The Chronicler apparently omitted *haššᵉlāmîm 'ᵃšer zābaḥ lᵉYHWH* from 1 Kgs 8.63 in order to depict these sacrifices as thank-offerings rather than as mere peace offerings.

thanksgiving by David and the organization of the temple services by Solomon.

According to 2 Chron. 29.31-33, Hezekiah arranged for the presentation of private thank-offerings after the completion of the public burnt offering.[1] Whether this was viewed as an innovation or merely the regularization of existing practice for the centralization of worship at Jerusalem, we cannot tell. But it was almost certainly the custom in the postexilic period.[2] The thank-offerings were offered in the slot allotted to the individual sacrifices at the festivals (2 Chron. 29.31b-33). The voluntary burnt offerings for thanksgiving, which were clearly distinguished from the peace offerings in being totally burnt, were probably offered first.[3] Then came the peace offerings for thanksgiving, which are called 'consecrated offerings' in 2 Chron. 29.33. So the Chronicler held that, from the reform of Hezekiah, the thank-offerings occupied a fixed position at the head of the private sacrifices.

Scholars disagree whether the persons presenting the thank-offerings sang the song of thanksgiving,[4] or whether it was sung for them by the temple musicians.[5] The mention of musical instruments in connection with thanksgiving (Pss. 33.2-3; 71.22-23; 92.1-3) and the reference to musical accompaniment in the vows of thanksgiving (Pss. 7.17; 21.13; 27.6; 57.7, 9; 59.17; 61.8; 71.22-23; 144.9) and in the psalms of thanksgiving (Pss. 18.49; 30.4, 12; 33.2; 66.4; 75.9; 92.1; 138.1) argue for their customary performance by the musicians. It could well have been a matter of choice depending either on the initial vow or on the ability to make the requisite payment to the musicians.

---

1.   The sense of $z^e b\bar{a}h\hat{i}m$ varies in Chronicles, depending on its context. It can be the term for all animal sacrifices (1 Chron. 29.21a; 2 Chron. 7.4-5; cf. 7.12). When it is paired with '$\bar{o}l\hat{o}t$, it refers to all the peace offerings (1 Chron. 29.21b; 2 Chron. 7.1). The peace offerings can be designated more generally as $zibh\hat{e}$ $\check{s}^e l\bar{a}m\hat{i}m$ (2 Chron. 30.22), or more specifically as $zibh\hat{e}$ $\check{s}^e l\bar{a}m\hat{i}m$ $w^e t\hat{o}d\hat{a}$ (2 Chron. 33.16), i.e. sacrifices of peace offerings as a thank-offering (cf. Rendtorff 1967: 70). The phrase $z^e b\bar{a}h\hat{i}m$ $w^e t\hat{o}d\hat{o}t$ in 2 Chron. 29.31 embraces the two classes of thank-offerings—the peace offerings, later defined as $haqq^o d\bar{a}\check{s}\hat{i}m$ in 29.33, and the freewill burnt offerings, whose numbers are given in 29.32.

2.   See Mayer 1986: 437.

3.   The structure of 2 Chron. 29.31, with its command to present thank-offerings followed by the account of its fulfilment makes it quite clear that the burnt offerings mentioned in 31b are to be taken as thank-offerings.

4.   See Gunkel 1933: 266; Fohrer 1970: 269.

5.   Mowinckel 1967: II, 31; Seidel 1989: 99, 103.

The performance of the thanksgiving by the temple musicians is evidently presupposed in 2 Chron. 30.21-22, which has already been analysed on pages 76 and 77 in the previous chapter. Now while this account could refer to the performance of the regular choral service together with the presentation of the public burnt offering, its context implies that the singing of praise with the thank-offerings is under discussion in this segment, and that for three reasons. First, in 2 Chron. 30.22 *mᵉzabbᵉḥîm zibḥê sᵉlāmîm* parallels the unusual *hithpael* participle *mitwaddîm* which describes their presentation with thanksgiving. Thus these peace offerings are presented with songs of thanksgiving to the LORD. Secondly, the chiastic structure of vv. 21-22 combines the joy of the people in presenting their peace offerings and eating the sacrificial meal with the performance of praise by the musicians. Consequently, the people too 'gave thanks to the LORD, the God of their fathers', just as the musicians 'gave praise to the LORD'. Thirdly, Hezekiah's commendation of the musicians for their skill in teaching the goodness of the LORD makes best sense if it refers to the songs of thanksgiving with their prominent element of proclamation to the assembled congregation.

According to 2 Chron. 30.21-22, the temple musicians were involved in the performance of praise for the individual thank-offerings as well as for the public burnt offering.[1] Nothing, however, is said about how this happened. They may have been involved in one of three ways. First, they could have sung a general call to present the thank-offerings such as is found in Psalm 107.[2] This would then have been sung before their presentation as an introduction to this part of the sacrificial ritual. Secondly, they could have taught an appropriate song of thanksgiving to the people who presented the sacrifice and have sung it together with them at the sanctuary. Thirdly, they could have performed the thanksgiving for them. If this was the case, then the people could well have joined in with the recurring refrain for thanksgiving as is attested in Jer. 33.11. But, whatever their involvement was, the musicians assisted the people in presenting their thank-offerings with songs of thanksgiving to the LORD.

---

1. This is confirmed by 2 Chron. 31.2, where the ministry of the Levites in performing thanks and praise is associated with both the burnt offerings and the peace offerings.

2. See Mowinckel 1967: II, 42. Ps. 100 may also have been used for this purpose.

The Significance of the Rite for Thanksgiving. The author of Chronicles shows that Hezekiah had a special interest in the performance of liturgical song. This interest was not restricted to the regular choral music for the public burnt offering but also included the songs of thanksgiving for the individual thank-offerings. After providing a regular slot for the thank-offerings in the sacrificial ritual, he is said to have commended the musicians for their skill in helping the people present their thank-offerings. He seems then to have encouraged this presentation and to have lent his weight to the development of its musical side by the temple choir.

It therefore comes as no surprise that the only two other references to the presentation of the thank-offerings come after 2 Chronicles 29–30. By means of two contrasting incidents, the significance of thanksgiving is presented, first negatively in 2 Chron. 32.24-26, and then positively in 2 Chron. 33.12-13 and 16. In both these cases, which are not taken from 2 Kings but are unique to Chronicles, the narrative recalls the divine promise about the temple as the house of sacrifice in 2 Chron. 7.12-14.

In 2 Chron. 32.24-26 the case for the presentation of the thank-offering is made negatively with remarkable brevity. It alludes to the events described at some length in 2 Kgs 20.1-11. While 2 Chron. 32.24 merely summarizes the events of Hezekiah's sickness and recovery, 32.25-26 adds the Chronicler's own postscript to this event:

> But Hezekiah did not pay back according to the benefit done to him, for his heart was proud; and wrath came upon him and Judah and Jerusalem. Then Hezekiah humbled himself together with the citizens of Jerusalem for the pride of his heart, so that the wrath of YHWH did not come upon them during the reign of Hezekiah.

At first glance the passage is rather puzzling with its mention of Hezekiah's pride, his failure to make repayment, his repentance, and the delay of the LORD's wrath. Curtis and Madsen (*1910: 491) believe that it all refers to Hezekiah's pride in displaying his treasures to the Babylonian emissaries and the delay of the Babylonian invasion after his acceptance of Isaiah's prophecy of judgment. Yet that overlooks the plain sense of the passage. It does not deal with Hezekiah's behaviour with the Babylonian envoys, which in any case is mentioned quite separately later in 2 Chron. 32.31, but with his lack of repayment to the LORD. This failure arose out of his pride, which was also disclosed later in his treatment of the envoys.

In this segment the Chronicler seems to draw on the same strand of tradition as the psalm of Hezekiah in Isa. 38.9-20. This may account for the later mention of Isaiah's vision in 2 Chron. 32.32. According to this tradition, the fault of Hezekiah lay in his failure to repay the LORD after his escape from certain death. The idiom *kigᵉmul 'ālāyw hēšîb* does not, as Rudolph (*1955: 310) implies, just refer to Hezekiah's subjective lack of gratitude, but to his failure to offer the thanksgiving which he had vowed in Isa. 38.20, for only if he had made such a vow would he be bound to make any such payment and be culpable if he did not do so. His pride then is shown not so much in his failure to acknowledge God's involvement in his deliverance from death as in his refusal to pay what he had vowed to the LORD.

2 Chron. 32.24-26 touches upon four aspects of the thank-offering. First, it was given in response to the experience of rescue by God from the threat of death. Secondly, the wrath of the LORD came upon those who, like Hezekiah, failed to fulfil their vows. Hezekiah's fault lay in his failure to fulfil his vow to make music on stringed instruments in the temple for the duration of his life. The use of the first person plural imperatives in Isa. 38.20 shows that he would not have done this by himself but would have endowed the temple musicians to do so for him. The neglect of this vow led to disaster both for the king and the people. Thirdly, since the king represented the people in worship, he offered thank-offerings for them on the occasion of their national deliverance. Lastly, the wrath of the LORD could be delayed but not averted by the subsequent acknowledgement of the failure to fulfil the vow. This would undoubtedly have included the presentation of the thank-offerings which had been previously promised.

What was expressed negatively in 2 Chron. 32.25 is expressed positively in 2 Chron. 33.16. Because of his apostasy which led to the establishment of an idol in the temple, Manasseh was taken as a prisoner to Babylon. There he sought the LORD's favour in petition and supplication. The Lord heard his prayer and brought him back to Jerusalem. Consequently, he not only rectified the idolatrous practices which he had introduced but also restored the altar of the LORD at the temple in Jerusalem. There he sacrificed peace offerings in thanksgiving to the LORD.[1] After his deliverance from death in exile he

---

1.   The *waw* in *zibḥê šᵉlāmîm wᵉtôdâ* is epexegetical, as in 2 Chron. 29.31. The terminology in 33.16 differs from 29.31, because Manasseh only presented peace offerings as his personal thank-offering. Hence the singular form of *tôdâ*.

came to know the LORD (2 Chron. 33.13) and so presented thank-offerings to him, even though he was under no obligation to do so.

In response to the onesided stress of Mosis (1973: 192-94) on this story of Manasseh's repentance as a paradigm for the return of Israel from exile, Williamson (*1982: 389) argues that it is 'the most explicit and dramatic example of the efficacy of repentance in the whole of the Chronicler's work'. It is also an example of the proper response to individual and corporate deliverance from death by the presentation of sacrifices with thanksgiving to the LORD. While Israel as a nation thanked the LORD for its salvation in the choral service performed during the presentation of the burnt offerings, its individual members did so by the presentation of the sacrifices for thanksgiving in the place reserved for them. In this way the people of Israel served the LORD as commanded by Manasseh in 2 Chron. 33.16 with the help of the Levitical musicians as described in 2 Chron. 30.21-22.

Summary. By their performance of thanksgiving, the people of Israel acknowledged the LORD's blessing, as they had experienced it in their own lives, repaid his generosity to them by their own generosity in presenting thank-offerings for the benefit of their invited guests, and proclaimed the LORD's goodness to those who were present with them at the temple. The Levitical musicians were both the supervisors and beneficiaries of the thanksgiving. With the help of their musical expertise, those who enjoyed the benefits which they had received from the LORD also rejoiced in the LORD as their benefactor. Thus through the performance of music and song, the great festivals became times of rejoicing for the ordinary people, as they presented their thank-offerings at the temple in their family groups.

Conclusion

According to Chronicles the order of service for the sacrifices at the temple unified all the various sacrifices and their rites in a single complex system of ritual enactments. The basic pattern was given by the order for the regular burnt offerings which was enacted twice each day. This order was expanded to include the public preparatory offerings for purification, the additional public burnt offerings for special occasions with their cereal offerings, and the individual burnt offerings and peace offerings. This order, in turn, determined the function and revealed the significance of the whole service and its main parts.

The sacrifices proceeded in an orderly sequence which clearly separated the public sacrifices from the individual sacrifices and grouped
the rites for the public sacrifices according to their ritual function.
Thus the application of blood from all the public sacrifices in the rite
of atonement, which coincided with the burning of incense and its
associated activities in the holy place, preceded the presentation of the
public burnt offering, which was burnt on the altar together with all
the parts for burning from the other public offerings. By the rite of
atonement the LORD forgave the unwitting sins of the congregation
and cleansed them of their impurity, so that it could appear before
him without incurring his wrath. By the presentation of the burnt
offerings, the LORD met with his people, so that he could receive them
and attend to their petitions. After that had been accomplished, the
people presented their individual thank-offerings and peace offerings.

In keeping with the instructions of David, the choral rite was
designed to fit exactly into the centre of this complex pattern, so that
its place within the ritual order would determine its function and
significance. It was performed during the presentation of the public
burnt offering which came after the rite for atonement. The musicians
therefore did not induce the LORD to accept his people but rather
announced his acceptance of them through his acceptance of their
burnt offering. Through the singing of the LORD's song, they praised
the LORD for his goodness and acknowledged his presence with them
in their worship. As they sang their song, they rejoiced in the LORD
and moved the people to rejoice in his presence with them at the temple.

The choral service was also associated ritually with the prostration
of the congregation during the presentation of the burnt offering. It
not only signalled the times for prostration by sounding the trumpets,
but also motivated the people to respond appropriately to the LORD's
meeting with them in the daily burnt offering by praising him for his
manifest goodness to them. Thus the choral performance during the
burnt offering announced the LORD's appearance to his people, which
was duly greeted by the homage of his people during the pauses in the
song of praise.

Under the influence of Hezekiah, a regular slot was set apart on
festive occasions for the presentation of individual sacrifices. Chief
among these were the thank-offerings. They were presented together
with songs of thanksgiving to the LORD. The musicians were also

involved in this part of the service. By singing the songs of thanksgiving for them or with them, they taught the people about the LORD's
goodness and so moved them to rejoice in him for the benefits
received from him. Through the musicians, their thanksgiving and joy
was linked with the thanksgiving and joy of the whole congregation.

The choral service did not exist by itself as a separate entity within
the worship at the temple but was closely coordinated with the public
burnt offering. It had no independent ritual function but was part and
parcel of the sacrificial ritual. As such it both proclaimed and
acclaimed the LORD as he came to be with his people and bless them.
Likewise the songs of thanksgiving were performed by the singers for
the people during the presentation of the thank-offerings. The praise
of each family group thereby became the praise of the congregation
and vice versa. These two settings then determined the ritual function
of the songs sung by the choir at the temple in Jerusalem.

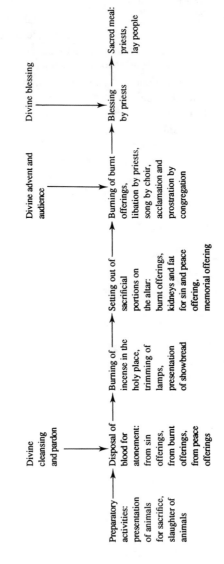

A. The Rite of Atonement

B. The Rite for Burnt Offering

C. The Sacrificial Meal

Preparatory → Disposal of → Burning of → Setting out of → Burning of burnt → Blessing → Sacred meal:
activities: blood for incense in the sacrificial offerings, by priests priests,
presentation atonement: holy place, portions on libation by priests, lay people
of animals from sin trimming of the altar: song by choir,
for sacrifice, offerings, lamps, burnt offerings, acclamation and
slaughter of from burnt presentation kidneys and fat prostration by
animals offerings, of showbread for sin and peace congregation
from peace offering,
offerings memorial offering

Divine Divine advent and Divine blessing
cleansing audience
and pardon

God's Activity in the Ritual Sequence for Public Sacrifice

Chapter 5

THE THEOLOGICAL SIGNIFICANCE OF THE LORD'S SONG

As described in Chronicles, the LORD's song was a part of the comprehensive ritual of sacrifice at the temple. It had no independent significance, since it both elucidated and was elucidated by the more general ritual with which it was associated. Since that ritual had been instituted by the LORD for him to interact with his people for their benefit, choral music too gained its significance in large measure from its involvement in that interaction.

The significance of choral music was therefore largely implicit, since it was determined by its ritual context and the tradition of worship in Israel. In his narrative, the Chronicler, however, takes up what was theologically implicit and makes it more explicit. He is particularly interested in showing its theological significance as a ritual performance in the LORD's presence at his temple in Jerusalem.

Sacred Song as Proclamation in 1 Chronicles 16.7-36

Introduction

The occurrence of the psalm of thanksgiving in 1 Chron. 16.8-36 is without parallel in Chronicles. Elsewhere, whenever the Chronicler specifies the content of sacred song, he either cites the thanksgiving refrain or some part of it. The question therefore arises why he inserted this rather lengthy composition here.

In all, four answers have been given. Keil (*1870: 153) proposes that the psalm was a hymn composed by David for the liturgical song in the public worship. While this proposal does justice to the narrative context of the psalm, it fails to note that 1 Chron. 16.7 does not claim that David gave this psalm to the Asaphites but that he appointed them to give thanksgiving to the LORD. Most modern scholars hold the view expressed by Myers (*1965a: 121):

> The Chronicler here illustrates what he believed was the origin and prac-
> tice in the time of David, by a concrete example from his own time and in
> so doing gives us an insight into certain liturgical usages in post-exilic
> times.

That view, however, does not consider how the psalm functions here
in its narrative context. Loader (1976: 74) notes the incorporation of
the song into the account of the singers' appointment and argues that
the psalm describes the place of Israel as God's chosen people among
the nations and the role of Jerusalem as 'the centre of salvation for
Israel in the world of the nations'. Butler (1978) and Hausmann
(1987) similarly argue that the psalm explains why choral music was
established in Jerusalem.

In what follows I shall investigate how 1 Chron. 16.8-36 functions
in its present narrative context. After considering the origin, redaction and structure of the psalm, I shall examine what it has to say
about the theological significance of sacred song.

The Origin and Redaction of 1 Chronicles 16.8-36
All scholars agree that the material in this psalm was not originally
composed by the Chronicler, but existed in some form before he
compiled it and placed it here. They also agree that this psalm is in
some way related to Psalms 105, 96 and 106. Yet how it is related has
been a matter of some discussion. Keil (*1870: 153, 160) argues that
the psalm was composed by David himself in its present form. Parts
of it were then later used to compose the three subsequent canonical
psalms. Apart from Goettsberger (*1939: 128, 131), who, however,
ascribes only vv. 8-22 to David, since these verses alone fit the occasion,
no major modern commentator has accepted his position.

Macy (1975: 110) holds that, since neither the text of the canonical
psalms nor the text of the psalm in Chronicles is demonstrably dependent on the other, this psalm 'is an example of parallel transmission of
songs which later became canonical'. If that were so, then the Chronicler
probably cited a liturgical text currently in use in his own day.

Like most scholars, Williamson (*1982: 128) considers that this
psalm was composed by the Chronicler from Psalms 96, 105 and 106
to illustrate the kind of praise which began in Jerusalem with the
establishment of choral music there by David. It is held that, since
most of the divergences from the canonical psalms are consistent with
the concerns of the Chronicler, they are best taken as coming from his

hand. That too is the position which I take.

The discussion on the origin of this psalm has been complicated by the claim of some critical scholars that, since 1 Chron. 16.7-36 interrupts the flow of narrative from 1 Chron. 16.4-6 to 37-42, it cannot stem from the Chronicler but must be a later interpolation.[1] Since David is supposed to have addressed the Levites in 1 Chron. 15.11, Rudolph (*1955: 115) takes 16.5b-38 as a secondary pro-priestly addition. He follows Rothstein and Hänel (*1927: 297) in their conjecture that v. 38 with its mention of Obed-edom belongs together with vv. 5b-6. He also argues that, had the Chronicler wished to say something more about Asaph, he would have added it most naturally to the data in v. 5. 1 Chron. 16.7-37 must then be an even later insertion than vv. 5-6 and 38 to show that the LORD was praised vocally as well as instrumentally.

None of these arguments is at all compelling. As I have already argued in Chapter 2, there are sound ritual reasons for the mention of the priests in 16.6 as in 15.4, 11, 14, 24. With Williamson (*1982: 122, 128), I would also argue that the disruption in the narrative stems from the compositional activity of the Chronicler (cf. Kittel *1902: 70). In all he combined three bodies of material in 1 Chron. 16.1-43. First, he received the narrative from 2 Sam 6.17-20a, which provided the framework in 1 Chron. 16.1-3 and 43 for the insertion of his material on the choral service. Within this framework he then placed the description of David's arrangement for the two-part choral service at Jerusalem and Gibeon now found in 16.4-6 and 37-42. Lastly, he inserted the psalm of thanksgiving with its introduction and conclusion into the description of David's arrangements for the choral service in Jerusalem in 16.7-36.

Three reasons can be advanced to support the contention that the Chronicler was responsible for the insertion of vv. 7-36 in its present context. First, in 1 Chron. 16.4 the Levites are said to have been appointed to 'proclaim', 'thank' and 'praise' 'YHWH', 'the God of Israel'. Now all these terms feature prominently in the following psalm with its introduction and conclusion. *zākar* (16.12, 15); *hôdâ* (16.7, 8, 34, 35; cf. 41); *hillēl* (16.10, 25, 36; cf. *tᵉhillâ* in 35); YHWH (16.7, 8, 10, 11, 14, 23, 25, 26, 28, 29, 31, 33, 34, 36; cf. 16.41); and

---

1. Rothstein and Hänel *1927: 297, 312-18; Noth 1943: 116; Galling *1954: 51; Rudolph *1955: 115, 127.

ᵉlōhê yiśrā'ēl (16.36).[1] While this correspondence may not prove
beyond doubt that the psalm is included by the Chronicler, it does
show that the content of the psalm is consistent with his statement
about the purpose of the choral service.

Secondly, the important term *tāmîd*, which is used by the Chronicler
to describe the synchronization of the choral service at Jerusalem with
the sacrificial service at Gibeon in 1 Chron. 16.6, 37, 40, is repeated
in the introductory call to praise in 16.11.

Thirdly, 16.7 was obviously composed by whoever inserted the
psalm. It contains three terms which anchor it in this context and the
thought world of the Chronicler. *nātan* is a deliberate echo of 16.4;
'Asaph and his kinsmen' is repeated immediately after the psalm in
16.37; and the notion of David's performance of praise 'by the hand'
(*bᵉyad*) of the musicians recurs at 2 Chron. 7.6 in the description of
the position and function of the singers in Solomon's temple.

It is, therefore, likely that this psalm comes from the Chronicler,
who uses it to advance his views of the choral service and its significance. If that is so, then it is valid to examine the redactional activity
of the Chronicler to discover the function of the psalm in its present
context. His choice of material, its rearrangement into its present
poetic shape, and the changes made by him to the received text all help
to clarify what this psalm has to say about the significance of liturgical
song.

The song of thanksgiving begins with the first part of Psalm 105.
Even though this historical psalm recounts the LORD's dealings with
Israel from the making of his covenant with the patriarchs to the gift
of the promised land, the Chronicler uses only the patriarchal introduction. The people of Israel are therefore called to praise the LORD
for the promise of the land in his eternal covenant with the patriarchs
and for his protection of them against the nations. By concentrating on
these two factors, he focuses by contrast on the period of David and
by analogy on the postexilic period. On the one hand, the promise of
the land and of security for his landless people reached its fulfilment
in the reign of David with his placement of the ark in Jerusalem and
his victories over Israel's enemies.[2] On the other hand, the people of
Israel in the Chronicler's day were scattered like the patriarchs among

---

1.   See Hill 1983: 99.
2.   See Goettsberger *1939: 129.

the nations and no longer fully possessed the promised land.[1] In this
situation they were then called to praise God not only for what he had
once done but also for what he would yet do for them.[2] Thus the promise of the covenant with the patriarchs was the cause of their praise.

This shift of focus, brought about by the selection of material from
Psalm 105, is emphasised by three changes to its text. First, there is
the change, obscured by the RSV, from Abraham to Israel in v. 13,
which is rather puzzling in view of the reference to God's covenant
with Abraham in v. 16. That covenant, however, is said to have
culminated in the grant of the land to Israel in vv. 17-18. The point is
made that not all of Abraham's descendants were given the land but
only the descendants of Jacob. They alone had a legal right to God's
land and access to his presence in it. This change is then in line with
the Chronicler's emphasis on the origin of Israel in Jacob rather than
Abraham as well as on his concern for the inclusion of all twelve
tribes in the liturgical community of his day.[3]

Secondly, there is the change from the indicative to the imperative
of *zkr* in v. 15.[4] Whereas the cause for praise in Ps. 105.8 had been the
LORD's remembrance of his covenant in delivering them from Egypt
and giving them the land, here the people are called to remember the
LORD's covenant with them in order to motivate them in their praise,
just as in 16.12 they were urged to remember his miraculous deeds.
They are thus regarded as recipients and heirs of the covenant like the
patriarchs. Thirdly, there is the change of person in 16.19 from 'they'
(*biheyôtām*) to 'you' (*biheyôtekem*), which is not followed by the RSV,
NEB and NIV. In this way the Chronicler identified his contemporaries
with the patriarchs, whose experience was of vulnerability as a landless
minority.[5] Like their ancestors they were aliens in their own land which
was ruled by the Persians. Yet like them they were also protected by
the LORD as a people with royal status and a prophetic mission.[6]

1.   Japhet (1979: 217-18) notes that when the Chronicler traces the continuity
between the patriarchs and the postexilic community in their relationship to the land of
Canaan, he proclaims the consummation of the covenant with the patriarchs to his
contemporaries; cf. Japhet 1989: 352-93.
2.   Cf. Williamson *1982: 129.
3.   See Williamson *1982: 129; cf. 40-41, 43-44.
4.   For support of *zikerû* in the MT, see Keil *1870: 158; Curtis and Madsen
*1910: 224; Loader 1976: 73; Williamson *1982: 129; Hausmann 1987: 84.
5.   Myers (*1965a: 116) rightly includes v. 19 in the promise of the covenant.
6.   While Ps. 105.15 may echo Gen. 20.7 in calling the patriarchs 'prophets',

To the introduction of Psalm 105 the Chronicler adds Psalm 96 and in doing so makes such a smooth transition in the development of ideas that the joint is barely noticeable. Thus 16.14-22 meshes in well with 23-26 by means of the mention of 'the earth' in 14 and 23 (cf. 18), 'the nations' in 20 and 24, and 'the peoples' in 20, 24 and 26. In fact vv. 23-24 could be taken as the positive counterpart to the LORD's warning to the pagan kings in v. 22, since the masculine plural imperatives in 23-24 agree with the masculine plural prohibitions in v. 22.

To achieve this match, the Chronicler makes a few significant alterations to Psalm 96. These are of two kinds. First, he clarifies the address of the psalm, so that 16.23-30 addresses the whole earth with its peoples, while 16.31-33 invites the cosmos with all its parts to praise the LORD.[1] Thus he begins with 96.1b, which makes it quite clear that there is a shift of address from the land of Israel to the whole world. Since the nations are addressed, it makes little sense to invite them to sing a new song in place of their previous song of praise to the LORD. The call then is for those who have never praised the LORD to begin to do so. Ps. 96.1a was therefore omitted as out of place. Once it was excluded, v. 2a was also omitted to restore the parallelism. The Chronicler also placed 96.10a after 11a and changed the imperative *'īmᵉrū* to the jussive *wᵉy'ōmᵉrû* to fit this reinterpretation. Thereby he assigns the task of proclaiming the LORD's kingship among the nations to the cosmos rather than the earth and its people. This distinction between the praise of the earth with its nations and the praise of the cosmos led to the omission of 96.10c and 13c with their mention of God's judgment of the peoples on the earth.[2] So by these omissions and the rearrangement of some lines, the Chronicler distinguishes between international and cosmic praise.

Secondly, he made some changes in the wording of Psalm 96 to fit his narrative context and to show the progression of praise from Israel to the nations. Thus he generalizes the specific references to the temple. Instead of 'his sanctuary', he speaks of 'his place' in 16.27,

---

there is no precedent for calling them 'anointed'. Kraus (1961: 721) argues that the terms have been democratized in Ps. 105.15. This is definitely the case in 1 Chron. 16.22; like the patriarchs, all the people of Israel are God's prophets and anointed people. Yet the terms are hardly synonymous, since for the Chronicler *māšîaḥ* is always a royal term.

1. See Becker *1986: 72-74; Hausmann 1987: 86-87.
2. For the last two points, see Becker *1986: 73-74.

which is probably meant to refer to his heavenly residence (cf. 2 Chron. 6.21). With this comes the change from *tip'eret* to *ḥedwâ*. The Chronicler thereby aligns v. 27b with the contents of vv. 10-11 and so transforms it from a statement about the nature of the temple to a statement of the Creator's gifts to all people. He also replaces the command for the peoples to enter 'his courts' with the command to come 'before him'. These changes are not just required by the narrative context which tells of choral praise in Jerusalem before the construction of the temple there, but also by the address of vv. 23-30 to the peoples of the world, whose praise need not be hampered by their lack of access to the temple in Jerusalem.

The Chronicler finished his psalm with the introduction and conclusion of Psalm 106. Three things stand out in his adaptation of this material for his psalm. First, he clearly separates the introductory call to thanksgiving from the final petition by the rubric w^e'$im^er\hat{u}$ and uses it to conclude his song of thanksgiving. Secondly, the change of address from YHWH '$^el\bar{o}h\hat{e}n\hat{u}$ to '$^el\bar{o}h\hat{e}$ $yi\check{s}'\bar{e}n\hat{u}$ together with the addition of $w^eha\d{s}\d{s}\hat{i}l\bar{e}n\hat{u}$ emphasizes that Israel needed to be saved by the LORD from foreign domination as well as brought back to its land. Thirdly, the rubrics in Ps. 106.48b are made part of the narrative in 1 Chron. 16.36b to show the validity of congregational involvement in the choir's praises by finding a precedent for it in the inauguration of the choral service in Jerusalem.

The Chronicler therefore created a new psalm from Psalms 96, 105 and 106. In his new compendium of praise he took pains to distinguish thanksgiving from petition. In it he also extended the call to praise from Israel to all the nations of the earth and the whole cosmos. Lastly, he embedded the psalm firmly into its present context verbally and thematically.

A Translation of 1 Chronicles 16.8-36

v. 8	Give thanks to YHWH, proclaim his name!
	Publicize his deeds among the peoples!
v. 9	Sing about him, make music about him![1]
	Muse on all his marvellous achievements!
v. 10	Glory in his holy name!
	Let those who seek YHWH rejoice in their hearts!

---

1. De Boer (1981) shows that the use of the preposition l^e with these verbs in the psalms means not that the psalmist sang 'to' the LORD, but rather 'about' him.

v. 11   Look for YHWH and his strength!
         Seek his presence regularly!
v. 12   Remember the wonders which he has done,
         his signs and his spoken judgments,
v. 13   you descendants of Israel,[1] his servant,
         you sons of Jacob, his chosen people!
v. 14   YHWH is our God;
         his judgments are everywhere on earth.
v. 15   Remember[2] his covenant always,
         the word he decreed for a thousand generations,
v. 16   which he made with Abraham,
         his vow to Isaac;
v. 17   he confirmed it as a statute to Jacob,
         as an everlasting covenant to Israel:
v. 18   'I shall give you the land of Canaan
         as the allotted portion of your inheritance,
v. 19   although you are[3] only a few people,
         insignificant and aliens in it'.
v. 20   When they moved from nation to nation,
         from one kingdom to another people,
v. 21   he did not allow anyone[4] to oppress them
         and warned kings about them:
v. 22   'Do not touch my anointed people!
         Do not harm my prophets!'[5]
v. 23   Sing about YHWH, all the earth!
         Announce his salvation from day to day![6]
v. 24   Relate his glory among the nations,
         his marvellous achievements among all the peoples!
v. 25   For YHWH is great and most praiseworthy;
         he is more awesome than all the gods.
v. 26   Indeed all the gods of the peoples are nonentities,
         but YHWH made the heavens.
v. 27   Splendour and grandeur are in his presence;
         strength and joy[7] are in his place.[8]
v. 28   Ascribe to YHWH, you families of peoples,
         ascribe to YHWH glory and strength!

1. Ps. 105.6 *'abrāhām* rather than *yiśrā'ēl*.
2. Ps. 105.8 *zākar* rather than *zik^{e}rû*.
3. Ps. 105.12 *bih^{e}yôtām* rather than *bih^{e}yôt^{e}kem*.
4. Ps. 105.14 *'ādām* rather than *l^e'îš*.
5. Ps. 105.15 *w^{e}lin^{e}bî' ay* rather than *ûbin^{e}bî' ay*.
6. Ps. 96.1a and 2a are omitted.
7. Ps. 96.6 *w^{e}tip'eret* rather than *w^{e}ḥedwâ*.
8. Ps. 96.6 *b^{e}miqdāšô* rather than *bim^{e}qômô*.

v. 29   Ascribe to YHWH the glory belonging to his name;
         take up an offering and enter his presence![1]
v. 30   Make prostration to YHWH in (his) holy splendour;
         tremble before him,[2] all the earth![3]
         Truly the world is secure; it cannot be shaken.[4]
v. 31   Let the heavens rejoice and the earth be glad;
         let them say[5] among the nations, 'YHWH is King!'
v. 32   Let the sea roar, and all that fills it!
         Let the countryside[6] exult, and everything in it!
v. 33   Then[7] the trees of the forest will be jubilant
         before[8] YHWH,
         for he comes[9] to judge the earth.[10]
v. 34   Give thanks to YHWH! Truly he is good,
         Truly his generosity is for ever!'
v. 35   And say:
         'Save us, God our saviour;[11]
         gather us and deliver us[12] from the nations,
         so that we may give thanks to your holy name,
         and glory in your praise.
v. 36   Blessed be YHWH, God of Israel,
         for ever and ever.'
         Then all the people said,[13] 'Amen!' and
         praised YHWH.

The Structure of 1 Chronicles 16.8-36a

The composite character of this psalm has led some scholars to assert that it is a rather superficial pastiche of material without any inner unity.[14] As a result of this rather dismissive judgment and the assump-

---

1. Ps. 96.8 *leḥaṣrôtāyw* rather than *lepānāyw*.
2. Ps. 96.9 *mippānāyw* rather than *millepānāyw*.
3. Ps. 96.10a is found in 1 Chron. 16.31b.
4. Ps. 96.10b is omitted.
5. Ps. 96.10 *'īmerû* rather than *wey'ōmerû*.
6. Ps. 96.12 *śāday* rather than *haśśādeh*.
7. Ps. 96.12 adds *kol*.
8. Ps. 96.13 *lipenê* rather than *millipenê*.
9. Ps. 96.13 repeats *kî bā'*.
10. Ps. 96.13b is omitted.
11. Ps. 106.47 YHWH *'elōhênû* rather than *'elōhê yiš'ēnû*.
12. Ps. 106.47 lacks *weḥaṣṣîlēnû*.
13. Ps. 106.48 *we'āmar* rather than *wayy'ōmerû*.
14. Gunkel (1926: 422) dismisses it as a rather superficially constructed combination, while Goettsberger (*1939: 131) reckons that its three parts lack in unity.

tion that portions reassembled by the Chronicler still functioned as
they had formerly, little attention has been given to this psalm as a
literary unit in its own right until recent times.

Already in the last century Keil (*1870: 157) had argued for the
coherence and symmetry of the psalm as a whole, which for him was
evidence of its creation by David. But since most scholars rejected his
position on the derivation of the canonical psalms from this psalm, his
literary observations were overlooked. Recently, however, a number
of scholars, utilizing the new methods of literary analysis, have again
argued for its inner unity. First came the work of Loader (1976). He
noted its thematic unity and argued for the psalm's functional coherence
in its narrative context. Then Butler (1978: 149) demonstrated that the
content and intention of the psalm as a liturgical text was consistent
with 'the content and intention of the Chronicler's history as a whole'.
In response to his work, Hill (1983) noted that the composition of this
psalm was governed by the main conventions and devices of classical
Hebrew poetry. Thus, even though it was a composite psalm, it nevertheless exhibited 'deliberate and skilful poetic arrangement' (p. 100).

A number of devices are used by the Chronicler to unify the psalm
and to distinguish its chief parts. First, there is the liturgical rubric in
v. 35a that separates the song of thanksgiving from the petition with
its doxology. Secondly, there is the use of inclusion with *hôdû
l^eYHWH* in vv. 8 and 34.[1] This marks off these verses as an introduction and conclusion and unifies the material in the psalm under the
notion of thanksgiving. The occurrence of *kol-hā'āreṣ* in vv. 23 and
30 demarcates the intervening verses as separate unit. Thirdly, apart
from *hôdû*, two other imperatives are repeated: *šîrû* in vv. 9 and 23[2]
and *zik^erû* in vv. 12 and 15. In each case they introduce new parallel
units of poetry. Fourthly, certain common terms act as catch words to
unify the material from the three former psalms.[3] They are: *'am* in
vv. 8, 20, 24, 26, 28; *gôy* in 20, 24, 31, 35; *šēm* in 8, 10, 29, 35;
qōdeš in 10, 29, 35; *hôdâ* in 8, 34, 35; and *hillēl, t^ehillâ* in 10, 25, 35.
It is thus evident from the recurrence of these key terms that the

   1.   Keil (*1870: 157) was the first to realize the significance of this inclusion; cf.
Hill 1983: 99-100.
   2.   Even though v. 8 does correspond with v. 34 and v. 9 with v. 23, this does
not allow us to speak about the chiastic arrangement of the psalm, as Hill does (1983:
99-100).
   3.   See Hill 1983: 100.

psalm has to do with the praise of the LORD and Israel's relationship with the nations.[1]

Apart from these verbal devices the psalm is built up around the repeated call to praise expressed in imperative and jussive forms. These introduce each new section and subsection. After ten initial calls to praise (vv. 8-11) comes a single imperative (12) which is then repeated a little later (15). A cluster of three imperatives (23-24) is followed by six imperatives (28-30a), five jussives (31-32) and a final imperative (34). As these calls to praise proceed, their audience, which is not initially specified, is first identified and then extended.[2] The singers first call on the Israelites (v. 13), then the earth (23, 30) with all its ethnic groups, and finally the whole cosmos (31-32) to praise the LORD. In contrast to this, the three imperatives in v. 35 are addressed as petitions to the LORD which serves to distinguish 35 from 8-34.

On the basis of these considerations, the following is the structure of the psalm:

A. *The Psalm of Thanksgiving: 1 Chron. 16.8-34*

    1.   *General Call to Thanksgiving*: 16.8
    2.   *Israel's Praise*: 16.9-22
        a.   Call to musical praise (9-11)
        b.   Double call to remembrance (12-22)
            (1)   remembrance of the LORD's works
                (a)   call to remember the LORD (12)
                (b)   identity and status of audience (13)
                (c)   content of remembrance (14)
            (2)   remembrance of the LORD's covenant
                (a)   call to remember the covenant
                       with the ancestors (15-18)
                (b)   protection of Israel as a result
                     of this covenant (19-22)
    3.   *International Praise*: 16.23-30
        a.   The praise of the whole earth (23-27)
            (1)   call to singing (23-24)
            (2)   reasons for song (25-27)
        b.   The praise of its peoples (28-30)
            (1)   call to prostration in sacrificial
                worship (28-30a)
            (2)   reason for prostration (30b)

---

1. See Loader 1976: 70-74.
2. See Keil *1870: 157; Becker *1986: 72-74; Hausmann 1987: 86-87.

4. *Cosmic Praise*: 16.31-33
    a.   Command for jubilant, universal proclamation
        of the LORD's kingship (31-32)
    b.   Result of proclamation (33)
5. *Final Call to Thanksgiving*: 16.34

B. *Summary Petition*: 16.35-36a
   1.   Petition for Israel's Deliverance (35)
   2.   Doxology (36a)

Proclamation through Praise in 1 Chronicles 16.4-42

In 2 Samuel 6 the climax of the transferral of the ark to Jerusalem
came with David's inauguration of sacrificial worship before it there.
After offering sacrifices for the people, David blessed them and provided food for their sacrifical banquets. The narrative in Chronicles,
however, shifts the climax away from the inauguration of sacrificial
worship in Jerusalem to David's establishment of a choral service
there in 1 Chron. 16.4-42.

There are, most likely, two reasons for this shift of emphasis. On
the one hand, the Chronicler wished to correct the belief that the
regular public sacrifices began there on that occasion. As far as he was
concerned, the public sacrifices could only be presented at the altar
before the tent of meeting at Gibeon (1 Chron. 16.39-40). Moreover,
since the LORD designated the place for the altar at Jerusalem only
later, as described in 1 Chron. 21.18–22.1, David could only begin to
offer his own sacrifices there after that event. On the other hand, the
Chronicler wished to show that David transferred the ark to Jerusalem
in order to inaugurate the choral performance there. The ark and the
LORD who sat enthroned on it had to be 'sought' in the proper way
(1 Chron. 13.3; 15.13). This was the responsibility of the Levites who
'ministered' to the LORD by ministering to the ark (1 Chron. 15.2;
16.4, 37). The Lord was then to be sought by the performance of praise
rather than by the mere presentation of the public sacrifices. The
Lord's presence and power, symbolized by the ark, was to be solicited
and announced in praise. Thus the choral service, instituted by David
for the care of the ark, distinguished the sanctuary in Jerusalem from
all the other sanctuaries which were primarily places of sacrifice.

This new emphasis by the Chronicler on sacred song is evident in
his arrangement of the material in 1 Chronicles 16. Into the story
from 2 Samuel 6 which had dealt with David's role in presenting sacrifices before the newly installed ark, the Chronicler inserted his

account of David's establishment of choral music. The significance of this is evident from the chiastic arrangement of the material. The two parts of outer narrative bracket, consisting of 16.1-3 and 43, were linked thematically by the mention of David's conferral of blessing in vv. 2 and 43. This frames the legislation of David for the two-part choral performance in Jerusalem and Gibeon in 16.4-6 and 37-42. These parts are joined thematically by the words *hôdâ* in vv. 4 and 41, *tāmîd* in 6, 37 and 40, *šērēt* in 4 and 37, and by the mention of the 'ark' in 4, 6, 37, the 'cymbals' in 5 and 42 and the 'trumpets' in 6 and 42. The centre of the chiasm is the psalm of thanksgiving in vv. 7-36 which now stands between David's decree for the performance of praise in 4-6 and its fulfilment in 37-38. Thus the transferral of the ark to Jerusalem culminates in the inauguration of the choral service there.

David is said to have appointed the musicians to minister before the ark by proclaiming, thanking and praising the LORD (1 Chron. 16.4). While 1 Chron. 16.4-6 and 37-42 tells how, when, where and by whom that was to be done, the psalm of thanksgiving explains why choral music was performed there. In all it gives two reasons for the performance of praise.

The first is by far the more important. In its song of thanksgiving, the choir proclaimed the name of the LORD and called on its audience to do likewise. This is evident from the repeated calls to praise, in which 'proclaim' (v. 8), 'publicize' (v. 8), 'muse on' (v. 9), 'announce' (v. 23), 'relate' (v. 24) and 'say' (v. 31) are used as synonyms for 'singing' and 'making music' to the LORD. Praise was therefore basically a matter of proclamation. Thus the song of thanksgiving was not addressed to the LORD but to human beings and his creation; it did not flatter the deity in order to extract favourable treatment from him but was performed for the benefit of his creatures who lacked what he was ready to give. Hence, as P.A.H. de Boer (1981) has argued, the preposition *lᵉ* with the various terms for the performance of praise in 16.8, 9, 23 means that it was done 'about' him rather than 'to' him.

The Lord and his name were the basic content of this proclamation. The holy name was to be proclaimed (16.8) in thanksgiving (16.35), so that his people could glory in it (16.10) and the gentiles could also honour it (16.29). But that praise was not limited to the mere recitation of his name; it related his acts (8b, 9b, 12, 14, 21, 23, 26b, 31b, 33c), his words (15-19, 22), his gifts (11a, 27b, 34b), his status (25), and his attributes (27a, 34a). All these were part of his name and so were to be proclaimed with it as they revealed his nature and will.

This proclamation of the LORD's name was a performative enactment.[1] It did not merely impart information about the LORD but actually effected his presence, for wherever his name was proclaimed, he was present with his people, as he had promised in Exod. 20.24.[2] Through their performance of praise, the singers introduced the LORD to his people and announced his presence among them. The people could therefore seek him, since he was present with them there (1 Chron. 16.10-11). Through the proclamation of his name in word and song, the LORD presented himself to his people at Jerusalem.

In the choral performance David acted as a herald of the heavenly King to Israel and the nations on earth. He had appointed the musicians as his representatives and had given them the psalm to perform for him. They were commissioned to exercise a double function for him. On the one hand, they announced the LORD and his presence to the assembled congregation. On the other hand, they called on their hearers to join them in proclaiming his name. This call went out first to their fellow Israelites, who were summoned to proclaim the LORD's name and praise his dealings with them in their history on the international arena. Both the singers and the Israelites, in turn, called on the whole world with all its many peoples to praise the LORD, rather than their deities, as the creator of the cosmos, their saviour, and the source of their strength and joy.[3] They also urged the whole cosmos to use its total resources to proclaim the universal reign of the LORD on the international stage. The proclamation of praise by the singers then looked back to his election of Israel as his chosen people and forward to the demonstration of his universal sovereignty.

To motivate them in proclaiming the LORD's name, the singers called on the Israelites to remember the LORD's dealings and covenant

1. See Austin 1975 for an analysis of the nature and function of performative utterances and Grimes 1988 for the application of his ideas to ritual criticism; cf. Assmann 1975: 87-91 for the performative use of divine names in Egyptian hymns.

2. See Niles 1974: 193-96; Mettinger 1982: 125-26; 1988: 8-9; Tournay 1991: 101-102; cf. Eichrodt 1967: 41-42; Kraus 1979: 21-22.

3. Loader (1976: 73-74) argues that, since the nations have no part in the LORD's salvation, they are called merely to acknowledge his glory in choosing and preserving his people. He can, however, only maintain this position by taking vv. 23-27 as addressed to Israel, by excluding the gentiles from Israel's praise, and by interpreting vv. 28-30 as a general, non-cultic call to submission.

with them (16.12-22). His deeds on their behalf and the promises of his covenant demonstrated his commitment to them as their God and the scope of his rule (16.14); his deeds and promises were the grounds of their praise that maintained their hope for their possession of the promised land as well as for their protection from their pagan enemies. At the same time they were to remember their status and function as descendants of Jacob and heirs of the covenant (16.13). As the chosen people of the LORD they had a divinely given royal status and exercised a prophetic function in their praise of him (16.22). As members of his royal choir they were sacrosanct and protected by him.

As they announced the LORD's sovereign presence and called on the congregation to remember the LORD by praising him, the singers also invited the Israelites to worship him as he had ordained. They urged the Israelites to seek the LORD's presence and strength regularly (16.11). They also invited the peoples of the world to relinquish their reverence for their deities and to recognize the sovereignty of the LORD by offering sacrifices to him and prostrating themselves as suppliants before him (16.28-29). In their praise the singers then invited the Israelites and all nations to receive strength and joy from the LORD in their common worship of him, which would lead to the proclamation of him and his goodness in their common praise.

The second reason for the performance of the choral service was to present Israel's petitions to her Lord (16.35). The focus in this, as in the psalm of thanksgiving, was on the relationship of Israel with the nations. Here, however, they are not envisaged as potential partners in praise but as enemies who threatened Israel's very existence as God's people. On behalf of his people, the singers therefore asked him to deliver them from their enemies and gather them from their dispersion among the nations.

The combination of petition with thanksgiving in this psalm is rather unexpected. Hausmann (1987: 89) believes that the two belonged closely together. She maintains that through their praise the singers moved the LORD to receive the petition of his people and to act on their behalf by reminding him of his past dealings with them. 1 Chron. 16.35 is therefore regarded by her as the climax of the psalm; the song of thanksgiving was merely the prelude to the petition for deliverance. This interpretation, however, ignores the obvious separation of petition from thanksgiving. As a piece of literature and as a liturgical text, 16.35 acts as an appendix rather than the culmination of an enactment. Moreover, the result clauses in the petition, which promise further praise as a result of the LORD's requested intervention, clearly subordinate this petition, to the performance of praise.

Thus the choral service begins and ends in praise. Yet that praise does shape the nature of Israel's petitions by reminding it of the LORD's covenant promises and by recalling the LORD's past dealings with them. Petitionary prayer is thus associated with the proclamation of praise. Its requests are motivated by the content of praise, just as the granting of its requests result in renewed praise.

According to the evidence from 1 Chron. 16.4-42, choral music was instituted to proclaim the LORD's name and announce his presence to the congregation and the whole world at Jerusalem. While this was basically the task of the singers, they performed it for David and the people. They not only proclaimed the LORD's name but also called upon the congregation to remember him by joining them in their praise. In their praise they invited both the Israelites and the peoples of the world to seek the LORD's presence and his benefits in their common worship of him. Motivated by the LORD's promises and manifest goodness to his people as expressed in their praise, they petitioned him for their deliverance. Thus, with the transferral of the ark to Jerusalem and the appointment of the singers, provision was made for the public proclamation of the LORD's name there together with the presentation of petitions for Israel.

Sacred Song as Prophecy in 1 Chronicles 25.1-6

Introduction

It is now widely acknowledged that the Chronicler had a special interest in the nature and function of prophecy.[1] In fact, the power of the prophetic word is a major theme of his work. Thus in 2 Chron. 20.20 trust in the LORD is equated with trust in his prophets with the result that obedience to their message is said to ensure national security and success. On the other hand, disobedience to prophecy led to disaster (2 Chron. 24.17-26). Just as the Davidic monarchy had been founded (1 Chron. 11.3) and confirmed dynastically by prophecy

---

1.   After the initial work by Welch (1939: 42-54), this theme has been explored by Willi (1972: 216-29), Newsome (1973), Petersen (1977: 55-96), Seeligmann (1978), Weinberg (1978), Micheel (1983) and Tournay (1991: 34-45).

(1 Chron. 17.3-14), so the rejection of prophecy led to the downfall of the kingdom (2 Chron. 36.15-16).

A number of prophets were particularly prominent in the establishment by David of public worship at Jerusalem. While Nathan had decreed that David's son would build the temple there (1 Chron. 17.12), Gad commanded David to build an altar at the site which the LORD had designated for the temple (1 Chron. 21.18; cf. 22.1). Whereas Samuel organized the gatekeepers for their duties (1 Chron. 9.22), Nathan and Gad instituted sacred song at the LORD's command (2 Chron. 29.25). Prophecy was therefore responsible for the establishment of the temple and the arrangement of its personnel, just as it had founded and confirmed the Davidic dynasty.

The choral rite was thus regarded as a product of prophecy. Yet the interaction between the two did not end there. The three original heads of guilds were called 'seers' (1 Chron. 25.5; 2 Chron. 29.30; 35.15). While their designation as the king's seers shows that they held some office in the royal court, 1 Chron. 25.1-6 asserts that they and all the musicians acted as prophets for the king in the worship at the temple. The question to be considered in this section is how the musicians prophesied at the temple, and why their performance of sacred song was regarded as prophecy.

Problems in the Interpretation of 1 Chronicles 25.1-6
These verses are notorious for the difficulties which they present to their reader. The first problem is the sense of *mispārām* in 25.1. Since this noun normally means 'number' or 'total', some scholars have argued that it is out of place here and belongs to 25.7, because the number of musicians is not stated apart from the six in 25.3 and the fourteen in 25.5.[1] Williamson (1979a: 256), however, is right in arguing that both here and in 1 Chron. 11.11 *mispār* means a 'list'.[2]

---

1.   See Rothstein and Hänel *1927: 447; Welch 1939: 88-89; Petersen 1977: 66. These scholars therefore postulate that vv. 2-6 was added by a later redactor. Peterson (1977: 66-68) goes so far as to argue for three levels of redaction in vv. 1-7, with an initial report of the Asaphites' appointment in vv. 1-2, which was expanded to include the three guilds of singers and was completed by the references to the singers as prophets and by the inclusion of the last nine Hemanite names, to arrive at 24 courses.

2.   Williamson also argues for the unity and originality of 1 Chron. 25.1-6. See 1 Chron. 27.1 for an additional example of *mispār* as 'list'.

This then is the list of names for the casting of lots mentioned in 25.9-31.

The second problem is the list of names from Hananiah to Mahazi-oth in v. 4b. Since the work of Ewald (1870: 680) from the last century, scholars have noted that the rather odd names here can be read as a poem, after a few words have been redivided and a few syllables have been repointed. But whatever the origin of this material, it is quite apparent that the Chronicler took this as a list of names which is how it functions here.

The third problem is whether to construe *b^edibrê hā'^elōhîm* in 25.5 with the preceding or following phrase. Some scholars take the phrase together with *ḥōzēh hammelek*. Thus Rothstein and Hänel (*1927: 450) and Ehrlich (1914: 350) assume that it describes the task of Heman to act as an adviser to the king 'in religious affairs', while Curtis and Madsen (*1910: 278) believe it could also mean that he had become a seer 'by the LORD's commands'.[1] Johnson (1962: 70-71 n. 3; 1979: 78), however, does not take the phrase to refer to Heman's call to be a seer but rather to the words of prophecy spoken by him as the king's seer. Like Johnson, Zalewski (1968: 301) holds that the LORD's words were spoken by Heman. Yet, since he rejects the opinion that Heman acted as a prophet in the strict sense of the word, he understands these words as the lyrics of the psalms. Most scholars, however, construe *b^edibrê hā'^elōhîm* together with the following infinitive as a statement about Heman's sons.[2] They take the phrase as a reference to the LORD's promise to increase the power and influence of Heman by giving him many children.[3] This interpretation is, on balance, to be preferred, since it best fits the immediate context. The emphasis in 25.5a then is not on Heman as the king's seer, but on his sons as given by God.

The fourth problem is whether 1 Chron. 25.6a should be taken to refer to the three guilds or just to the Hemanites. Those scholars who

---

1.   Cf. Petersen 1977: 90 n. 43; Braun *1986: 241.

2.   See Rudolph *1955: 166; Williamson *1982: 168.

3.   Zalewski (1968: 303) considers that the phrase refers to the exaltation of David. Zalewski takes *l^ehārîm qāren* as an abbreviated form of *l^ehārîm qāren m^ešîḥô*. The duty of Heman as the King's seer was to sing royal psalms of praise. While there is much to commend this interpretation, the reference in the first part of the verse to Heman's sons tilts the balance in favour of the more usual interpretation as found in the RSV.

advocate the former solution argue that, since '*ᵃbîhem* may be used distributively for each father, 1 Chron. 25.6 summarizes the content of vv. 2-5 (e.g. Keil *1870: 201). Those who advocate the latter solution base their view on the singular form of '*ᵃbîhem* and the need for a parallel statement to vv. 2b and 3b on the role of the Hemanites. Moreover, *kol-'ēlleh* which occurs both in vv. 5 and 6 is best taken to refer to the same group in both verses. 25.6a then probably refers to the Hemanites.

The fifth problem is how to construe the three names 'Asaph and Jeduthun and Heman' at the end of 1 Chron. 15.6. Three interpretations have been advanced. First, the LXX and T add a copula before Asaph and so take the names together with '*al-yᵉdê hammelek*.[1] Yet this is possible only if the first part of the verse refers to the three guilds rather than just the Hemanites. Secondly, the names are understood as a misplaced gloss on *kol-'ēlleh* earlier in the verse (Rothstein and Hänel *1927: 451). Those scholars who hold that the Hemanites are spoken of here therefore argue that this gloss quite mistakenly changes the subject of the sentence (Rudolph *1955: 166; Williamson *1982: 168). Thirdly and most likely, the names are construed with '*al yᵉdê hammelek* as a summary for 25.2-6a. It describes the general subordination of the three heads of guilds to the king, just as Asaph had earlier been subordinated to him (RSV; NEB; NIV; Braun *1986: 241).

A Translation of 1 Chronicles 25.1-6

v. 1   David and the officers of the army set apart for ritual service the sons of Asaph, Heman and Jeduthun, who were to prophesy[2] with lyres, harps and cymbals.
Their list was—workmen for ritual service:

v. 2   Of the sons of Asaph[3]—Zakkur, Joseph, Nethaniah and Asharelah; the sons of Asaph were under[4] Asaph who prophesied under the king.

---

1.   Cf. Petersen 1977: 64.

2.   K has the noun *hannᵉbî'îm*. Since its *yodh* probably comes from a detached stroke from *aleph*, and since it is qualified by the mention of musical instruments, I follow Q together with many MSS, LXX, T and V, all no doubt influenced by the forms in vv. 2 and 3, and take it as a verb.

3.   The lack of an initial reference to Asaph, in contrast with Jeduthun in v. 3 and Heman in v. 4, may, as Keil (*1870: 200) suggests, be because his guild did not bear his name, but was always called 'the sons of Asaph' (2 Chron. 20.14; 35.15; Ezra 2.41; 3.10; Neh. 7.44).

4.   Or 'at the side of'; cf. vv. 3, 6. See Braun *1986: 246-47.

v. 3   Of Jeduthun—the sons of Jeduthun were Gedaliah, Zeri, Jeshaiah, Shimei,[1] Hashabiah and Mattithiah, that is, six men;
they were under their father Jeduthun who prophesied with the lyre and were in charge of[2] giving thanks and praise to YHWH.

v. 4   Of Heman—the sons of Heman were Bukkiah, Mattaniah, Uzziel, Shebuel and Jerimoth; Hananiah, Hanani, Eliathah, Giddalti and Romamti-ezer; Joshbekashah, Mallothi, Hothir, Mahazi-oth;

v. 5   all these were the sons of Heman, the king's seer, according to the promise of God to raise up his[3] horn;
God gave Heman fourteen sons and three daughters;

v. 6   all these were under their father in the song sung at YHWH's house with cymbals, harps and lyres for the service of God's house.
Asaph and Jeduthun and Heman were under the king.

The Context and Structure of 1 Chronicles 25.1-6

The passage under consideration is part of a chapter on the organization by David of musicians for Solomon's temple. This chapter follows the record of his organization of the Levites and priests in 1 Chronicles 23–24. It is followed by the record of his organization of the gatekeepers and the other Levitical officials in 1 Chronicles 26.

The material in ch. 25 is itself divided into two parts: vv. 1-6 and vv. 7-31. These two parts are not only linked by their common subject matter but also by the catch phrase *way^{e}hî mispārām* in vv. 1 and 7.[4] Both have to do with David's organization of the musicians for their ritual responsibilities at the temple. While the first part deals with the choice of 24 leaders, the function of their music and their relationship to the three heads of guilds and their royal patron, the second part records the number of master musicians eligible for the choral service and the allotment of the 24 leaders into their watches with their members for service at the temple.

1 Chron. 25.1-6 consists of a narrative introduction followed by a

---

1.   Inserted from v. 17 as required by the number six.

2.   As Braun (*1986: 242) notes, the use of the *'al* with an infinitive is unique. It does not, however, substitute for a *lamedh* attached to an infinitive of purpose, as he maintains; rather the punctuation of the MT shows that the infinitives are the activity of the six leaders and not just of Jeduthun. *'al* would therefore indicate their area of responsibility. The *'al* could also be used, as in Lev. 7.12, 13; Num. 6.20; 15.9; 28.10, 15, 24, for what is done in addition to the set ritual; cf. BDB, 755; König (1882: 88).

3.   Read *qarnô* from haplography in the MT.

4.   See Williamson 1979ᵃ: 256; *contra* Rothstein and Hänel *1927: 447.

list in three parts with a conclusion. The material in each of these parts is arranged after a common pattern which is repeated with minor variations. The elements in this pattern are the designation of the guild according to its 'father', the enumeration of those 'sons' who were chosen as leaders of the 24 watches, and their subordination to their 'father'.

There are three significant variations from this pattern. First, only in 25.2 and in the summary in v. 6b are the heads of guilds subordinated to the king, even though all the leaders of the watches are made subordinate to their respective fathers. Secondly, while Asaph and Jeduthun are appointed to prophesy, Heman is put in charge of the liturgical song and its accompaniment at the temple. Lastly, only 25.5 mentions the status of a head of guild as the king's seer as well as God's gift of numerous progeny.

We thus arrive at the following outline of structure for the passage, in which the irregular features are italicized:

A.   David's Organization of the Musicians for their Ministry
     at the Temple: 1 Chron. 25.1

B.   The List of Appointees; 1 Chron. 25.2-6
     1.   Asaph and his sons
          (a)   the four leaders (2a)
          (b)   Asaph's authority, *prophetic task* and
                responsibility (2b)
     2.   Jeduthun and his sons
          (a)   the six leaders (3a)
          (b)   Jeduthun's authority, *prophetic task* and
                musical function (3b)
     3.   Heman and his sons
          (a)   the fourteen leaders (4)
          (b)   *the position of Heman and the reason for his*
                large family (5)
          (c)   Heman's authority *and musical function* (6a)
     4.   The responsibility of Asaph, Jeduthun and Heman
          to the king (6b)

The Prophetic Function of Sacred Song

1 Chron. 25.1-6 reports that David and his generals organized the singers to act as prophets at Solomon's temple. This involved two separate pieces of organization. On the one hand, the 24 leaders of watches from the three guilds were all appointed to prophesy (1 Chron. 25.1).

On the other hand, Asaph and Jeduthun were also set aside to act as prophets in a more specific way, while Heman was merely designated as the king's seer. The Chronicler thereby distinguishes a more general kind of prophecy by all the musicians from a more specific sort of prophecy by Asaph and Jeduthun.[1] Both of these, however, are connected in some way with the ritual performance of sacred song at the temple.

The sense of the commission given to the musicians in 1 Chron. 25.1 has been the matter of some controversy. Generally speaking, there have been two predominant schools of interpretation which vary in taking the term 'prophesy' figuratively or literally.

Those who argue for a figurative sense fall into two groups. Köberle (1899: 4) takes 'prophesy' as a technical term for the performance of sacred song. Yet that hardly does justice to the choice of this verb here. It would indeed be a rather obscure way of saying what could be said more clearly by means of the verbs *šîr* or *zimmēr*. Others hold that this verb qualifies the manner of performance. Thus the verb is taken to refer to the practice of improvization (Ehrlich 1914: 350), or the inspiration of the musicians (Keil *1870: 199), or their ecstatic singing (Slotki *1952: 133), or the power to arouse religious enthusiasm in their audience (Kretzmann *1923: 684). All these interpretations are rather unlikely for two main reasons. First, while the verb *nibbā'* is indeed used elsewhere in the *niphal* and *hithpael* to describe ecstatic behaviour or inspiration by the divine spirit, it is never used figuratively elsewhere in Chronicles. Secondly, these interpretations simply do not match the context. Since the matter under discussion is the organization of personnel for service at the temple, one would expect some mention of what the singers were meant to do rather than of how they were to perform their music.

---

1.   The discussion on the sense of the verb 'prophesy' in 1 Chron. 25 has been overshadowed by the debate on the related and yet separate historical question of the supposed derivation of the postexilic singers from the cult prophets in the monarchical period. The chief advocate of this view has been Mowinckel (1922: 14-22). He has been followed by the influential studies of von Rad (1930: 113-15) and Gese (1963: 222-23). De Vaux (1961: 384-86) has opposed this view by arguing that they descended from the pre-exilic singers at the temple, while Petersen (1977: 55-96) argues that the singers did not derive from pre-exilic prophetic guilds but were given prophetic status by the Chronicler and his compatriots. Zalewski (1968: 296-310) maintains that the singers themselves assumed prophetic and priestly attributes to enhance their status, but does not postulate when this occurred.

Even though most scholars agree that the Chronicler regarded the songs sung in the choral service as a kind of prophecy, there is some disagreement on exactly how they functioned as prophecy. In all, three points of view have been propounded. First, some of those who hold that the musical guilds evolved or took over from the cultic prophets in the pre-exilic period argue that the musicians delivered inspired prophetic utterances either as free musical compositions or, more likely, in prescribed liturgical forms (von Rad 1930: 114-15; Galling *1954: 73). Arens (1961: 52) even maintains that they not only addressed God in praise and petition for the congregation, but also, like the cultic prophets, addressed the congregation with God's word in a blessing, or declaration of forgiveness, or an oracle given in answer to their prayer. Such an interpretation, however, is too broad. It goes beyond the evidence in 1 Chron. 25.1, which refers merely to the prophetic character of the regular choral service.

Secondly, in reaction to this view, Zalewski (1968: 301-302, 305, 309-10) maintains that, since the words of the psalms were regarded as words of God given by divine inspiration, they had prophetic power, when accompanied by musical instruments, to create success and well-being for those who heard them. In support of this he postulates that *b^edibrê hā'^elōhîm* in 25.5 refers to the lyrics of the psalms, as do 'the words of David and Asaph the seer' in 2 Chron. 29.30. Even though this interpretation of 1 Chron. 25.5 is, as has already been shown, rather unlikely, his argument for the prophetic power of the psalms sung in the choral service is valid, though a little too limited in scope.

Thirdly and most likely, Rudolph (*1955: 171) maintains that the singing of the psalms by the temple choir was a form of prophetic proclamation. The verb *nibbā'* describes the ritual function and significance of sacred song. Even though the singers did not receive prophetic oracles directly from the LORD to deliver to the people, they did proclaim the LORD to them in music and song, just as the prophets in 1 Sam. 10.5-6 had prophesied to musical accompaniment. Rudolph, however, does not go beyond these rather brief assertions, nor does he explain how and why their proclamation was considered prophetic.

In the light of the data on the nature of the choral service elsewhere in Chronicles, the proclamation of the singers could be regarded as prophetic in four ways. First, since they stood in God's presence at the

temple and mediated between him and his people, their status and
authority was prophetic, in that they spoke for God to his people. Like
some of the prophets they were authorized to intercede for the people
in their songs. Yet such intercession was not associated with the
delivery of a corresponding prophetic oracle, as is evident from
1 Chron. 16.35. Secondly, the manner of their proclamation was prophetic. Like many of the classical prophets they addressed the people
in poetry and song. Thirdly, and most significantly, by its association
with the burnt offering their proclamation was prophetic in purpose.
They proclaimed the LORD's acceptance of his people with their burnt
offering and admonished them to act appropriately. Thus they not
only proclaimed the LORD's name and his benefits in their praise but
also urged the people to remember him and seek his help in their
worship. Furthermore, by praising the LORD as the only God, they
also passed judgment on the pagan gods and proclaimed his salvation
to the nations (cf. 1 Chron. 16.23-27). Fourthly, their proclamation
was prophetic in power, since it was empowered by the LORD himself.
It did not merely speak about him and his strength but actually communicated him and his strength to the people (cf. 2 Chron. 30.21).
Like the prophetic oracles of salvation, their praise presupposed the
LORD's acceptance of his people and brought his salvation to them.
Their praise was effectual, because in it they proclaimed the LORD's
name and announced his goodness to the people. Thus the proclamation of the singers was prophetic in status, manner, function and power.

In 1 Chron. 25.1-6 the Chronicler explains the significance of the
choral service by treating it as a species of prophecy.[1] All the singers
exercised a prophetic role in their singing at the temple. Even though
the singers did not usually act as prophets by communicating divine
oracles to the people, their regular musical performance was regarded
by the Chronicler as a 'kind of ritualized prophecy' 'in which God
spoke to his people' (Newsome 1973: 224-25).[2] It announced his

---

1.   This connection between the LORD's acceptance of his people with their
sacrifices and the singing of his praises is not restricted to Chronicles. Thus just as
the LORD's rejection of his people's sacrifices had resulted in his silencing of their
songs in Amos 5.21-23, so in Jer. 33.10-11 his future acceptance of them would
lead to a renewal of song (cf. Isa. 42.10-13; 44.22-23; 51.3).

2.   For evidence of further development of the belief that the proclamation of
praise, when empowered by God's spirit, was a kind of prophecy, see Lk. 1.67-79
and 2.27-32 as well as the rabbinical material collected by Grözinger (1982: 99-107).

gracious acceptance of their burnt offering and his favourable disposition to them.

The Proclamation and Celebration of the LORD's Presence through Sacred Song in 2 Chronicles 5.2–7.11

Introduction

With the story of the consecration of the temple in 2 Chron. 5.2–7.11, we come to 'one of the major climaxes' in Chronicles (Williamson *1982: 213). It is the culmination of the narrative which began with the capture of Jerusalem by David in 1 Chronicles 11 and his transferral of the ark there in 1 Chronicles 15–16, the fulfilment of the promises made to David in 1 Chronicles 17 about the construction of the temple by his successor, and the goal of his preparations in 1 Chronicles 22–26 and 28–29. It therefore comes as no surprise that the choral rite, which had been instituted by David with the coming of the ark to Jerusalem, should figure so prominently in its ceremonial installation in the temple. In fact, the Chronicler uses this occasion to give us an epitome of his theology of praise by showing the role of choral music in evoking and celebrating the LORD's presence at his temple in Jerusalem.

This interest in sacred song is evident from the changes and additions made to the text from 1 Kgs 8.1-66. While the Chronicler retains most of his received text, he does shift the focus and purpose of the narrative significantly by making some additions and so altering the structure of the account.

First, he leaves out Solomon's address at the conclusion of his prayer in 1 Kgs 8.54-61 which had, together with the corresponding initial address in 1 Kgs 8.14-21, framed his prayer for the confirmation of the Davidic dynasty and the acceptance of Israel's petitions at the temple. It is replaced by the public manifestation of divine glory to the assembled congregation with the descent of fire on the altar in 2 Chron. 7.1-3, which thus forms a parallel to the secret filling of the temple with the LORD's glory in 2 Chron. 5.11-14, taken from 1 Kgs 8.10-11. This change focuses attention on the altar and its sacrifices which is, as Rudolph (*1955: 217-18) has noted, consistent with the Chronicler's understanding of the temple as 'a house of sacrifice' (2 Chron. 7.12) as well as a place of prayer.[1] We are thus given to

---

1. The same interest in the altar and the sacrifices presented there is evident in

understand that Solomon offered his prayer in connection with the
presentation of the public sacrifices on the altar. The same concern is
evident in the Chronicler's interpretation of the first week in the
fortnight of celebrations at Jerusalem as 'the inauguration of the altar'
in 2 Chron. 7.9. Thus, whereas Kings had taken the LORD's manifestation of his glory in the temple as the presupposition for his acceptance
of Israel's prayers there, the Chronicler associates both the manifestation of divine glory and the acceptance of prayer with the presentation
of the public sacrifices at the altar.

Secondly, in 2 Chron. 6.41-42 he adds a new conclusion from
Ps. 132.8-10 to the prayer of Solomon.[1] Taken together with the new
material in 2 Chron. 7.1-3, this conclusion changes the point of the
whole prayer. The ritual function of Solomon's prayer in Kings had
been to secure the LORD's acceptance of Israel's prayers at the temple
in the time to come. Ritually speaking, it had nothing to do with the
consecration of the temple which was accomplished by the installation
of the ark in the temple (1 Kgs 8.2-11), Solomon's presentation of the
temple to the LORD (1 Kgs 8.12-13), and the offering up of sacrifices
there (1 Kgs 8.62-64). The Chronicler, however, changes the ritual
function of the prayer by associating it with the consecration of the
altar. He distinguishes between the consecration of the temple in
2 Chron. 5.11-14 by the entry of God's glory and the consecration of
the altar in 2 Chron. 7.1-3 by the descent of fire. With this came
certain changes in the ritual, by which this was accomplished. Thus,
whereas the temple was dedicated to the LORD by the insertion of the
ark and the choral performance in 2 Chron. 5.2-14, the altar was
dedicated by Solomon's prayer and the presentation of the public
sacrifices upon it in 2 Chron. 6.12–7.3.

The addition of 6.41-42 ties the prayer closely to the subsequent
manifestation of divine glory by the descent of fire on the altar. In
these verses Solomon makes two main requests. First, he asks the LORD
to manifest his divine power to and for his people by making the
temple his permanent residence. Secondly, he asks the LORD to exercise
his power there for the benefit of his people through the ministry of
his priests. Both these requests are answered publicly by the subsequent theophany, for, by the acceptance of their sacrifices, the LORD

the Chronicler's additions at 1 Chron. 21.28-22.1; 2 Chron. 2.3-5; 4.1; 5.12; 8.13.

1.   For discussion on this addition, see Myers *1965[b]: 37-38; Williamson
*1982: 220-21; Welten 1979.

intervened on his people's behalf and so demonstrated his powerful presence with them there.

Thirdly, in addition to the mention in 2 Chron. 7.3 of the congregation's involvement in sacred song, the Chronicler inserts more material on the choral service at two significant points in the account taken from 1 Kings. On the one hand, he introduces a rather detailed description of the full choral service performed by the priests and Levitical singers in 2 Chron. 5.11b–13a.[1] This comes in the account of the appearance of the glory cloud in the temple after the insertion of the ark. On the other hand, between the mention of the animals slaughtered for peace offerings in 2 Chron. 7.4-5 and the reference to the consecration of the inner court in 2 Chron. 7.7, he adds a note on the relative positions of the priests and singers for performing their songs of thanksgiving. By the addition of these three passages the Chronicler associates the choral service with the presence of the LORD's glory in the temple, the presentation of sacrifices there, and the manifestation of the LORD's glory in fire during the presentation of the sacrifices.

The Structure of 2 Chronicles 5.2–7.11

The most recent and ambitious attempt to account for the literary arrangement of 2 Chron. 5.2–7.11 comes from R.B. Dillard (*1987: 5-7; 1980[a]: 299-300; 1984). He contends that the whole of 2 Chronicles 1–9 was arranged as an elaborate chiasm with a pattern of correspondence between 1 Chron. 1.1-17 and 9.13-28, 2.1-16 and 8.17–9.12, 2.17–5.1 and 8.1-16, 5.2–7.10 and 7.11-22. I shall therefore consider his case to see whether it can supply a literary key to identify the main concerns of the Chronicler in this account.

The part of his argument which has some bearing on this discussion is his analysis of 2 Chron. 5.2–7.22, which forms the centre of his proposed chiasm. Yet, as he himself admits, this crucial section is 'most convoluted in its general structure' (1984: 89). There is no direct echo of 5.2–7.10 in 7.11-22 but rather two separate patterns of arrangement.

First, he claims that the two speeches of Solomon in 6.1-42 to the people and then to God correspond with the twofold reply of God to Solomon and the people in 7.11-22. This, however, can only be

---

1.   For the refutation of Rudolph's argument (*1955: 211) on the addition of 5.11b-13a by a later redactor, see Zalewski 1968: 357-58 n. 3; Williamson *1982: 215-16; Dillard *1987: 40-41.

sustained by ignoring the address to the LORD in 6.1-2 and the literary unity of 7.12-22 as a single oracle from the LORD. Moreover, the second appearance of the LORD to Solomon corresponds more readily with his first appearance in 2 Chron. 1.7-13. Thus, even though God's answer echoes Solomon's prayer thematically and terminologically as could well be expected, the case for a chiastic match is rather weak.

Secondly, the proposed correspondence between 6.1-42 and 7.11-22 is complicated by 5.2-14 and 7.1-10 which are said to form their own separate chiastic bracket around 6.1-42. On the face of it, the case here seems much stronger. Thus the summons by Solomon in 5.2-3, the presentation of sacrifices in 5.4-10, the performance of music in 5.11b-13 and the glory cloud in 5.13b-14 are said to be matched by the glory cloud in 7.1-2, the sacrifices in 7.4-5 and 7, the choral service in 7.3 and 6 and the dismissal in 7.8-10. Yet even here there is no clear chiastic pattern. There are no common markers for the opening and closing of each unit. Moreover, if 7.1-10 was supposed to echo 5.2-14, the Chronicler could easily have rearranged his material, so that the references to the sacrifices would be separated from the references to the choral service in 7.1-7 to round off the chiasm.

The case of Dillard for the chiastic arrangement of 2 Chron. 5.2–7.22 is thus rather forced. In his concern to discover a chiastic structure, he has not delineated the limits of each literary unit correctly, nor has he noticed the relation of the units to each other. This has been done more satisfactorily by Braun (1973: 510-11) and Williamson (*1982: 212-13). On the one hand, Williamson notes that, just as 5.1 rounds off the account of the temple's construction, so 7.11 rounds off the account of its dedication (p. 224). 7.12-22 must therefore be taken as a separate unit of narrative. On the other hand, he observes that the words of Solomon in 6.1-11 do not belong together with his prayer in 6.12-42 but with what precedes it (p. 216). Thus, whereas the first two speeches in 6.1-11 comment on the transferral of the ark into the temple, the prayer before the altar in 6.12-42 has to do with the consecration of the altar in 7.1-3.

Taking this into account, we therefore arrive at the following two-part arrangement of this section:

A. *The Consecration of the Temple by the LORD*: 5.2–6.11

    1.   The assembly of Israel at Solomon's command (5.2-3).
    2.   The transferral of the ark into the temple (5.4-10).
    3.   The advent of the LORD's glory during sacred song (5.11-14).

4. Solomon's presentation of the temple to the LORD (6.1-2).
5. Solomon's explanation of his reasons for building the temple (6.3-11).

B. *The Consecration of the Altar by the LORD*: 6.12–7.10

1. Solomon's prayer for the dedication of the altar
   (a) introduction (6.12-13)
   (b) petition for the confirmation of the Davidic dynasty (6.14-17)
   (c) petition for the acceptance of Israel's prayers (6.18-40)
   (d) petition for the LORD's intervention for his people (6.40-41).
2. The manifestation of God's glory by the descent of fire on the altar and the people's response (7.1-3).
3. The presentation of sacrifices with songs of praise (7.4-6).
4. The consecration of the inner court (7.7).
5. The fortnight of celebration (7.8-9).
6. Solomon's dismissal of the people (7.10).

The Theological Significance of Sacred Song in 2 Chronicles 5.2–7.11
The Importance of Precedent. In this section of Chronicles the choral performance is mentioned three times. None of these references are found in 1 Kings 8, but they have all been introduced by the Chronicler at certain key points of the narrative. Whether these passages came from sources at his disposal or whether they were his own composition, they nevertheless together present the most complete statement in Chronicles on the nature and significance of liturgical song at the temple.

The weight of these passages does not just come from their content but also from their setting. They are contained within the account of the inauguration of worship at the temple in Jerusalem. This itself is, as has already been argued, the climax of the story of its establishment which began with the conquest of Jerusalem. The Chronicler concentrates on the foundation of worship at the temple, because for him its foundation not only determined its nature and significance but also set precedents for its subsequent operation and development.

This story sets precedents in three areas of ritual activity. First, it sets certain social precedents by determining who was involved in worship at the temple, where, and with whom. Thus the Chronicler deliberately includes the Levitical singers in the company of celebrants which had previously consisted of the king, the elders and the priests. It also sets certain ritual precedents in contentious areas for subsequent observance. The Chronicler describes exactly who performs what aspect of ritual and when. So, for example, while

Solomon presented the temple to the LORD, blessed the people, and offered petitions for himself and his people, the singers performed their song together with the priestly trumpeters, after the ark had been installed in the temple by the priests and as the sacrifices were presented on the altar. Most importantly, the account sets certain theological precedents. The Chronicler takes the activity of God in occupying the temple with his glory and in manifesting his glory to the people at the high point of the sacrificial ritual as an indication of his ongoing involvement in the sacrificial ritual at the temple. These three sets of precedents are all equally important, since God's inter-action with his people in their regular worship depended on the per-formance of the proper ritual by the rightly authorized ministrants.

This notion of ritual precedent in this foundational story is presup-posed in the following discussion of how the choral rite was involved in the interaction between God and his people in their worship at the temple and why.

The Evocation of God's Glory in 2 Chronicles 5.11-14

v. 11   Now when the priests came out of the holy place, for all the priests present had consecrated themselves without regard[1] for any divisions,

v. 12   and all[2] the Levitical musicians—Asaph, Heman and Jeduthun, with their sons and kinsmen—were standing east of the altar, dressed in linen, with[3] cymbals, harps and lyres,[4] and with them 120 priests were playing with trumpets,

v. 13   and[5] together[6] the trumpeters and musicians

---

1.   See GKC §114 k and l.

2.   See Kropat 1909: 7 for the emphatic use of l^e with nouns in apposition with the nominative case, and for the position of $l^e kull\bar{a}m$ (49).

3.   For the *beth* of concomitance in Chronicles, see Driver 1913: 539 and Kropat 1909: 39.

4. b^e may be excluded for euphonic reasons before a k^e.

5.   The main problem in translating v. 13a is how to construe its relationship with the preceding and following clauses. Two solutions have been proposed. First, Curtis and Madsen (*1910: 340) take $way^e h\hat{i}$ as a resumption of the same verb in the previ-ous verse. They therefore construe 13a as the first of three temporal clauses, all intro-duced by a preposition with an infinitive construct. The difficulty with this is that, while b^e or k^e may be used as temporal prepositions with an infinitive construct, l^e never has this temporal sense. Secondly, like the LXX, Rudolph (*1955: 210) seems to take 13a as another circumstantial clause with the other two participial clauses in v. 12. This is the better solution, for we then have a logical progression from separate descriptions of the musicians and trumpeters in v. 12 to their common task in v. 13a.

were making proclamation[1] with one sound[2] by praising and thanking[3] YHWH; and when they raised[4] a sound with trumpets, cymbals, and the instruments of song, and praised YHWH, 'Truly he is good! Truly his generosity is for ever!', the temple[5] was filled with the cloud of[6] YHWH's house,[7]

v. 14   so that the priests could not stand to minister before the cloud, because the glory of YHWH filled the house of God.

What we have here is a single complex sentence which stems largely from the Chronicler. Into the simple sentence from 1 Kings consisting of a temporal clause followed by two main clauses, he has made two

6.   The LXX takes k^e'$eh\bar{a}d$ as the subject of $way^eh\hat{i}$. It was probably derived from k^e'$\hat{i}\check{s}$ '$eh\bar{a}d$ (Num. 14.15; Judg. 20.1, 8, 11; 1 Sam. 11.7) in classical Hebrew, and was used adverbially in postexilic Hebrew with a verb (Ezra 3.9; Isa. 65.25) or adjective (Ezra 6.20; Eccl. 11.6) as a synonym for the older word $yahd\bar{a}w$, as seen in the replacement of $yahd\bar{a}w$ (Isa. 11.6) by k^e'$eh\bar{a}d$ in Isa. 65.25.

1.   The use of l^e and an infinitive after $way^eh\hat{i}$ is rather unusual. Its nearest parallel is found in 2 Chron. 26.5. It could be construed in one of three ways. First, Rudolph (*1955: 210) seems to take it as an infinitive of obligation (cf. Driver 1892: 275; Kropat 1909: 24). The problem with this is that v. 13a then becomes a prescription after the apparent descriptions in v. 12. Secondly, and more likely, it could be taken as the subject of $way^eh\hat{i}$ and used with l^e for the doer of the action, as in 2 Chron. 13.5; 20.17; 22.9; Ezra 4.3; cf. 1 Chron. 5.1; 29.12. But $h\bar{a}y\hat{a}$ is not used in any of these cases. Lastly, and most likely, it could be used, like the participle with $h\bar{a}y\hat{a}$, here as in 2 Chron. 26.5, to describe continued action (see BDB, 227; Holl, 78).

2.   Since $ha\check{s}m\hat{i}a$' is used intransitively elsewhere in Chronicles (1 Chron. 15.16, 19, 28; 16.5, 42; cf. Neh. 12.42), $q\hat{o}l$ '$eh\bar{a}d$ is best construed here as an adverbial accusative.

3.   These infinitives could also indicate the purpose of the performance.

4.   See Polzin 1976: 56-57 for the Chronicler's use of k^e and b^e on infinitive constructs without $h\bar{a}y\hat{a}$ in temporal clauses.

5.   The Chronicler also uses a disjunctive waw for the apodosis to a temporal clause in 1 Chron. 15.29, 2 Chron. 7.1 and 26.19.

6.   In 1 Kgs 8.10 'the cloud' is the subject rather than 'the house'. Isa. 6.4 and Ezra 10.4 may have influenced this change.

7.   As Keil (*1870: 243) notes, the indefinite form of the noun suggests that it be taken as a construct and revocalized accordingly. There would otherwise be no reason for the change from Kings. Apart from this there are three other possibilities, listed in order of probability. (1) $b\hat{e}t$ YHWH could be omitted as a marginal gloss on $b\hat{e}t$ $h\bar{a}$'$^el\bar{o}h\hat{i}m$ in 5.14 taken from 1 Kgs 8.11 and mistakenly reintroduced here. (2) It may be construed as an appositional expansion on $habbayit$, which, however, hardly seems necessary. (3) $b\hat{e}t$ may be emended to $k\bar{a}b\hat{o}d$ from the LXX, which, however, was probably influenced by the wording of the following verse.

major insertions. First, there are the four parenthetical clauses in 11b-
13a. While the first of these is a causal clause which explains why the
whole priesthood was involved in the ceremony, the next three are
circumstantial clauses which mention the position of the musicians, the
cooperation of the trumpeters with them, and the united performance
of both these groups. Secondly, there are two additional temporal
clauses in 13a, each introduced by an infinitive construct with a
preposition. These clauses describe the actual musical performance.
The skeleton of the new sentence then consists of three temporal
protases followed by two apodoses.

The Chronicler makes these changes in order to expound his theology of sacred song. Both Kings and Chronicles place equal weight on
the occupation of the temple by God's glory on the day of its dedication. Yet they differ on the nature of the ritual enactment through which
this occurred. The author of Kings held that it was accomplished by
the introduction of the ark into the temple. Hence the glory of the
LORD would presumably remain there as long as the ark was still present. The Chronicler, however, modifies this view in the light of the
absence of the ark from the second temple. He presents a concept of
the divine presence in the temple which was less localized and more
closely linked to the regular performance of the sacrificial ritual.

Now the Chronicler could very easily have connected the choral
service with the transferral of the ark into the temple in 2 Chron. 5.5-
7, as he had done with its transportation to Jerusalem in 1 Chronicles
15. This would have satisfied any need to include the singers in this
foundational event but would not have indicated their continuing
involvement in the ritual at the temple. He therefore makes it quite
clear that liturgical song began only after the ark had been deposited
in the temple, and that its performance was associated with the entrance
of the LORD's glory into the temple. Thus, while he does not entirely
dissociate the divine glory from the ark, he links its advent with the
performance of choral music. The transferral of the ark was a pre-
condition for the appearance of the LORD's glory, but its actual
entrance into the temple occurred during the singing of sacred song.

There has not been much reflection on this remarkable feature of
Chronicles. So, for instance, Curtis and Madsen (*1910: 339) merely
note that the appearance of the glory-cloud coincides with the outburst
of sacred song. It has received five different explanations. First, it is
taken to refer anachronistically to what used to happen at the temple

in the postexilic period (Coggins *1976: 163). Yet this is rather unlikely, since all the priests and musicians were not involved on any single occasion in the regular worship at the temple. Nor did the glory of the LORD ever again visibly appear at the temple during the choral performance.

Secondly, other commentators merely take it as further evidence of the Chronicler's delight in pageantry and choral music (Williamson *1982: 215; Dillard *1987: 42). That may well be the case, but it does not by itself account for the association of sacred song with the presence of God's glory in the temple.

Thirdly, the entrance of God's glory into the temple during the singing of sacred song is taken by Sendrey (1969: 538) as a mark of God's approval of the choral service, just as its entrance in Kings demonstrated his approval of the temple. There may be an element of truth in this, but it seems to apply more readily to the manifestation in 2 Chron. 7.1-3 which, as Arens (1961: 47-48) has shown,[1] confirmed the legitimacy of both the temple and its services as instituted by David.

Fourthly, while Roubos (*1972: 67) claims that sacred song was the prelude to the LORD's appearance, Arens (1961: 46) and Becker (*1988: 24) hold that its performance produced the divine theophany. This also misses the mark, for the actual theophany occurred only later after Solomon's prayer (7.1-3). The emphasis here is not on the public appearance of God's glory but on its veiled presence and hidden occupation of the temple.

Lastly, Rudolph (*1955: 211) and a few scholars after him[2] maintain that the choral service evoked the divine glory. This interpretation best fits the context. The divine glory was evoked by the enunciation of the LORD's name and the proclamation of his virtues in sacred song. It was not produced by the music itself, however grand it may have been, but rather by the singing of the common refrain for thanksgiving by the whole choir with full musical accompaniment. This refrain was the most significant element in the performance of the choral service on that momentous occasion, for by it the LORD's

1. Keil (*1870: 247) takes it only as the divine confirmation of sacrificial worship there.
2. See Koch 1961: 541; Mayer 1986: 437. Zalewski (1968: 357) maintains that the common performance of the singers and trumpeters ensured 'the presence of the glory of God in the Temple'.

glory was evoked. While the harps and lyres accompanied the singing of the refrain, the trumpets and cymbals announced the LORD's entrance into his temple and proclaimed his veiled presence to the congregation who knew about it only through the choral performance.

Several features of this account show that in it the Chronicler meant to reveal the significance of the regular choral performance. First, the choir did not sing a special anthem composed for the occasion but the refrain for thanksgiving which was the epitome of the regular choral service (1 Chron. 16.8, 34, 41; 2 Chron. 7.3, 6). Secondly, the choral service was performed in front of the altar, after the priests had performed their ministry within the temple, as was the case in the daily ritual. Thirdly, the note taken from Kings about the exclusion of the priests from the temple seems to be aetiological in its intent. The author of Kings had explained why the priests were absent from the temple at the height of the daily ritual. The Chronicler, however, puts the choral performance in this slot and so contrasts the regular ministry of the musicians with the regular ministry of the priests by associating it with the hidden presence of the LORD in his temple.[1] The incident from 1 Kgs 8.10-12 lends itself to this reinterpretation, because it does not have to do with the visible manifestation of the LORD's glory as in 2 Chron. 7.1-3, which was an extraordinary event, but with the presence of the LORD in the temple with his glory veiled in a cloud.

In 2 Chron. 5.11-14 the Chronicler sketches out his theology of the choral service in a simple narrative. In the service for the dedication of the temple as well as in the regular services at the temple, the appointed musicians evoked the LORD's glory by proclaiming his name in sacred song. That glory was veiled in a cloud and hidden within the recesses of the temple away from the sight of the congregation. It was, however, announced to the people in the songs which glorified the LORD. His glory, which was evoked by sacred song, was thus made known to them verbally rather than visually in the choral performance. U.S. Leupold (1969: 180) may therefore be justified in making this claim:

> Here then lies the rationale for the hymn of praise to Yahweh. In a sense
> he himself is its author. He demands the *tehillah*. He needs it in order to

---

1. The absence of the priests from the temple is mentioned again in 2 Chron. 7.2 by the Chronicler, as if to underline the importance of this matter. Like Exod. 40.35, 2 Chron. 7.2 mentions their inability to *enter* the temple, as opposed to an ability to stand in service within it as in 2 Chron. 5.14.

maintain and make public his *kabod*. It is a reflection of his *kabod*. The song of praise is part and parcel of his epiphany.

The Choral Celebration of God's Glory and Goodness in 2 Chronicles 7.1-3. The mention of sacred song in 2 Chron. 7.1-3 not only echoes but also stands in contrast to 5.10-14. In both cases the same refrain was sung, while the priests were excluded from the temple by the glory cloud. Both were also associated with the presentation of the public sacrifices at the altar. Yet, despite these similarities, the two performances of sacred song differ in two respects. First, while the choral music evoked the LORD's glory in 5.10-14, it was, as Roubos (*1972: 88) observes, performed in response to the public manifestation of his glory in 7.1-3. Secondly, whereas the refrain was sung by the choir in the former case, the whole congregation joined in the singing of it in the latter. In this way the Chronicler explores the theological significance of the choral service from two different angles.

First, the song of thanksgiving came in response to the descent of fire on the altar and the appearance of the LORD's glory over the temple. The reaction of the people to this parallels what happened at the inauguration of sacrificial worship at the tabernacle in Lev. 9.24.[1] This account, however, has an additional element which has no parallel there or elsewhere in the Old Testament. The glory of the LORD which had previously filled the temple was revealed to the people by appearing 'over' the temple.[2] This was God's answer to Solomon's request in 2 Chron. 6.41 for the LORD to settle in the temple. The appearance of the LORD's glory 'over' the temple showed that this had in fact occurred. Thus the descent of fire from heaven coincided with the manifestation of the LORD's glory as it settled 'over' the temple, just as the glory cloud had once settled 'over' the tabernacle.

By treating the descent of fire on the altar and the appearance of God's glory over the temple as a single event, the Chronicler shows

1. In 1 Chron. 21.26 the Chronicler also mentions the descent of fire from heaven in answer to David's invocation of the LORD at the inaugural sacrifices in Jerusalem. Mosis (1973: 150-55) rightly notes that both these cases differ from Lev. 9.24, where fire is said to 'proceed' from the LORD's presence, and 1 Kgs 18.38, where it is said to have 'fallen'. He, however, uses the parallel account in 2 Macc. 2.4-10 to argue that in 7.1-3 the Chronicler foreshadows the future manifestation of divine glory at the final restoration of Israel.

2. The nearest parallels to this are found in Exod. 40.35, 38 and Num. 9.18-19, 22, where the cloud is said to have settled over the tabernacle.

that the LORD accepted both the temple and the sacrificial worship there. The temple therefore became his place of residence where he would subsequently receive the sacrifices and answer the prayers of his people. Moreover, by coupling the fire on the altar with the disclosure of the LORD's glory, the Chronicler seems to suggest that, just as the fire burnt up the daily burnt offerings on the altar, so the LORD also met daily with his people to accept their sacrifices and their prayers there. Thus, as the temple was the place for the LORD's daily audiences with his people, the sacrificial ritual at the altar was the means by which he met with his people, pardoned their transgressions and granted their petitions.

The people reacted to this manifestation by prostrating themselves and breaking out into thanksgiving. They thereby acknowledged that they were in the presence of the LORD, and that he was favourably disposed to them. In their song they also thanked him for taking the temple as his residence and accepting their sacrifices as the ritual agency for approaching him there in prayer. This unique event then established a precedent for the LORD's daily acceptance of his people's sacrifices and prayers. It also established a precedent for their regular response to his acceptance in prostration and thanksgiving.

Secondly, by means of their involvement in sacred song, the people rejoiced in the LORD's goodness. In the conclusion to Solomon's prayer which had come from Ps. 132.8-10, the Chronicler makes an apparently unwarranted change to the text by replacing $y^e rann\bar{e}n\hat{u}$ with $yi\acute{s}m^e\d{h}\hat{u}$ $ba\d{t}\d{t}\hat{o}b$ in 2 Chron. 6.41. It is unlikely that he did so because he regarded the verb as obscure and archaic, since he used it quite readily in 1 Chron. 16.33 as well as its noun in 2 Chron. 6.19 and 20.22. There must then be some other reason for the change.

The term itself is not common. It is found elsewhere only in Deut. 26.11, where it occurs in the legislation for the presentation of firstfruits. After they had been set down at the altar, the Israelite was to perform an act of prostration and 'rejoice in all the goodness' of the LORD to him and his family. It is, however, uncertain whether the Chronicler alludes to this verse or not. At the very least, the use of the term in Deut. 26.11 and its rarity suggest that the reasons for the change are theological.

This change seems to have been influenced by $\acute{s}^em\bar{e}\d{h}\hat{i}m$ $w^e\d{t}\hat{o}b\hat{e}$ $l\bar{e}b$ $`al...ha\d{t}\d{t}\hat{o}b\hat{a}$ $^{`a}\check{s}er$ $`\bar{a}\acute{s}\hat{a}$ YHWH $l^ed\bar{a}w\bar{i}d$, which was taken from 1 Kgs 8.66 and included in 2 Chron. 7.10 with the addition of $w^eli\check{s}^el\bar{o}m\bar{o}h$.

With the addition of *ṭôb* in 7.3, the Chronicler thus establishes a link by catch word between the rejoicing of God's people in 6.41, their song of thanksgiving in 7.3, and their persistent jubilation at his goodness in 7.10.

The argument implied in this seems to run as follows. In 2 Chron. 6.41-42 Solomon asked the LORD to make the temple his resting place, so that his people could 'rejoice' there in his 'goodness'. This joy in his 'goodness' comes from the 'help' (*tᵉšû'â*) given to them through the ministry of the priests as established by David and Solomon, his anointed kings,[1] and from the LORD's acceptance of their intercession. His acceptance of their intercession rests upon his promised mercies to David.[2] So that the LORD's people could rejoice in his 'goodness', Solomon asked the LORD to accept his prayer and the temple with its sacrificial apparatus, which both he and David had established.

This came to pass in 7.3 with the thanksgiving of the people for the LORD's 'goodness' to them in accepting their sacrifices at the altar. By his theophany, the LORD indicated that he would henceforth be present with them in their worship and grant his help to them. This was as certain as his covenant with David, for, through the establishment of the temple and its services, Solomon not only fulfilled the basic condition for the permanency of his dynasty,[3] but the people also began to enjoy the benefits of the LORD's covenant with David. They benefited materially and spiritually from the king's patronage of the sacrificial ritual and choral music at the temple, for through it they could feast on the sacrifices for thanksgiving offered for them by the king as their host (2 Chron. 7.4-5, 7-9), approach the LORD in prayer, and praise him in sacred song. Thus, as a result of their involvement in the sacred services, established by David and Solomon, all Israel returned home 'rejoicing' in the LORD's 'goodness' to them through David and Solomon (7.10), which was why choral music had been instituted (1 Chron. 15.16; 2 Chron. 23.18; 29.30; cf. 30.21- 26).

By their participation in the song of thanksgiving sung during the presentation of the burnt offering, the people acknowledged the

---

1. Dillard (*1987: 51) argues that, just as the Chronicler added the name of Solomon to David in 7.10, he also altered the singular *mᵉšîḥekā* from Ps. 132.10 to a plural to give equal weight to both kings in 6.42.

2. Williamson (1978) argues for this as an objective genitive, while Dillard (*1987: 51-52) takes it as a subjective genitive; cf. Adinolfi 1966.

3. See Williamson 1977[b]: 138-42; 1983: 313-18.

LORD's presence with them there and reacted gratefully to his acceptance of their prayers. They were also filled with joy as they rejoiced in his goodness in granting his help to them through the ministry of the priests at the temple, and in commissioning David and Solomon to establish the temple with its services. Thus through sacred song they celebrated God's glory and rejoiced in his goodness to them.

The Proclamation and Celebration of Deliverance in Sacred Song in 2 Chronicles 20.1-30

Introduction

In Chronicles warfare is associated with the performance of public worship at the temple. This association of martial activities with cultic matters is shown in a number of ways which are rather puzzling to the modern reader.

First, martial imagery and terminology are at times used to describe the temple and its officials. Thus, while the temple was pictured as the LORD's camp with his military headquarters in 2 Chron. 31.2, the four chief gatekeepers who formed his palace guard (1 Chron. 9.18-19), were called *gibbōrê haššō'ʿarîm* in 1 Chron. 9.26, that is, 'champion gatekeepers'.[1] The heads of the priestly families in charge of the ritual at the temple were called 'champions in the work of service at the LORD's house' in 1 Chron. 9.13. Just as there was a 'division' of soldiers on active duty in the army each month of the year (1 Chron. 27.1-15), so 'divisions' of priests (1 Chron. 24.1; 28.13, 21; 2 Chron. 5.11; 8.14; 23.8; 31.2, 15-16), Levites (1 Chron. 23.6; 28.13, 21; 2 Chron. 23.8; 31.2, 17; 35.4, 10) and gatekeepers (1 Chron. 26.1, 12, 19) were rostered for service at the temple. The clergy at the temple were therefore envisaged as the LORD's soldiers, his palace guard.

Secondly, David involved the leaders of the army in the organization of the cult.[2] He not only consulted them about what to do with the

---

1. Some of the gatekeepers are also called *gibbōrê ḥayil* in 1 Chron. 26.6, *'îš ḥayil* in 26.8, and *bᵉnê ḥayil* in 26.7, 9, though this may indeed refer to their military status and prowess, which qualified them to police the temple. See Zalewski 1968: 434-41 for an examination of these terms as applied to the gatekeepers.

2. Cf. Jehoshaphat's consultation of his people in 2 Chron. 20.21, and Hezekiah's involvement of his princes on matters of ritual in 2 Chron. 29.20, 30; 30.2, 6, 12; 31.8.

ark (1 Chron. 13.1), but also included them in its transferral to Jerusalem (1 Chron. 15.25) and in his appointment of the temple musicians (1 Chron. 25.1). They were present at David's commissioning of Solomon to build the temple (1 Chron. 28.1), and contributed to its construction (1 Chron. 29.6). Whatever the political reasons for these measures, the Chronicler seems to suggest by this that public worship was not only a social matter involving the king, the tribal leaders and the nation, but also a military matter involving the army and its leaders.

Thirdly, success or failure in battle impinged directly on the welfare of the temple through the addition to or depletion of its treasures. Thus booty from battle helped construct the temple and also provided animals for the sacrifices there (1 Chron. 18.8, 10-11; 26.26-28), while defeat led to its plunder (2 Chron. 12.9; 25.24; 36.7, 10, 18). Moreover, the payment for alliances with pagan nations for their support in war often came from the temple and its treasury (2 Chron. 16.2; 28.21). Thus both lack of faith in God at the threat of attack and defeat in battle diminished the glory of the temple.

Fourthly, just as heterodoxy in worship led to defeat in battle, so orthodoxy in worship led to victory. This theology which is implicit in many of the accounts of warfare in Chronicles is expressed most clearly in 2 Chronicles 13 both by the speech of Abijah and the outcome of the battle with the northern Israelites. As long as God's people faithfully performed the ritual of sacrifice as prescribed in the law of Moses (2 Chron. 13.10-11) and cried out to the LORD for help (13.14; cf. 6.34-35; 14.10; 20.9), the LORD led them as his army into battle (13.12; cf. 14.12), fought for them (cf. 20.28; 32.8), defeated their enemies (13.15; cf. 14.11; 20.22) and gave them the victory (13.16; cf. 1 Chron. 18.6, 13; 2 Chron. 20.17). The secret of success in battle therefore lay in the LORD's presence, which was granted to them through their invocation of him.

Now much of this could be evidence of the survival and perhaps even revival of ancient notions of holy warfare under the influence of Deuteronomy.[1] Yet it is obviously more than just that. The Chronicler is not interested in the conditions for success in a holy war, but rather in the place of worship in the establishment and maintenance of peace.

---

1. See the influential proposals of von Rad (1952) on the nature and setting of holy war in Israel, which have been challenged and modified by Smend (1963), Stolz (1972), Weippert (1972), Miller (1973) and G.H. Jones (1975).

With his presentation of Solomon as a man of peace in 1 Chron. 22.9, he recommends orthodoxy in worship as the best recipe for the peace and security of Israel (2 Chron. 13.23–14.6; 15.15, 19; 20.30). The cult and its officials were involved in the defence of the realm, for, by the acceptance of the nation's sacrifices and prayers at the temple, the LORD not only defended his people by forgiving them (2 Chron. 6.24-25) and so preventing their defeat in battle (cf. 2 Chron. 6.36), but also championed their cause by giving them victory in battle (2 Chron. 6.34-35) and delivering them from captivity (2 Chron. 6.36-39).

Within this general framework of thought, the Chronicler also advocated the exercise of prayer and the performance of praise in 2 Chron. 20.1-30 as a form of supernatural warfare which involved no overt military activity on their part but only faith in the prophetic word of God.

The Context of 2 Chronicles 20.1-30

The story of the miraculous victory in 2 Chronicles 20 should not be isolated from its context. It is in fact the climax of the narrative which stretches from 2 Chronicles 14 to 2 Chronicles 20. Although some of the material in these chapters comes from Kings, the Chronicler has combined it with much additional material and has reshaped it to serve his own ends.

As Dillard (*1987: 129-30) has observed, the units of this narrative have been so arranged that the reign of Jehoshaphat in chs. 17–20 parallels and yet contrasts with the reign of Asa in chs. 14–16. After the notice of accession in both sections (13.23; 17.1-2), the Chronicler mentions the first reform of the king (14.1-4; 17.3-9). This had to do with the implementation of the *tôrâ* (14.3; 17.9), and is characterized as 'seeking the LORD' (14.3; 17.4). Related are the fortification of cities (14.5-6; 17.10-13a), the strength of the army (14.7; 17.13b-19), the first war (14.8-14; 18.1–19.3), the second period of reform (15.1-19; 19.4-11), the second war (16.1-10; 20.1-30), an assessment of the reign (16.11; 20.31-34), and the punishment for transgression followed by the notice of death and burial (16.12-14; 20.35–21.1a). In both reigns we have the parallel activities of two prophets, one who encourages (15.1-7; 20.14-17), and another who condemns the king (16.7-10; 20.37). Within this pattern of parallel incidents the two reports of battle stand in inverse contrast to each other with a reversal in chs. 17–20 of the initial sequence in chs. 14–16 of victory through reliance on the LORD and defeat through reliance on aliens. 2 Chron. 20.1-30 forms the climax of the Chronicler's discussion on seeking the LORD both in the performance of worship and the administration of justice.

As Williamson (*1982: 291) has noted, this story is also the climax of the Chronicler's presentation of Jehoshaphat's reign. Just as his reforms in 17.7-9 are completed in 19.4-11, so his failure against the Syrians in 18.1–19.3 is rectified by his success against the three armies in 20.1-30.

The prominence of 20.1-30 is highlighted by the connections established thematically by three key motifs.[1] First, we have the occurrence of *dāraš*. Since Jehoshaphat 'sought' the LORD rather than the baals (17.3-4), the LORD's wrath was averted (19.3). Then when he was threatened by the invasion from the south, he 'sought' the LORD by proclaiming a national fast (20.3). Secondly, there are the variations in the idiom *hāyâ 'im*. Even though the LORD was 'with' Jehoshaphat because of his rejection of the baals (17.3), he decided to go 'with' the wicked King Ahab in his war against the Syrians (18.3). After that fiasco, he assured the judges appointed by him that the LORD would be 'with' them in giving judgment (19.6), if they were just (19.11). If Jehoshaphat and his people relied on the LORD in battle, Jahaziel assured them that the LORD would be 'with' them and give them the victory (20.17). Thirdly, we have the term *pahad YHWH*.[2] The dread of the LORD which had struck the nations as a result of Judah's indoctrination in the *tôrâ* (17.10), and which was to motivate the judges in their administration of the LORD's justice (19.7), culminated in the nation's reaction to the defeat of the armies through the performance of praise by the choir (20.29). Thus the three themes of seeking the LORD, his presence with his people, and the resultant dread of the LORD by the nations are all drawn together by our story and related to the performance of praise by the Levitical choir.

The Structure of 2 Chronicles 20.1-30

  A. *The Attack on Judah by her Enemies*: 20.1-2
  B. *The National Fast*: 20.3-19
      1.   Its convocation by Jehoshaphat (3-4)

---

   1. See Allen 1988 for a discussion of the use of recurring and contrasted motifs in Chronicles.
   2. See Mosis 1973: 70-72 for a discussion of this term here in Chronicles.

This story thus exhibits a clear narrative pattern. Apart from an introduction and conclusion, there are three blocks of narrative for the three separate episodes in the story. Each of these has a different temporal and spatial setting, and each culminates in a musical performance.

The Martial Significance of Sacred Music and Song

The conclusion of each of the major episodes in 20.1-30 with some form of praise serves to highlight this feature. In each instance a different point is made about the martial significance of sacred song in a situation where Judah and Jerusalem are threatened with certain and disastrous defeat.

Praise for the Promise of Divine Victory in 20.18-19. In his lament on the fast at Jerusalem, Jehoshaphat asked the LORD to execute judgment on the enemies of Judah (20.12). The Lord answered with an oracle delivered by Jahaziel, a Levitical singer belonging to the guild of Asaph, whose founder had been commissioned to prophesy at the king's direction. In his oracle the prophet not only assured the people that the LORD would gain the victory for them but also excluded them from direct participation in the battle. As was the case with their ancestors in the exodus (Exod. 14.13-14, 30-31), they were to be passive witnesses of his victory over their enemies.

The reaction of the congregation to this message is given in vv. 18-19:

Then as Jehoshaphat bowed down with his face to the ground, all Judah
and the citizens of Jerusalem fell down before YHWH to make prostration
to YHWH.[1] The Korahites who were Levites belonging to the Kohathites[2]
stood up to praise YHWH, the God of Israel, with a loud voice.

By leading the people in the act of prostration at the temple,
Jehoshaphat acknowledged that the LORD had heard his petition and
would save his people. While the congregation still lay prostrate
before the LORD, some Korahite Levites stood up and praised the
LORD in loud song. They were most likely not part of the regular
choir but belonged to the general company of the Levites.[3] According
to 1 Chron. 9.19, they were gatekeepers at the entrance to the temple,
where they would have worked together with the singers.[4]

This performance of praise by these Levites was an extraordinary
occurrence, since the Levitical choir had been appointed by David to
offer praise during the presentation of sacrifices at the temple. Here
then we have a new group leading the praise. In response to the
prophetic oracle, they praised the LORD for the promise of victory
and in so doing anticipated the victory. They expressed their faith in
the prophetic oracle by breaking out into praise.

Victory during the Performance of Praise in 20.21-22. The next
morning Jehoshaphat addressed the army, before it went out to

1.   As Kropat notes (1909: 25), the word order forms a chiastic pattern here.
This would indicate that the two actions occurred simultaneously; cf. Andersen 1974:
120-22.

2.   Despite the assertion of Köberle (1899: 91), the *waw* in *ûmin-b^enê haqqorhîm*
is a *waw explicativum*. See Rudolph *1955: 262; Gese 1963: 232; Williamson
*1982: 299; cf. GKC §154a n. 1(b).

3.   Since Gese (1963: 230-34) assumes that they were singers, he postulates that
this account must reflect the second of three stages in the development of the musical
guilds during the postexilic period. To fit them into his scheme for their development, therefore, he includes the Korahites in the guild of Jeduthun, from which they
later split to form the guild of Heman. Their descent was then later traced by the
Chronicler back to Korah and Kohath in 1 Chron. 6.133b-38. In contrast with this
rather forced reconstruction, Miller (1970) argues that they were never singers in
Jerusalem, but came from Hebron during Josiah's reform to serve at the temple as
gatekeepers and bakers.

4.   Cf. 1 Chron. 26.1-19, where they are associated with Obed-edom, who was
both a gatekeeper and a singer. See Zalewski 1968: 414-26 on the relationship
between singers and gatekeepers in Chronicles.

witness the LORD's victory, as instructed in 20.16-17. In his address
he urged his troops to put their faith in God and in his prophets to
keep them safe and give them success on the battlefield. The narrative
then continues:

> After consulting with the people, he appointed those who were to sing[1] to
> YHWH, and those who were to praise (his) holy splendour[2] as they went
> before the armed troops, and those who were to say, 'Give thanks to
> YHWH! Truly his generosity is for ever!'

The moment that they began with jubilant praise, YHWH laid
ambushes for[3] the Moabites, the Ammonites and the people of Mount

1.   Only here and in 2 Chron. 29.28 is the *polel* participle of *šîr* used without an
article.

2.   *hadrat qōdeš* is found elsewhere only in Pss. 29.2; 96.9 and 1 Chron. 16.29.
Traditionally, the phrase has been taken to refer either to God's splendour (AV, NEB,
NIV, REB), or the attire of the celebrants (RSV). Cross (1950) challenges these inter-
pretations by arguing that, since *hdrt* occurs in Ugaritic in CTA 14, 155 as a parallel
term for the vision of a deity in a dream, it should be understood as 'manifestation'.
He therefore proposes that in Ps. 29.2 the phrase be translated 'when he appears in
his holiness'. His proposal has won the approval of Kraus (1961: 233, 664-65),
Ackroyd (1966) and Margulis (1970: 337). It received a further refinement from
Freedman and Hyland (1973: 243-45), who, like Vogt (1960: 24 n. 1), argued that
qōdeš should be understood as 'holy place' and that the phrase should be translated
as 'the holy place of his appearing'. These etymological arguments have, however,
been called into question by Caquot (1956), Donner (1967: 331-33) and Loretz
(1974: 185-86). This means that context and usage must decide the matter. In
asserting that the phrase must refer to the vestments of the singers, Warmuth (1978:
340) fails to observe that it is here introduced by *lᵉ* rather than *bᵉ* as elsewhere. Now
this preposition can be construed in one of two ways. First, with Freedman and
Hyland (1973: 245), it may be taken to indicate direction or location, as is often the
case in Chronicles (see Kropat 1909: 43-44). It would then be translated by 'to his
theophanic holy place' (Freedman and Hyland) or 'in the splendour of the sanctuary'
(Vogt). Neither of these senses, however, suits the activity of a choir leading an
army to battle. Secondly, as Saalschütz (1829: 35-36 n. 37) observes, the regular use
of *lᵉ* for the object of *hillēl* and the parallel with *mᵉšōrᵉrîm lᵉYHWH* makes it most
likely that *lᵉhadrat* is to be taken as the object of *mᵉhalᵉlîm*, so conveying the idea of
'splendour' rather than 'attire'; cf. Ehrlich 1914: 367.

3.   Since the armies were not ambushed, but rather destroyed each other, Ehrlich
(1914: 367) proposes that we read *maᶜᵃrābîm*. His proposal, however, has not been
taken up, even though Galling (*1954: 128) agrees with him that the word refers to
the confusion of the armies by the LORD. *mᵉᵃrᵉbîm* could be construed abstractly as
'ambushes', like the *qal* plural participle (see BDB, 70), or personally as 'men in
ambush', which is the sense in Judg. 9.25 and so most likely here. It could refer to

Seir, who were invading Judah, so that they were routed.

There is one difficulty in the interpretation of 20.21. Its main verb governs three participles as its object. These could be taken nominally and verbally. Thus they could refer to the appointment of three groups: the musicians who were to play their instruments to the LORD, the trumpeters who were to lead the army out by sounding the trumpets in his praise, and the vocalists who were to sing the thanksgiving refrain. They could also be taken verbally to describe three activities. They thus either refer to three different groups or, more probably, to three aspects of a single performance.

Now the martial character of sacred song is shown here in three ways. First, in consultation with his people, Jehoshaphat appointed the choir to act as the vanguard of the army. Whereas the choir could have been composed of the Korahites mentioned in v. 19, the use of the participle *mᵉšōrᵉrîm*, which is the term for the temple musicians in Chronicles, and the mention of the refrain for thanksgiving, which was a regular part of their repertoire, make it likely that the temple choir was appointed to this task. Ritually speaking, that was a remarkable innovation. It had previously been the practice for the priests to lead the army with their trumpets (2 Chron. 13.12; cf. Num. 10.9; 31.6) and for the people to sound the battle cry at the blast of the trumpets (2 Chron. 13.15; cf. Josh. 6.5, 16, 20). Moreover, in the past, the ark had been brought into battle by the Levites (Num. 14.44; 1 Sam 4.3-11; 14.18). On this occasion, however, the priestly trumpeters were supplemented by the temple musicians,[1] while the refrain for thanksgiving supplanted the battle cry.[2] The Levitical choir thus acted as the vanguard of the army. With them the LORD himself stood at the head of his army. His attendance, however, was secured by the invocation of his name in sacred song rather than by the presence of the ark.

---

one of two groups: (1) the Seirites or some other detachments from the enemy armies (Keil *1870: 291-92; Goettsberger *1939: 290; Japhet 1989: 131); (2) angels or other supernatural powers (Rudolph *1955: 261; Williamson *1982: 300; Dillard *1987: 159). While the latter interpretation seems most likely, it should be noted that the account is deliberately vague on the details of the battle.

1.   Büchler (1899: 100-101), followed by Zalewski (1968: 360), argues that the musicians replaced the trumpeters. This, however, is rather unlikely in view of the mention of trumpets in 20.28.

2.   See Williamson *1982: 300; Petersen 1977: 75; Dillard *1987: 159.

Secondly, this arrangement was made in response to the prophecy of Jahaziel and the admonition of Jehoshaphat. Through the performance of sacred song, the LORD himself was with them, as he had promised in 20.17, and gave them the victory without any material assistance from them in the battle. By appointing the choir as their vanguard, they put their faith in the LORD and his prophets. They showed their faith in his prophets both by acting on the prophetic word of Jahaziel and by relying on the prophetic power of the words sung by the Levites to give them the victory.

Thirdly, the moment the choir began to sing their praises at the head of the army, the LORD intervened on their behalf. The soldiers of the three invading armies were induced to attack and destroy each other. How this happened we do not discover, since the account is remarkably reticent about the details of the battle, which was, in any case, not witnessed by the Judahites. While the Chronicler clearly asserts that the LORD's intervention occurred as the song began, he does not claim that the army attacked the enemy with song,[1] or that the song caused the divine intervention.[2] The latter may indeed be implied, but the matter is not stated quite so unambiguously. Rather the connection between the performance of song and the LORD's intervention is veiled in mystery. All this, however, serves to highlight the LORD's achievement and the importance of his people's praise. By their praise they showed their faith in him as their champion and relied on him for their deliverance. Praise was their chief defence against the enemies who threatened their survival. The power of praise lay in its connection with the prophetic word of God and in its proclamation of his holy name.

Praise for the LORD's Victory in 20.26-28. When the people of Judah arrived at the battlefield, all that was left for them to do was to view the scene of the battle and to spend three days in collecting the spoil. Then came the celebration:

---

1. The witty jibe by Stinespring (1961: 209) that 'the choir puts the foe to flight and causes great slaughter with a few well-directed psalms' is based on a misreading of the situation, since the Judahites never came into contact with the enemy.

2. So Büchler 1899: 100; Arens 1961: 50; Micheel 1983: 53; cf. Petersen 1977: 75.

On the fourth day they assembled in[1] the Valley of Blessing where they blessed YHWH; hence the name of the place is the Valley of Blessing to this day. Then all the men of Judah and Jerusalem, with Jehoshaphat at the head, returned to Jerusalem with joy, for YHWH had given them cause to rejoice over their enemies. They entered YHWH's house in Jerusalem[2] with harps, lyres and trumpets.

These verses describe the triumphal procession of the victorious army from the battlefield back to the temple in Jerusalem where they had first assembled on the day before the battle. They celebrated their triumph in three ways. First, in an assembly on the battlefield they blessed the LORD, just as David and his princes had done (1 Chron. 29.10, 20) and Hezekiah and his princes would do (2 Chron. 31.8) in response to the contribution of the people to the temple. In doing this, they ascribed the victory to the LORD and acknowledged him as the giver of their spoil. Secondly, led by the king, they returned with their spoil to Jerusalem full of jubilation at what the LORD had done for them. Lastly, the triumph culminated in a musical procession of the whole army into the temple. The mention of the temple and the trumpets seems to indicate that the same choir was involved in the return from battle as in the advance. In their praise, they proclaimed how the LORD had fought for them and had triumphed over their enemies without any military assistance from them. As a result of this celebration, the surrounding kingdoms dreaded the LORD and refrained from attacking them. In the final count, therefore, sacred song was not so much a supernatural weapon in war as a supernatural deterrent against attack. It helped to preserve the peace of the realm.

Summary. This story explores the martial significance of praise. It focuses on Jehoshaphat's appointment of the temple choir to lead the army of Judah into battle. There is, however, no indication that this was meant to be a regular feature of their warfare.[3] This was, after all, an extraordinary occasion, in which the placement of the choir as

---

1. For use Chronicler's use of *l^e* in a local sense, see Kropat 1909: 44.
2. Literally, 'they entered Jerusalem to YHWH's house'.
3. Even the books of Maccabees, which often mention sacred song, only once report an attack 'with trumpets and battle songs' in 2 Macc. 15.25-27, after the request of Judas for an angelic manifestation against the enemy with their elephants; music and song are, however, mentioned as part of triumphal celebrations in 1 Macc. 4.24; 14.5; 2 Macc. 10.38.

the vanguard of the army came as a result of the prophetic promise in 20.15-17. Rather, the Chronicler uses this story to convince his post-exilic audience, who had no army to protect them against their enemies, that their best defence lay in their reliance on the words of the prophets and the performance of praise by the temple choir. By their performance of the LORD's praises, the choir anticipated the victories promised by the LORD through his prophets, secured his intervention against their enemies in times of peril, and rejoiced in the victories which the LORD had given them against their enemies. Praise of the LORD's victories in sacred song was their best deterrent against foreign attack, for it proclaimed that the LORD needed no military assistance from his people to vanquish their enemies. As is shown by 1 Chron. 16.31-33, such songs of praise anticipated the universal triumph of their heavenly king.

The theology of praise in Chronicles is thus ultimately universal and perhaps even eschatological in scope. While the LORD's praise is located in the worship of Israel at the temple in Jerusalem, it transcends both the temple and the people of Israel; it not only reaches out to subdue the nations hostile to the LORD but also includes them and all cosmic powers in its proclamation of his universal judgment and rule.

Conclusion

By his additions to the narrative he has inherited from Kings, the Chronicler develops the outline of a theology of praise which explains the significance of sacred song.

Since liturgical song was instituted by the LORD himself as part of the sacrificial ritual at the temple in Jerusalem, it was involved in his interaction with his people there. Through the ritual performance of choral music during the oblation of the burnt offering, the singers presented the LORD to his assembled people. They evoked the LORD and announced his presence to the congregation. They accomplished this by pronouncing his name and by proclaiming him with his virtues and achievements to their audience. In doing this, they acted in a prophetic capacity, for they spoke for God to his people. As they sang their songs of praise, they announced the LORD's acceptance of his people and declared his favourable disposition to them; they also proclaimed the LORD's deliverance of his people and secured his intervention against their enemies.

At the same time, sacred song served to articulate the response of the people to the LORD's presence with them, for the singers acted on behalf of the king and his people before the LORD. By their performance of choral music, they expressed the people's gratitude for his benefits to them, articulated their jubilation at his goodness, enunciated their amazement with him, voiced their adoration of him, confessed their faith in him and interceded on their behalf before him.

Thus the theological significance of sacred song was determined by its ritual function. It proclaimed the LORD's gracious presence to his people at the temple and articulated their response to his presence with them there.

Chapter 6

CONCLUSIONS

Matters for Further Consideration

As a result of the research undertaken in this study, a number of matters have arisen that have not been possible to investigate because of necessary limitations of scope, but which merit further consideration in the light of its findings.

The Difference between the Presentation of the Musicians in Chronicles and in Ezra–Nehemiah

The books of Ezra and Nehemiah resemble the books of Chronicles in making frequent mention of the temple musicians. There is indeed much that these books have in common with Chronicles, such as the use of the term $m^e \check{s}\bar{o}r^er\hat{i}m$ for the musicians (e.g. Ezra 2.41, 70; 7.7; 10.24), their designation as Levites (Ezra 3.10; Neh. 11.17; 12.24b-25a, 27-29), their division into three groups under three heads (Neh. 11.17; 12.8b-9, 24b-25a), the appointment of these heads by David and his arrangement of the musicians into watches for praise and thanksgiving (Neh. 12.24, 46), the organization of the choral service as part of the temple ritual by David and Solomon (Neh. 12.45), the combination of the priestly trumpeters with the Levitical musicians (Ezra 3.10; Neh. 12.35-36, 41-42), the use of cymbals, harps and lyres with sacred song (Neh. 12.27), the singing of the refrain for thanksgiving (Ezra 3.11), the connection of thanksgiving with prayer (Neh. 11.17), and the reference to the chambers (Neh. 10.40) and the station of the singers (Neh. 13.11).

Yet, despite these many resemblances, there appear to be four differences which call for further investigation. First, the books of Ezra and Nehemiah do not explicitly mention the coordination of the choral service with the presentation of the burnt offering, even where one would expect it, such as at the re-establishment of sacrificial worship at Jerusalem in Ezra 3.1-6. The only possible allusions to it may be in the mention of rejoicing in connection with the sacrifices presented at the dedication of the temple in Ezra 6.16-17 and at the dedication of the city wall in Neh. 12.43. Secondly, whereas the Chronicler understood the performance of sacred song as a proclamation of the LORD's presence and an announcement of his acceptance of his people, in Ezra and Nehemiah it seems to be taken as a means of sanctification. Thus in Neh. 12.27-43 the wall of Jerusalem was sanctified by sacred song (cf. Ezra 3.10-11). Thirdly, the Persian king seems to have replaced the Davidic monarch as the patron of sacred song after the restoration (Neh. 11.23). If that is so, were the singers then responsible for praying for him and his sons as commanded by Darius in Ezra 6.10? Fourthly, Mattaniah, the leader of the Asaphites, is termed *rō'š haťᵉhillâ yᵉhôdeh latťᵉpillâ* in Neh. 11.17 (cf. the *ketib* of Neh. 12.46). Does this refer to his precedence over the other two heads of guilds, or to his liturgical function, when all three heads officiated together?

The Connection between the Theology of Praise in Chronicles and Isaiah

While scholars have recognized that the book of Isaiah was strongly influenced by the theology of Zion as elaborated in some of the oldest psalms in the psalter, no one has yet considered whether the tradition of Isaiah may in some way have influenced the theology of praise in Chronicles. Two points may warrant some further investigation. First, does Isa. 55.4 refer to David's role as the founder of sacred song in Jerusalem, when it speaks of him as a witness to the peoples and a commander of the nations, and has this tradition influenced the Chronicler in his composition of 1 Chron. 16.7-36? Secondly, was the Chronicler influenced in part by the book of Isaiah in his understanding of the choral service as a species of prophecy? In the tradition of Isaiah, songs of praise figure prominently in the prophetic proclamation of salvation. Thus Isaiah contains songs sung by the prophet (25.1-5; 61.10-11), songs to be sung by the citizens of Zion after their deliverance (12.1-6; 26.1-19), and hymns calling on the whole world to praise the LORD for Israel's redemption (42.10-13; 44.23; 49.13). By joining the prophet in his praise, Israel and the world joined him in proclaiming his message of salvation. Moreover, Isa. 30.29-33 claims that by singing the LORD's praises, Israel would promulgate the LORD's judgment upon its enemies; indeed through the 'sound' of the people's song, the LORD's 'voice' would speak out his judgment against the enemies. As a proclamation of salvation, the songs of praise in Isaiah were therefore meant to effect the deliverance of Israel. Thirdly, was the Chronicler also influenced by Isaiah's prophecies that the nations would not only join Israel in prostrating themselves before the LORD (Isa. 45.22-23; 66.23) and in presenting sacrifices to him (Isa. 18.7; 19.19-23; 56.6-7), but also in praising him (Isa. 42.10-13; 60.6; cf. 61.11) and in declaring his glory among the nations (Isa. 66.19)?

The Information in Chronicles about the Cultic Setting of the Psalms
Since the appearance of Mowinckel's *Psalmenstudien* (1921–1924), the debate on the cultic setting of the psalms has been dominated by discussion of whether the *Sitz im Leben* of many psalms was to be found in the liturgy for the New Year's Festival in the pre-exilic period. The debate has proved to be inconclusive for want of concrete evidence. In view of the evidence in Chronicles that psalms of thanksgiving and praise were performed during the presentation of the burnt offerings and thank-offerings, it might be worthwhile to investigate whether some of the psalms were not only used in the sacrificial ritual of the postexilic period but also actually came to be composed for this ritual purpose, as seems to be claimed by the Chronicler.

The Understanding of Praise as Prophecy in Later Writings
While the interpretation of the choral music in 1 Chron. 25.1-6 as a kind of ritualized prophecy is without parallel in the literature of the Old Testament, it does crop up in the New Testament as well as later Jewish literature. We find this equation of praise with prophecy in Lk. 1.67 and in the rabbinical material collated by Grözinger (1982: 99-107). It seems also to be implied by the connection between inspiration by the Spirit and praise in Lk. 2.27-35, 10.21-22 and Eph. 5.18-20. Similar ideas seem to lie behind the description of David as a prophet in Mk 12.36, Acts 2.20 and 4.25 and of Asaph as a prophet in Matt. 13.35. There is also a close connection between apocalyptic prophecy and praise in the book of Revelation. The praise of Almighty God and the Lamb by the saints together with the heavenly host seems to set in motion the great eschatological deeds envisaged by the seer. Hence the unsealing of the seven seals by the Lamb in Rev. 6.1–8.1, the victory of Michael over Satan in heaven and the appearance of the

two beasts on earth in 12.1–13.18, the pouring out of God's wrath from seven bowls in 16.1-21, and the final victory over all the powers of evil in 19.11–20.15 all occur after, and apparently as a result of, acts of praise in the heavenly liturgy. By singing the victory song of the Lamb to Almighty God the saints then conquer the beast. Further research could therefore investigate whether these later writers were influenced by Chronicles or not, and why they equated some kinds of praise with prophetic utterances.

The Replacement of David by Jesus as the Leader of Praise in the New Testament

It seems to me that the tradition of David as the patron of praise at the temple in Jerusalem may have influenced the belief of the early Christians that Jesus was the leader of praise in their worship. Thus in Heb. 2.12 the words of Ps. 22.23, which are ascribed to David, describe how Jesus proclaims the name of his Father and praises him in the liturgical assembly (cf. Rom. 15.9). Just as David had given his words to the Levitical singers in 1 Chron. 16.7-36 for them to use in praise, so the word of Jesus is said in Col. 3.16 to provide the content of the songs sung by his disciples in their instruction and encouragement of each other. The idea that they were to thank and praise God the Father through Jesus in such passages as Rom. 1.8; 7.25; 16.27; Col. 3.17; Heb. 13.15, 1 Pet. 4.11 and Jude 25, and that they were to give thanks for kings and the whole human race (1 Tim 2.1-2), may also have been influenced by the tradition of David as the founder of the choral service at the temple and his institution of vicarious praise in Chronicles.

Summary of Findings

The Royal Foundation of Sacred Song

In his work the Chronicler sets out to describe the origin and development of the LORD's song as a ritual enactment, from its embryonic beginnings with David to the attainment of its full stature in the measures undertaken by Hezekiah.

a. Just as David is counted with Solomon as the founder of the temple in Jerusalem with its services and the orders for its clergy, so the choral rite is derived in essence from the ritual legislation and patronage of David.

b. David is said to have organized the choral rite in three stages.

> 1. He ordered the heads of the Levitical families to appoint an orchestra consisting of Levites and of priests for the transportation of the ark to its tent in his palace at Jerusalem.
> 2. After the ark had been deposited in Jerusalem, he arranged for the performance of praise at the times for the daily burnt offering with choirs in two separate places, one choir under the leadership of Asaph before the ark in Jerusalem, and the other under the leadership of Heman and Jeduthun before the altar in Gibeon.
> 3. In his preparations for the construction of the temple by Solomon, David established a pool of four thousand Levites as potential musicians, determined that the musicians should praise the LORD during the presentation of the daily burnt offerings, and fixed the method for their allotment into 24 courses.

c. Solomon assigned a prominent place to the choir in the ritual for the dedication of the temple and implemented David's plans for the regular praise after the completion of the temple.

d. The development of liturgical song culminated in the reforms of Hezekiah after the apostasy of Asa, with his re-establishment of it according to its divine institution, his authorization of the psalms of David and Asaph for performance in the sacrificial ritual and his promotion of the choir's involvement in the presentation of the individual thank-offerings.

The Divine Institution of Sacred Song

The Chronicler aims to prove the legitimacy of choral music by showing that it was commanded by the LORD and was wholly consistent with the ancient pattern of worship which the LORD had ordained through Moses.

a. At the command of the LORD through his prophets, Gad and Nathan, David organized the choral rite for the temple at Jerusalem.

b. Even though the choral rite had not been instituted in the Pentateuch, it is held to have fulfilled three commands of the LORD in the law of Moses:

> 1. his instruction to the priests in Num 10.10 to proclaim the LORD during the presentation of the public burnt offerings and peace offerings;
> 2. his commission to the Levites in Deut. 10.8 and 18.5 to stand before him at the ark and to minister there in his name;

3. his call to all the Israelites in Deuteronomy to rejoice in his presence as they presented their sacrifices to him at his chosen sanctuary.

c. The Lord demonstrated his acceptance of sacred song and the whole sacrificial ritual established by David and Solomon by the descent of fire from heaven upon the altar of burnt offering at the dedication of the temple.

Precedents for the Performance of Sacred Song
The Chronicler does not give us a history of the gradual formation of liturgical song as a result of particular impersonal causes and personal pressures but rather presents us with the stories of its foundation in fulfilment of a divine command, stories which establish ritual precedents for its subsequent operation and development.

a. These foundational stories tell how, where, when, why, with what and by whom the LORD's song was to be performed at the temple in Jerusalem.

b. They indicate how the LORD used sacred song to announce his presence at his regular meetings with his people during the performance of the sacrificial ritual at the temple.

c. The Chronicler shows that the liturgical reforms of Jehoiada, Hezekiah and Josiah merely restored and developed the choral rite which David had originally founded.

Sacred Song as a Ritual Enactment
The Chronicler uses the traditional priestly system of ritual symbolism to present sacred song as a ritual enactment with sacred words performed at a sacred place during sacred times on sacred instruments by sacred people.

a. The essence of sacred song consisted of the public announcement of the LORD's presence.

1. In their songs of praise the musicians proclaimed his holy name.
2. Through their proclamation of his holy name, the musicians announced the LORD's advent to his assembled people and his favourable disposition to them.

b. The song of the LORD was sung before the altar for burnt offering in the inner court of the temple.

1. The musicians occupied an intermediate position between the people in the outer court and the presence of the LORD at the altar in the inner court.
2. Their position defined their status over against the priests as well as their ritual function to mediate between the LORD and his people.

c. Sacred song was performed at the sacred times fixed for the daily burnt offering, when the LORD met with his people and their representatives.

1. The times for sacred song were set at the ritually significant points of transition from day to night, from week to week, from month to month and from season to season.
2. The performance of sacred song turned these occasions into times for rejoicing in the LORD and his manifest goodness.

d. The instruments for the performance of the LORD's song were regarded as 'temple vessels' whose status and power depended on their divine institution and ritual use.

1. Since the trumpets had been instituted by Moses to be sounded by the priests over the sacrifices offered to the LORD, they were regarded as 'holy vessels' for proclaiming the LORD's presence and summoning his people to prostrate themselves before him.
2. Since the cymbals, lyres and harps had been instituted by David at the LORD's command through his prophets Gad and Nathan for use by the Levitical musicians, they were regarded as 'vessels of service'.
   a. The cymbals announced the onset of sacred song as well as the Lord's acceptance of the sacrifices of his people.
   b. As 'vessels of song', the harps and lyres accompanied the songs of praise to the LORD and called on the assembled congregation to join the musicians in their praise.
3. All these instruments combined with the words of the songs to proclaim the gracious presence of the LORD with his people and to move them to rejoice in his goodness.

e. The Lord's song was instituted by David, the LORD's anointed king, to be performed for him and the people by the priests and the Levitical musicians.

1. David was regarded as the leader in praise.
   a. He appointed the musicians to offer praise for him and gave them his instruments to perform his song of praise.
   b. Through them he called on all God's people as well as the nations of the earth and the entire cosmos to join him in his praise.
2. The musicians who sang the songs of praise were taken from the ranks of the three Levitical clans and served as Levites at the temple.

a.   As Levites they represented the king and the people in their ministry of praise and prayer.

b.   As Levites they also represented the LORD and ministered to the people in the LORD's name through their performance of sacred song.

3. Ritually speaking, the priests legitimized the involvement of the musicians in the sacrificial ritual.

a.   They alone had access to the LORD's holy presence by virtue of their ordination and responsibility for the sacrificial ritual.

b.   Through the inclusion of the priestly trumpeters in the choir, the Levitical musicians were involved in the sacrificial ritual at the altar.

The Place of Sacred Song in the Sacrificial Ritual

The Chronicler presents liturgical song as part of a unified ritual performance within the general framework provided by the order for the presentation of the daily burnt offering at the temple.

a. The Lord's song was not performed during the rite for atonement in the preparatory section of the service, but during the subsequent central rite for the presentation of the burnt offering.

1. Sacred song was not meant to induce the LORD to accept his people but presupposed his acceptance of them in the rite for atonement.

2. Since the LORD held his daily audiences with his people at the temple during the public burnt offering, sacred song combined with it to proclaim his gracious presence with his people, his acceptance of their sacrifices and his readiness to receive their petitions.

b. The synchronization of singing with the presentation of the public burnt offering served two practical ritual purposes.

1. It announced the times for the prostration of the congregation in the LORD's presence.

2. It enlisted the involvement of the congregation at certain designated places in the ritual enactment.

c. The choir also performed songs of thanksgiving during the presentation of the public and private thank-offerings on festivals and other special occasions.

1. The presentation of the public thanksgiving by the king came after the completion of the burnt offering and involved the whole congregation in the jubilation of the occasion.

2. The private thank-offerings came first in the slot for the private sacrifices and involved the guests of those who presented them.

3. In both cases, the choir expressed the gratitude of those who presented the thank-offerings and proclaimed the LORD's goodness to the assembled congregation.

The Theology of Sacred Song

The Chronicler explains the significance of sacred song within the larger context of the sacrificial ritual at the temple.

a. By praising the LORD, the singers proclaimed his name and publicized his accomplishments.

1. They introduced the LORD to his people and announced his presence with them.
2. They disclosed his gracious character and benevolent disposition to his people.
3. They called on the congregation to remember the LORD's covenant with them and to base their petitions on his promises to them.
4. They invited the Israelites and all the nations of the world to seek the LORD's presence and strength in their worship of him.

b. By praising the LORD the singers acted as his prophets and prophesied in his name.

1. They stood in the LORD's presence and mediated between him and his people by speaking for him to them in their songs.
2. They proclaimed the LORD's judgment on his enemies and his salvation to his people.
3. They communicated the LORD's acceptance of them in his approval of their sacrifices and brought his help to them in their proclamation of his name.
4. Through them the LORD announced his salvation to his people.

c. By praising the LORD, the singers evoked his glorious presence at the temple in Jerusalem and responded to its manifestation there.

1. By proclaiming the LORD's name, the singers evoked the LORD's glory, hidden in a cloud in the temple, and revealed his veiled presence verbally to his people there in their song of praise.
2. They led the people in responding with awe, gratitude and jubilation to the LORD's acceptance of them and their sacrifices to him.

d. By praising the LORD, the singers engaged in supernatural warfare against the LORD's enemies.

1. They recounted the LORD's victories over their enemies and celebrated his power to defeat them with little or no military assistance from his chosen people.

2. They defended God's people and secured their deliverance by their proclamation of the LORD and of his salvation in sacred song.

3. They proclaimed his future acts of deliverance and his universal triumph over all evil powers as he had promised through his prophets.

4. By publicizing the LORD's prowess in defeating the greatest gods of the foreign nations and his military feats in defending his people, the singers intimidated their enemies and persuaded them to submit to his rule.

e. The nations of the world both benefited and suffered from Israel's performance of the LORD's song.

1. Like Israel they were beneficiaries of his royal generosity and so were bound to acknowledge him as their God.

2. Through the institution and performance of sacred song, the Davidic kings anticipated the revelation of the LORD's kingship over all his creation, proclaimed the name of the LORD to the nations, and called on them to acknowledge him in sacrifice, prostration and praise.

3. The performance of sacred song was both a proclamation of the LORD's benevolence to the nations and a pronouncement of his judgment on them and their deities.

4. The nations could therefore either become partners with Israel in the praise of his holy name, or else face defeat at his hands by their defiance of his name.

In the narratives which recount the foundation and development of sacred music and song the Chronicler explains the ritual status, function and significance of sacred song as an important part of the total sacrificial ritual at the temple in Jerusalem. Thus, since the Chronicler holds that sacred song was instituted by the LORD himself to announce his presence with his faithful people and to proclaim his acceptance of them, J.S. Bach may be considered justified in having understood 1 Chronicles 25 to be the foundation for all God-pleasing church music and in having used 2 Chron. 5.13 to assert that the ritual function of liturgical music was to proclaim the gracious presence of the LORD with his people in their worship of him.

BIBLIOGRAPHY

Commentaries on Chronicles are placed before the list of special studies and reference works. Where a book has more than one place of publication, only the first is listed.

Commentaries

Ackroyd, P.R.
1973   *1 & 11 Chronicles, Ezra, Nehemiah: Introduction and Commentary*, Torch Bible Commentary, London: SCM Press.
Allen, L.C.
1987   *1, 2 Chronicles*, The Communicator's Commentary, Waco, TX: Word Books.
Becker, J.
1986   *1 Chronik*, Die Neue Echter Bibel, Würzburg: Echter Verlag.
1988   *2 Chronik*, Die Neue Echter Bibel, Würzburg: Echter Verlag.
Benzinger, I.
1901   *Die Bücher der Chronik*, KHAT 20, Tübingen: Mohr.
Bertheau, E.
1854   *Die Bücher der Chronik*, Kurzgefasstes Exegetisches Handbuch zum Alten Testament 15, Leipzig: S. Hirzel.
Braun, R.L.
1986   *1 Chronicles*, WBC 14, Waco, TX: Word Books.
Cazelles, H.
1954   *Les livres des Chroniques*, La Sainte Bible, Paris: Cerf.
Coggins, R.J.
1976   *The First and Second Books of Chronicles*, CBC, Cambridge: Cambridge University Press.
Curtis, E.L. and A.A. Madsen
1910   *A Critical and Exegetical Commentary on the Books of Chronicles*, ICC, Edinburgh: T. & T. Clark.
Dillard, R.B.
1987   *2 Chronicles*, WBC 15, Waco, TX: Word Books.
Elmslie, W.A.L.
1954   'The First and Second Books of Chronicles', in G.A. Buttrick *et al.* (eds.), *The Interpreter's Bible*, III, Nashville, 341-548.
Galling, K.
1954   *Die Bücher der Chronik, Ezra, Nehemia*, ATD 12, Göttingen: Vandenhoeck & Ruprecht.

Goettsberger, J.
1939 *Die Bücher der Chronik oder Paralipomenon*, Die Heilige Schrift des Alten Testaments, Bonn: Peter Hanstein.
Keil, C.F.
1870 *Die Bücher der Chronik*, Biblischer Commentar über das Alte Testament 5/1, Leipzig: Dörffling & Franke.
Kittel, R.
1902 *Die Bücher der Chronik*, HKAT 1/6, Göttingen: Vandenhoeck & Ruprecht.
Kretzmann, P.E.
1923 'Chronicles', *Popular Commentary of the Bible*, I, St Louis: Concordia, 651-74.
Mangan, C.
1982 *1–2 Chronicles, Ezra, Nehemiah*, Old Testament Message 13, Wilmington, DE: Michael Glazier.
Merrill, E.H.
1988 *1, 2 Chronicles*, Bible Study Commentary, Grand Rapids: Eerdmans.
Michaeli, F.
1967 *Les livres des Chroniques, d'Esdras et de Néhémie*, Commentaire de l'Ancien Testament 16, Neuchâtel: Delachaux & Niestlé.
Myers, J.M.
1965[a] *1 Chronicles*, AB 12, Garden City, NY: Doubleday.
1965[b] *II Chronicles*, AB 13, Garden City, NY: Doubleday.
Rothstein, J.W. and J. Hänel
1927 *Das erste Buch der Chronik*, KAT 18/2, Leipzig: Deichert.
Roubos, K.
1969 *I Kronieken*, De Prediking van het Oude Testament, Nijkerk: Callenbach.
1972 *II Kronieken*, De Prediking van het Oude Testament, Nijkerk: Callenbach.
Rudolph, W.
1955 *Chronikbücher*, HAT 21, Tübingen: Mohr (Paul Siebeck).
Slotki, I.W.
1952 *Chronicles*, Soncino Books of the Bible, London: Soncino Press, 1952.
Williamson, H.G.M.
1982 *1 and 2 Chronicles*, NCB, London: Marshall, Morgan & Scott.

Special Studies and References Works

Abba, R.
1977 'The Origin and Significance of Hebrew Sacrifice', *BTB* 7, 123-38.
1978 'Priests and Levites in Ezekiel', *VT* 28, 1-9.
Ackroyd, P.R.
1958 'Two Old Testament Historical Problems of the Early Persian Period', *JNES* 17, 13-27.
1966 'Some Notes on the Psalms. 3. The Interpretation of *hadrat qodes*', *JTS* 17, 393-96.
1967 'History and Theology in the Writings of the Chronicler', *CTM* 38, 501-15.
1968[a] 'Historians and Prophets', *SEÅ* 33, 18-54.
1968[b] *Exile and Restoration: A Study of Hebrew Thought of the Sixth Century BC*, London: SCM Press.

1968[c]   'The Interpretation of Exile and Restoration', *CJT* 14, 3-12.
1970[a]   *The Age of the Chronicler: The Selwyn Lectures, Supplement to Colloquium—The Australian and New Zealand Theological Review*, Auckland: SPCK.
1970[b]   *Israel under Babylon and Persia*, Oxford: Oxford University Press.
1972   'The Temple Vessels. A Continuity Theme', in G.W. Anderson *et al.* (eds.), *Studies in the Religion of Ancient Israel*, VTSup 23, Leiden: Brill, 166-81 (= *Studies in the Religious Tradition of the Old Testament*, London: SCM Press, 1987, 46-60).
1973   'The Theology of the Chronicler', *LTQ* 8, 101-16.
1976   'Chronicles, I and II', *IDBSup*, 156-58.
1977   'The Chronicler as Exegete', *JSOT* 2, 2-32.
1988   'Chronicles–Ezra–Nehemiah. The Concept of Unity', in O. Kaiser (ed.), *Lebendige Forschung im Alten Testament*, BZAW 100, Berlin: de Gruyter, 189-201.
1991   *The Chronicler in his Age*, JSOTSup 101, Sheffield: JSOT Press.

Adinolfi, M.
1966   'Le "opere di pietà liturgica" di David in 2 Chron 6, 42', *BeO* 8, 31-6.

Albright, W.F.
1921   'The Date and the Personality of the Chronicler', *JBL* 40, 104-24.
1942   *Archaeology and the Religion of Israel: The Ayer Lecture of the Colgate–Rochester Divinity School 1941*, Baltimore: The Johns Hopkins University Press.
1950   'The Judicial Reform of Jehoshaphat (2 Chron. 19:5-11)', in S. Lieberman (ed.), *Alexander Marx Jubilee Volume*, New York: Jewish Theological Seminary of America, English Section, 61-82.

Allan, M.W.T.
1971   'The Priesthood in Ancient Israel with Special Reference to the Status and Function of the Levites', Doctoral Dissertation, Glasgow University.

Allen, L.C.
1988   'Kerygmatic Units in 1 & 2 Chronicles', *JSOT* 41, 21-36.

Amit, Y.
1981   'A New Outlook on the Book of Chronicles', *Imm* 13, 20-29.

Andersen, F.I.
1970   *The Hebrew Verbless Clause in the Pentateuch*, SBLMS 14, Nashville: Abingdon Press.
1974   *The Sentence in Biblical Hebrew*, Janua Linguarum, Series Practica 231, The Hague: Mouton.
1986   'Yahweh, the Kind and Sensitive God', in P.T. O'Brien and D.G. Peterson (eds.), *God who is Rich in Mercy*, Homebush, NSW: Lancer, 41-88.

Anderson, G.A.
1987   *Sacrifices and Offerings in Ancient Israel: Studies in their Social and Political Importance*, HSM 41, Atlanta: Scholars Press.
1991   'The Praise of God as a Cultic Event', in G.A. Anderson and S.M. Olyan (eds.), *Priesthood and Cult in Ancient Israel*, JSOTSup 125, Sheffield: JSOT Press, 15-33.

Anderson, G.W.
1986   'nae̩sah, lam[e]nas̩s̩eah', *ThWAT*, V, cols. 565-70.

Arens, A.
1961   *Die Psalmen im Gottesdienst des alten Bundes*, TTS 11, Trier: Paulinus
        Verlag.
Assmann, J.
1975   *Ägyptische Hymnen und Gebete*, Zürich: Artemis Verlag.
Aufrecht, W.E.
1988   'Genealogy and History in Ancient Israel', in L. Eslinger and G. Taylor
        (eds.), *Ascribe to the Lord: Biblical and Other Studies in Memory of Peter
        C. Craigie*, JSOTSup 67, Sheffield: JSOT Press, 205-35.
Augustin, M.
1982   'Beobachtungen zur chronistischen Umgestaltung der deuteronomistischen
        Königschroniken nach der Reichsteilung', in M. Augustin and J. Kegler
        (eds.), *Das Alte Testament als geistige Heimat: Festgabe für H.W. Wolff
        zum 70. Geburtstag*, EH 23/177, New York: Peter Lang, 11-50.
Austin, J.L.
1975   *How to do Things with Words: The William James Lectures Delivered at
        Harvard University in 1955*, ed. J.O. Urmson and M. Sbisa, Oxford:
        Clarendon Press.
Avigad, N.
1978   'The King's Daughter and the Lyre', *IEJ* 28, 146-51.
Bagley, T.J.
1987   'The Choral Work. A Presentation of 1 Chronicles 16 as an Indicator of the
        Chronicler's Method', Master's Thesis, Covenant Theological Seminary, St
        Louis.
Barker, D.G.
1984   'The Theology of the Chronicler. A Synoptic Investigation of Chronicles 13,
        15–17 and 2 Samuel 6–7', Doctoral Dissertation, Grace Theological
        Seminary.
Barth, C.
1980   '*zmr*', *TDOT*, IV, 91-98.
Bartlett, J.R.
1969   'The Use of *Rō'š* as a Title in the Old Testament', *VT* 19, 1-10.
Baudissin, W.W. von
1889   *Die Geschichte des alttestamentlichen Priesterthums*, Leipzig: S. Hirzel.
1902   'Priests and Levites', *HDB*, IV, 67-97.
Bayar, B.
1968   'The Biblical Nebel', *Yuv* 1, 89-161.
1982[a] 'Ancient Musical Instruments. The Finds That Could not Be', *BARev* 8/1,
        19-33.
1982[b] 'The Titles of the Psalms. A Renewed Investigation of an Old Problem', *Yuv*
        4, 29-123.
Bea, A.
1941   'Neue Arbeiten zum Problem der biblischen Chronikbücher', *Bib* 22, 46-58.
Beattie, J.
1966   'Ritual and Social Change', *Man* NS 1, 60-74.
Begg, C.
1988[a] 'Babylon and Judah in Chronicles', *ETL* 64, 142-52.
1988[b] 'The Classical Prophets in the Chronistic History', *BZ* 32, 100-107.

Berg, S.B.
1980   'After the Exile. God and History in the Books of Chronicles and Esther', in
            J. Crenshaw and S. Sandmel (eds.), *Divine Helmsman*, New York: KTAV,
            107-27.
Best, H.M. and D. Hullar
1975   'Music; Musical Instruments', *ZPEB*, IV, 311-24.
Beyerlin, W.
1967   'Die *toda* der Heilsvergegenwärtigung in den Klageliedern des Einzelnen',
            ZAW 79, 208-24.
1973   'Kontinuität beim "berichtenden" Lobpreis des Einzelnen', in H. Gese and
            H.P. Rüger (eds.), *Wort und Geschichte: Festschrift für K. Elliger*, AOAT
            18, Neukirchen–Vluyn: Neukirchener Verlag, 17-24.
Beyse, K.M.
1984   '$k^e l\hat{\imath}$', *ThWAT*, IV, cols. 179-85.
Bickermann, E.J.
1949   'The Historical Foundations of Postbiblical Judaism', in L. Finkelstein (ed.),
            The Jews, their History, Culture, and Religion, I, New York: Harper &
            Row, 70-112 (republished in M.E. Stone and D. Satran, *Emerging Judaism*,
            Minneapolis: Fortress Press, 1989, 19-45).
Bleek, F.
1869   *An Introduction to the Old Testament*, trans. G.H. Venables, London:
            T. & T. Clark.
Blenkinsopp, J.
1972   *Gibeon and Israel*, SOTSMS 2, Cambridge: Cambridge University Press.
1988   *Ezra–Nehemiah*, OTL, London: SCM Press.
Boer, P.A.H. de
1981   'Cantate Domino: An Erroneous Dative?', in van der Woude 1981, 55-67.
Böhmer, J.
1934   'Sind einige Personennamen in Chr 25:4 "kunstlich geschaffen"?', *BZ* 22,
            93-100.
Bornkamm, G.
1964   'Lobpreis, Bekenntnis und Opfer', in W. Eltester and F.H. Kettler (eds.),
            *Apophoreta: Festschrift für Ernst Haenchen zu seinem siebzigsten
            Geburtstag*, BZNW 30, Giessen: Töpelmann, 46-63.
Botterweck, G.J.
1956   'Zur Eigenart der chronistischen Davidgeschichte', *TQ* 136, 402-35.
Bourdillon, M.F.C. and M. Fortes (eds.)
1980   *Sacrifice*, New York: Academic Press.
Braulik, G.
1980   'Die Freude des Festes. Das Kultverständnis des Deuteronomium—die älteste
            biblische Festtheorie', in R. Schulte (ed.), *Leiturgia, Koinonia, Diakonia:
            Festschrift für Kardinal Franz König zum 75. Geburtstag*, Vienna: Herder,
            127-79.
Braun, R.L.
1971   'The Message of Chronicles: "Rally Round the Temple"', *CTM* 42, 502-14.
1973   'Solomonic Apologetic in Chronicles', *JBL* 92, 503-16.
1976   'Solomon, the Chosen Temple Builder: The Significance of Chronicles 22,
            28 and 29 for the Theology of Chronicles', *JBL* 95, 581-90.

| 1977 | 'A Reconsideration of the Chronicler's Attitude toward the North', *JBL* 96, 59-62. |

1977   'A Reconsideration of the Chronicler's Attitude toward the North', *JBL* 96, 59-62.

1979   'Chronicles, Ezra, and Nehemiah: Theology and Literary History', in J.A. Emerton (ed.), *Studies in the Historical Books of the Old Testament*, VTSup 30, Leiden: Brill, 52-64.

Brongers, H.A.

1965   'Die Wendung *bᵉšēm jhwh* im Alten Testament', ZAW 77, 1-20.

Brueggemann, W.

1988   *Israel's Praise: Doxology against Idolatry and Ideology*, Philadelphia: Fortress Press.

Brunet, A.M.

1953   'Le Chroniste et ses Sources', *RB* 60, 481-508.

1954   'Le Chroniste et ses Sources', *RB* 61, 349-86.

Budd, P.J.

1989   'Holiness and Cult', in R.E. Clements (ed.), *The World of Ancient Israel: Sociological, Anthropological and Political Perspectives: Essays for Members of the Society for Old Testament Study*, Cambridge: Cambridge University Press, 275-98.

Büchler, A.

1895   *Die Priester und der Cultus im letzten Jahrzehnt des Jerusalemischen Tempels*, Vienna: Alfred Hölder.

1899   'Zur Geschichte der Tempelmusik und der Tempelpsalmen', *ZAW* 19, 93-133, 329-44.

1900   'Zur Geschichte der Tempelmusik und der Tempelpsalmen', *ZAW* 20, 97-135.

Busink, T.A.

1970   *Der Tempel von Jerusalem*, I, Leiden: Brill.

1980   *Der Tempel von Jerusalem*, II, Leiden: Brill.

Buss, M.J.

1963   'The Psalms of Asaph and Korah', *JBL* 82, 382-92.

Buszin, W.E.

1968   'Religious Music among the Jews', *CTM* 39, 422-31.

Butler, T.C.

1978   'A Forgotten Passage from a Forgotten Era (1 Chr. XVI 8-36)', *VT* 28, 142-50.

Buttenwieser, M.

1926   '*bikᵉlē—'ōz lᵉYHWH*', *JBL* 45, 156-58.

Campbell, K.M.

1980   'The Role of Music in Worship', *EvQ* 52, 43-46.

Cancik, H.

1970   'Das jüdische Fest. Ein Versuch zur Form und Religion des chronistischen Geschichtswerkes', *TTQ* 150, 335-48.

Caquot, A.

1956   'In splendoribus sanctorum (Ps. 29, 2; 96,9; 1 Chr. 16,29)', *Syria* 33, 36-41.

1966   'Peut-on parler de messianisme dans l'oeuvre du chroniste?', *RTP* 16, 3rd ser., 110-20.

Carpenter, E.E.

1988   'Sacrifices and Offerings in the Old Testament', *ISBE*, IV, 260-73.

Carr, G.L.
    1973   'The Claims of the Chronicler for the Origin of the Israelite Priesthood',
                Doctoral Dissertation, Boston University.
Carson, D.A. and H.G.M. Williamson (eds.)
    1988   *It is Written: Scripture Citing Scripture: Essays in Honour of Barnabas
                Lindars, SSF*, Cambridge: Cambridge University Press.
Casetti, P.
    1977   'Funktionen der Musik in der Bibel', *FZ* 24, 366-89.
Chang, W.I.
    1973   'The Tendenz of the Chronicler', Doctoral Dissertation, Hartford University.
Charles, R.H.
    1913   *The Apocrypha and Pseudepigrapha of the Old Testament in English, with
                Introductions and Explanatory Notes to Several Books*. I. *The Apocrypha of
                the Old Testament*, Oxford: Clarendon Press.
Childs, B.S.
    1979   *Introduction to the Old Testament as Scripture*, London: SCM Press.
    1985   *Old Testament Theology in a Canonical Context*, London: SCM Press.
Clements, R.E.
    1965   *God and Temple: The Idea of the Divine Presence in Ancient Israel*, Oxford:
                Basil Blackwell.
Clines, D.J.A.
    1981   'Nehemiah 10 as an Example of Early Jewish Biblical Exegesis', *JSOT* 21,
                111-17.
    1984   *Ezra, Nehemiah, Esther*, NCB, Grand Rapids: Eerdmans.
Cody, A.
    1969   *A History of Old Testament Priesthood*, Rome: Pontifical Biblical Institute.
Cogan, M.
    1985   'The Chronicler's Use of Chronology as Illuminated by Neo-Assyrian Royal
                Inscriptions', in J. Tigay (ed.), *Empirical Models for Biblical Criticism*,
                Philadelphia: University of Pennsylvania Press, 197-210.
Cohn, R.L.
    1981   *The Shape of Sacred Space: Four Biblical Studies*, AARSR 23, Atlanta:
                Scholars Press.
Collins, M.
    1976   'Ritual Symbols and the Ritual Process. The Work of Victor W. Turner',
                Worship 50, 336-46.
Cooper, A.M.
    1983   'The Life and the Times of King David according to the Book of Psalms', in
                R.E. Friedman (ed.), *The Poet and the Historian: Essays in Literary and
                Historical Biblical Criticism*, HSS 26, Atlanta: Scholars Press, 117-31.
Cornill, C.H.
    1907   *Introduction to the Canonical Books of the Old Testament*, trans. G.H. Box,
                London: Williams & Norgate.
    1909   *Music in the Old Testament*, trans. L.G. Robinson, Chicago: The Open
                Court.
Croft, S.J.L.
    1981   Review of H.G.M. Williamson, *Israel in the Books of Chronicles*, *JSOT* 14,
                68-72.

Cross, F.M.
1950   'Notes on a Canaanite Psalm in the Old Testament', *BASOR* 117, 19-21.
1961   *The Ancient Library of Qumran and Modern Biblical Studies*, rev. edn, London: Greenwood Press.
1964   'The History of the Biblical Text in the Light of Discoveries in the Judaean Desert', *HTR* 57, 281-99.
1966   'Aspects of Samaritan and Jewish History in Late Persian and Hellenistic Times', *HTR* 59, 201-11 (republished in M.E. Stone and D. Satran [eds.], *Emerging Judaism*, Minneapolis: Fortress Press, 1989, 49-59).
1973   *Canaanite Myth and Hebrew Epic: Essays in the History of the Religion of Israel*, Cambridge, MA: Harvard University Press.
1975   'A Reconstruction of the Judean Restoration', *JBL* 94, 4-18 (*Int* 29, 1975, 187-201).

Crüsemann, F.
1969   *Studien zur Formgeschichte von Hymnus und Danklied in Israel*, WMANT 32, Neukirchen–Vluyn: Neukirchener Verlag.

Danby, H.
1933   *The Mishnah: Translated from the Hebrew with Introduction and Brief Explanatory Notes*, London: Oxford University Press.

Dauenhauer, B.P.
1975   'Some Aspects of Language and Time in Ritual Worship', *IJPR* 6, 54-62.

Davies, D.
1977   'An Interpretation of Sacrifice in Leviticus', *ZAW* 89, 387-99.

Davies, G.I.
1979   'A Note on the Etymology of *Histaḥᵃwāh*', *VT* 29, 493-95.

Delekat, L.
1964   'Probleme der Psalmenüberschriften', *ZAW* 76, 280-97.
1967   *Asylie und Schutzorakel am Zionheiligtum: Eine Untersuchung zu den privaten Feindpsalmen*, Leiden: Brill.

Delitzsch, F.
1894   *Biblischer Commentar über die Psalmen*, Biblischer Commentar über das Alte Testament 4/1, Leipzig: Dörffling & Franke.

Demsky, A.
1971   'The Genealogy of Gibeon (1 Chronicles 9.35-44)', *BASOR* 202, 16-23.
1973   'Geba, Gibeah, and Gibeon. An Historico-Geographic Riddle', *BASOR* 212, 26-31.
1986   'The Clans of Ephrath: Their Territory and History', *TA* 13, 46-59.

Dillard, R.B.
1980[a]   'The Chronicler's Solomon', *WTJ* 43, 289-300.
1980[b]   'The Reign of Asa (2 Chronicles 14–16). An Example of the Chronicler's Theological Method', *JETS* 23, 207-18.
1984[a]   'Reward and Punishment in Chronicles. The Theology of Immediate Retribution', *WTJ* 46, 164-72.
1984[b]   'The Literary Structure of the Chronicler's Solomon Narrative', *JSOT* 30, 85-93.
1985   'David's Census: Perspectives on Samuel 24 and 1 Chronicles 21', in W.R. Godfrey and J.L. Boyd (eds.), *Through Christ's Word: A Festschrift*

for Dr Philip G. *Hughes*, Phillipsburg, NJ: Presbyterian and Reformed Press, 94-107.

1986   'The Chronicler's Jehoshaphat', *TJ* 7, 17-22.

Dohmen, C.

1984   '*mizbeaḥ*', *ThWAT*, IV, cols. 787-801.

Dommershausen, W.

1977   '*gôrāl*', *TDOT*, II, 450-56.

Donner, H.

1967   'Ugaritismen in der Psalmenforschung', *ZAW* 79, 322-50.

Douglas, M.

1966   *Purity and Danger*, London: Routledge & Kegan Paul.

1968   'The Contempt of Ritual', *New Blackfriars* 49, 475-82, 528-35.

1970   *Natural Symbols: Explorations in Cosmology*, New York: Barrie & Jenkins.

1975   *Implicit Meanings*, London: Routledge & Kegan Paul.

1978   *Cultural Bias*, London: Royal Anthropological Institute.

Driver, S.R.

1913   *An Introduction to the Literature of the Old Testament*, 9th edn, Edinburgh: T. & T. Clark.

Duke, R.K.

1990   *The Persuasive Appeal of the Chronicler: A Rhetorical Analysis*, JSOTSup 88, Sheffield: JSOT Press.

Dumbrell, W.J.

1984   'The Purpose of the Books of Chronicles', *JETS* 27, 257-66.

Duschak, M.

1866   *Geschichte und Darstelling des jüdischen Cultus*, Mannheim: J. Schneider.

Eaton, J.H.

1981   *Vision in Worship: The Relation of Prophecy and Liturgy in the Old Testament*, London: SPCK.

1984[a]   'Music's Place in Worship. A Contribution from the Psalms', in A.S. van der Woude (ed.), *Prophets, Worship and Theodicy*, OTS 23, Leiden: Brill, 85-107.

1984[b]   *The Psalms Come Alive*, London: Mowbrays.

Ebeling, E.

1914   *Keilschrifttexte aus Assur religiösen Inhalts*, I, Wissenschaftliche Veröffentlichungen der Deutschen Orient-Gesellschaft 34, Leipzig: Hinrichs.

Edelman, D.

1985   'The Meaning of *Qiṭṭēr*', *VT* 35, 395-404.

Edersheim, A.

1950   *The Temple: Its Ministry and Services*, Grand Rapids: Eerdmans.

Eerdmans, B.D.

1912   *Das Buch Leviticus*, Alttestamentliche Studien 4, Giessen: Töpelmann.

1947   *The Hebrew Book of Psalms*, OTS 4, Leiden: Brill.

Ehrlich, A.B.

1914   *Randglossen zur hebräischen Bibel*, VII, Hildesheim: Georg Ohms.

Ehrlich, E.L.

1959   *Die Kultsymbolik im Alten Testament und im nach-biblischen Judentum*, SR 3, Stuttgart: Anton Hiersemann.

1965   'Der Aufenthalt des Königs Manasse in Babylon', *TZ* 21, 281-86.

Eichrodt, W.
1961   *Theology of the Old Testament*, I, trans. J. Baker, London: SCM Press.
1967   *Theology of the Old Testament*, II, trans. J. Baker, London: SCM Press.
Eising, H.
1980   'zākhar', *TDOT*, IV, 64-82.
Eissfeldt, O.
1965   *The Old Testament: An Introduction*, trans. P.R. Ackroyd, Oxford: Basil Blackwell.
Eliade, M.
1961   *The Sacred and the Profane: The Nature of Religion*, New York: Harper & Row.
Ellermeier, F.
1970   'Beiträge zur Frühgeschichte altorientalischer Saiten-instrumente', in A. Kuschke and E. Kutsch (eds.), *Archäologie und Altes Testament: Festschrift für K. Galling*, Tübingen: Mohr, 75-90.
Emerton, J.A.
1977   'The Etymology of *histahawah*', in A.S. van der Woude (ed.), *Instruction and Interpretation: Studies in Hebrew Language, Palestinian Archaeology and Biblical Exegesis*, OTS 20, Leiden: Brill, 41-55.
Engler, H.
1967   'The Attitude of the Chronicler toward the Davidic Monarchy', Doctoral Dissertation, Union Theological Seminary.
Eshkenazi, T.
1986   'The Chronicler and the Composition of I Esdras', *CBQ* 48, 39-61.
Eslinger, L.
1986   'Josiah and the Torah Book. Comparison of 2 Kgs 22.1–23.28 and 2 Chron. 34.1–35.19', *HAR* 10, 37-62.
Ewald, H.
1870   *Ausführliches Lehrbuch der hebräischen Sprache des alten Bundes*, 8th German edn, Göttingen: Dieterich'sche Buchhandlung.
1876   *History of Israel*, trans. R. Martineau, London: Longmans, Green & Co.
Fabry, H.-J. and M. Weinfeld
1987   'minḥāh', *ThWAT*, V, cols. 987-1001.
Faur, J.
1979–80   'The Biblical Idea of Idolatry', *JQR* 70, 1-15.
Finesinger, S.B.
1926   'Musical Instruments in the Old Testament', *HUCA* 3, 21-76.
1931–32   'The Shofar', *HUCA* 8-9, 193-228.
Fishbane, M.
1985   *Biblical Interpretation in Ancient Israel*, Oxford: Clarendon Press.
Fohrer, G.
1970   *Introduction to the Old Testament*, trans. D. Green, London: SPCK.
Follet, R. and P. Nober
1954   'Zur altorientalischen Musik', *Bib* 35, 230-39.
Foxvog, D.A. and A.D. Kilmer
1986   'Music', *ISBE*, III, 436-49.
Freedman, D.N.
1961   'The Chronicler's Purpose', *CBQ* 23, 436-42.

Freedman, D.N. and C.F. Hyland
1973   'Psalm 29: A Structural Analysis', *HTR* 66, 237-56.
Fricker, R.
1979   '*šîr* singen', *THAT*, II, cols. 895-98.
Friedrich, G.
1964   'σάλπιγξ, σαλπίζω, σαλπιστής', *TWNT*, VII, 71-88.
Fritz, V.
1977   *Tempel und Zelt: Studien zum Tempelbau in Israel und zu dem Zeltheiligtum der Priesterschrift*, WMANT 47, Neukirchen–Vluyn: Neukirchener Verlag.
Füglister, N.
1977   'Sühne durch Blut. Zur Bedeutung von Leviticus 17, 11', in G. Braulik (ed.), *Studien zum Pentateuch: Walter Kornfeld zum 60. Geburtstag*, Freiburg: Herder, 143-64.
Galling, K.
1951   'Königliche und nicht-königliche Stifter beim Tempel von Jerusalem', *BBLA* 68, 134-42.
Galpin, F.W.
1937   *The Music of the Sumerians*, Cambridge: Cambridge University Press.
Gennep, A. van
1960   *The Rites of Passage*, trans. M.B. Vizedom and G.L. Caffee, Chicago: University of Chicago Press.
Gerstenberger, E.
1980   *Der bittende Mensch: Bittritual und Klagelied des Einzelnen im Alten Testament*, WMANT 51, Neukirchen–Vluyn: Neukirchener Verlag.
Gertner, M.
1960   'The Masorah and the Levites. An Essay in the History of a Concept', *VT* 10, 241-84.
Gese, H.
1963   'Zur Geschichte der Kultsänger am zweiten Tempel', in O. Betz *et al.* (eds.), *Abraham unser Vater: Juden und Christen im Gespräch über die Bibel: Festschrift für Otto Michel zum 60. Geburtstag*, Leiden: Brill, 222-34 (= *Vom Sinai zum Zion: Alttestamentliche Beiträge zur biblischen Theologie*, Munich: Chr. Kaiser Verlag, 1974, 147-58).
1964   'Der Davidsbund und die Zionserwählung', *ZTK* 61, 10-26 (= *Vom Sinai zum Zion: Alttestamentliche Beiträge zur biblischen Theologie*, Munich: Chr. Kaiser Verlag, 1974, 113-29).
Gibson, J.C.L.
1978   *Canaanite Myths and Legends*, 2nd edn, Edinburgh: T. & T. Clark.
Goldingay, J.
1975   'The Chronicler as Theologian', *BTB* 5, 99-126.
Görg, M.
1967   *Das Zelt der Begegnung: Untersuchung zur Gestalt der sakralen Zelttraditionen Altisraels*, BBB 27, Bonn: Peter Hanstein.
1984   '*kinnôr*', *ThWAT*, IV, cols. 210-16.
1983   'Der Altar. Theologische Dimensionen im Alten Testament', in J. Schreiner (ed.), *Freude am Gottesdienst: Aspekte ursprünglicher Liturgie: Festschrift für J.G. Plöger*, Stuttgart: Katholisches Bibelwerk, 291-306.

Gorman, F.H.
1990   *The Ideology of Ritual: Space, Time and Status in the Priestly Theology*, JSOTSup 91, Sheffield: JSOT Press.

Goudoever, J. van
1959   *Biblical Calendars*, Leiden: Brill.

Goulder, M.D.
1974   *Midrash and Method in Matthew*, London: SPCK.

Gradenwitz, P.
1959   *The Music of Israel*, New York: Norton.

Graetz, H.
1872   'Die Doxologien in den Psalmen', *MGWJ* 21, 481-96.
1881   'Die musikalischen Instrumente im Jerusalemischen Tempel und der musikalische Chor der Leviten', *MGWJ* 30, 241-59.

Gray, G.B.
1925   *Sacrifice in the Old Testament: Its Theory and Practice*, Oxford: Clarendon Press (republished with 'Prolegomenon' by B.A. Levine, New York: KTAV, 1971).

Gressmann, H.
1903   *Musik und Musikinstrumente im Alten Testament: Eine religionsgeschichtliche Studie*, Giessen: Töpelmann.

Grether, O.
1934   *Name und Wort Gottes im Alten Testament*, BZAW 64, Berlin: de Gruyter.

Grimes, R.L.
1979   'Modes of Ritual Necessity', *Worship* 53, 126-41.
1982[a]   *Beginnings of Ritual Studies*, Lanham, MD: University Press of America.
1982[b]   'Defining Nascent Ritual', *JAAR* 50, 539-55.
1985   *Research in Ritual Studies: A Programmatic Essay and Bibliography*, London: Scarecrow.
1988   'Infelicitous Performances and Ritual Criticism', *Sem* 41, 103-22.

Grimme, H.
1940–41   'Der Begriff von hebräischen hodah und todah', *ZAW* 58, 234-40.

Groot, J. de
1924   *Die Altäre des salomonischen Tempelhofes*, BZAW 6, Stuttgart: Kohlhammer.

Gross, H.
1960   'Zur Wurzel *zkr*', *BZ* NF 4, 227-37.

Grözinger, K.E.
1982   *Musik und Gesang in der Theologie der frühen jüdischen Literatur—Talmud Midrash Mystik*, Tübingen: Mohr (Paul Siebeck).

Gruber, M.I.
1980   *Aspects of Nonverbal Communication in the Ancient Near East*, I, II, Studia Pohl: Dissertationes Scientificae De Rebus Orientis Antiqui 12, Rome: Biblical Institute Press.

Gunkel, H.
1913   'Die Psalmen', *Reden und Aufsätze, Göttingen*, 92-123 (republished in P.H.A. Neumann [ed], *Zur neueren Forschung*, Darmstadt: Wissenschaftliche Buchgesellschaft, 1976, 19-54).
1929   *Die Psalmen*, GHAT 2/2, 4th edn, Göttingen: Vandenhoeck & Ruprecht.

1933　　*Einleitung in die Psalmen*, completed by J. Begrich, Göttingen: Vandenhoeck & Ruprecht.

Gunneweg, A.H.J.
1965　　*Leviten und Priester*, FRLANT 89, Göttingen: Vandenhoeck & Ruprecht.
1981　　'Zur Interpretation der Bücher Ezra–Nehemiah. Zugleich ein Beitrag zur Methode der Exegese', in J.A. Emerton (ed.), *Congress Volume, Vienna 1980*, VTSup 32, Leiden: Brill, 146-61.

Guthrie, H.H.
1966　　*Israel's Sacred Songs: A Study of Dominant Themes*, New York: Seabury.

Haag, H.
1971　　*Vom alten zum neuen Pascha: Geschichte und Theologie des Osterfestes*, SBS 49, Stuttgart: Katholisches Bibelwerk.
1973　　'Das Mazzenfest des Hiskia', in H. Gese and H.P. Rüger (eds.), *Wort und Geschichte: Festschrift für Karl Elliger zum 70. Geburtstag*, Neukirchen–Vluyn: Neukirchener Verlag, 87-94.

Halpern, B.
1981b　　'Sacred History and Ideology: Chronicles' Thematic Structure—Indications of an Earlier Source', in R.E. Friedman (ed.), *The Creation of Sacred Literature: Composition and Redaction of the Biblical Text*, NES 22, Berkeley: University of California Press, 35-54.

Halter, C.
1963　　*God and Man in Music*, St. Louis: Concordia.

Hancher, M.
1988　　'Performative Utterance, the Word of God, and the Death of the Author', *Sem* 41, 27-40.

Handy, L.K.
1988　　'Hezekiah's Unlikely Reform', *ZAW* 100, 111-15.

Hanks, T.D.
1981　　'The Chronicler: Theologian of Grace', *EvQ* 53, 16-28.

Haran, M.
1959　　'The Ark and the Cherubim: Their Symbolical Significance in Biblical Ritual', *IEJ* 9, 89-94.
1961　　'The Complex of Ritual Acts Performed inside the Tabernacle', in C. Rabin (ed.), *Studies in the Bible*, ScrHier 8, Jerusalem: Magnes Press, 272-302.
1969　　'The Divine Presence in the Israelite Cult and the Cultic Institutions', *Bib* 50, 251-67.
1978　　*Temples and Temple Service in Ancient Israel: An Inquiry into the Character of Cult Phenomena and the Historical Setting of the Priestly School*, London: Clarendon Press.
1983　　'Priesthood, Temple, Divine Service. Some Observations on Institutions and Practices of Worship', *HAR* 7, 121-35.
1985　　'Book-Size and the Device of Catch-Lines in the Biblical Canon', *JJS* 36, 1-11.

Hasel, G.F.
1979　　'Chronicles, Books of', *ISBE*, I, 666-73.

Hauer, C.
1982　　'David and the Levites', *JSOT* 23, 33-54.

Hauge, M.R.
1990   'On the Sacred Spot. The Concept of the Proper Localization before God', *SJOT* 1, 30-60.

Hausmann, J.
1987   'Gottesdienst als Gotteslob. Erwägungen zu 1 Chr 16, 8-36', in H. Wagner (ed.), *Spiritualität: Theologische Beiträge*, Stuttgart: Calwer Verlag, 83-92.

Hermisson, H.-J.
1965   *Sprache und Ritus im altisraelitischen Kult. Zur 'Spiritualisierung' der Kultbegriffe im Alten Testament*, WMANT 19, Neukirchen–Vluyn: Neukirchener Verlag.

Hickmann, H.
1950   'Die kultishe Verwendung der altägyptischen Trompete', *WO* 1/5, 351-55.
1970   'Altägyptische Musik', in *Orientalische Musik, Handbuch der Orientalistik* 1/4, Leiden: Brill, 135-70.

Hill, A.E.
1983   'Patchwork Poetry or Reasoned Verse? Connective Structure in 1 Chronicles XVI', *VT* 33, 97-101.

Hoenig, S.B.
1979–80   'The Biblical Designation for Pupil', *JQR* 70, 176-77.

Houtman, C.
1981   'Ezra and Law', in van der Woude 1981, 91-115.

Hubert, H. and M. Mauss
1964   *Sacrifice: Its Nature and Function*, trans. W.D. Halls with a Foreword by E.E. Evans-Pritchard, Chicago: Cohen & West.

Humbert, P.
1946   *La 'terou'a', analyse d'un rite biblique*, Recueil de travaux publié par la Faculté des Lettres 23, Neuchâtel: Université de Neuchâtel.

Hummel, H.D.
1979   *The Word Becoming Flesh*, St Louis: Concordia.

Hummelauer, P.Fr.v.
1904   '1 Chr. 25. Ein Beitrag zum Gebrauch des Loses bei den Hebräern', *BZ* 2/3, 254-59.

Hurvitz, A.
1986   'The Term *lskwt srym* (Ezek 40:44) and its Place in the Cultic Terminology of the Temple', in S. Japhet (ed.), *Studies in Bible*, ScrHier 31, Jerusalem: Magnes Press, 49-62.

Idelsohn, A.Z.
1932   *Jewish Liturgy and its Development*, New York: Schocken Books.

Im, T.-S.
1985   *Das Davidbild in den Chronikbüchern: David als Idealbild des theokratischen Messianismus für den Chronisten*, EH 23, New York : Peter Lang.

Jackson, A.
1968   'Sound and Ritual', *Man* NS 3, 293-99.

Jacob, B.
1896   'Beiträge zu einer Einleitung in die Psalmen I. *sela*', *ZAW* 16, 129-81.
1897   'Beiträge zu einer Einleitung in die Psalmen II. *lhzkr*', *ZAW* 17, 48-80.

Janowski, B.
1982   *Sühne als Heilsgeschehen: Studien zur Sühnetheologie der Priesterschrift und*

zur Wurzel KPR im Alten Orient und im Alten Testament, WMANT 55, Neukirchen–Vluyn: Neukirchener Verlag.

1989 'Das Königtum Gottes in den Psalmen. Bemerkungen zu einem neuen Gesamtentwurf', *ZTK* 86, 389-454.

Japhet, S.

1968 'The Supposed Common Authorship of Chronicles and Ezra–Nehemiah Investigated Anew', *VT* 18, 330-71.

1972 'Chronicles, Book of', *EncJud*, V, 517-34.

1979 'Conquest and Settlement in Chronicles', *JBL* 98, 205-18.

1985 'The Historical Reliability of Chronicles', *JSOT* 33, 83-107.

1989 *The Ideology of the Book of Chronicles and its Place in Biblical Thought*, trans. A. Barber, BEATAJ 9, New York: Peter Lang.

Jenni, E.

1980 'Aus der Literatur zur chronistischen Geschichtsschreibung', *TRu* (NF) 45, 97-108.

Jennings, T.W.

1982 'On Ritual Knowledge', *JR* 62, 111-27.

Jenson, P.P.

1992 *Graded Holiness: A Key to the Priestly Conception of the World*, JSOTSup 106, Sheffield: JSOT Press.

Jeremias, J.

1970 *Kultprophetie und Gerichtsverkündigung in der späten Königszeit Israels*, WMANT 35, Neukirchen–Vluyn: Neukirchener Verlag.

1987 *Das Königtum Gottes in den Psalmen: Israels Begegnung mit dem kanaandischen Mythos in den Jahwe-König-Psalmen*, FRLANT 141, Göttingen: Vandenhoeck & Ruprecht.

Jetter, W.

1978 *Symbol und Ritual: Anthropologische Elemente im Gottesdienst*, Göttingen: Vandenhoeck & Ruprecht.

Johnson, A.R.

1962 *The Cultic Prophet in Ancient Israel*, 2nd revised edn, Cardiff: University of Wales Press.

1979 *The Cultic Prophet and Israel's Psalmody*, Cardiff: University of Wales Press.

Johnson, M.D.

1969 *The Purpose of Biblical Genealogies*, Cambridge: Cambridge University Press.

Johnstone, W.

1983 'Chronicles, Canons and Contexts', *AUR* 50, 1-18.

1986 'Guilt and Atonement. The Theme of 1 and 2 Chronicles', in J. Martin and P. Davies (eds.), *A Word in Season: Essays in Honour of William McKane*, JSOTSup 42, Sheffield: JSOT Press, 113-38.

1987 'Reactivating the Chronicles Analogy in Penateuchal Studies, with Special Reference to the Sinai Pericope in Exodus', *ZAW* 99, 16-37.

Jones, G.H.

1975 ' "Holy War" or "Yahweh War"?', *VT* 25, 642-58.

Jones, I.H.

1986 'Musical Instruments in the Bible Part I', *BT* 37, 101-16.

1987   'Musical Instruments in the Bible Part II', *BT* 38, 129-43.
Junker, H.
1927   *Prophet und Seher in Israel*, Trier: Paulinus Verlag.
Kaiser, W.C.
1989   'The Unfailing Kindnesses Promised to David: Isaiah 55:3', *JSOT* 45
            (1989), 91-98.
Kapelrud, A.S.
1963   'Temple Building, a Task for Gods and Kings', *Or* (NS) 32, 56-62 (*God and
            his Friends in the Old Testament*, Lommedalen: Universitetsforlaget, 1979,
            184-90).
Kartveit, M.
1989   *Motive und Schichten der Landtheologie in 1 Chronik 1–9*, ConBOT 28,
            Stockholm: Almqvist & Wiksell.
Kaufmann, Y.
1961   *The Religion of Israel from its Beginnings to the Babylonian Exile*, trans. and
            abridged from Hebrew by M. Greenberg, Chicago: The University of
            Chicago Press.
Kautsch, E.
1886   'Miscellen', *ZAW* 6, 260.
Keel, O.
1978   *The Symbolism of the Biblical World: Ancient Near Eastern Iconography and
            the Book of the Psalms*, trans. T.J. Hallett, London: SPCK.
Keet, C.C.
1928   *A Liturgical Study of the Psalter*, London: George Allen & Unwin.
Kegler, J.
1989   'Das Zurücktreten der Exodustradition in den Chronikbüchern', in R. Albertz
            et al. (eds.), *Schöpfung und Befreiung: Für Claus Westermann zum 80.
            Geburtstag*, Stuttgart: Calwer Verlag, 54-66.
Kegler, J. and M. Augustin
1984   *Synopse zum chronistischen Geschichtswerk*, BEATAJ 1, New York: Peter
            Lang.
Keil, C.F.
1887–88   *Manual of Biblical Archaeology*, I, trans. P. Christie, Edinburgh: T. & T.
            Clark; II, trans. A. Cusin, Edinburgh: T. & T. Clark.
Kellermann, D.
1984   '*lewî, l^ewijîm*', *ThWAT*, IV, cols. 499-521.
1987   '*ōlāh/'ōlāh*', *ThWAT*, VI, cols. 105-24.
Kellermann, U.
1988   'Anmerkungen zum Verständnis der Tora in den chronistischen Schriften',
            BN 42, 49-92.
Kitchen, K.A.
1980   'Music and Musical Instruments', *IBD* 2, 1031-40.
Kiuchi, N.
1987   *The Purification Offering in the Priestly Literature: Its Meaning and Function*,
            JSOTSup 56, Sheffield: JSOT Press.
Kleinig, J.W.
1988   'Witting or Unwitting Ritualists', *LTJ* 22, 13-22.
1992   'The Divine Institution of the Lord's Song in Chronicles', *JSOT* 55, 75-83.

Knoppers, G.N.
1990   'Reheboam in Chronicles: Villain or Victim?', *JBL* 109, 423-40.
Köberle, J.
1899   *Die Tempelsänger im Alten Testament: Ein Versuch zur israelitischen und jüdischen Cultusgeschichte*, Erlangen: Fr. Junge.
Koch, K.
1961   'Denn seine Güte währet ewiglich', *EvT* 21, 531-44.
1965   'Das Verhältnis von Exegese und Verkündigung anhand eines Chroniktextes (1 Chr. 10)', *TLZ* 90, 659-70.
Kolari, E.
1947   *Musikinstrumente und ihre Verwendung im Alten Testament: Eine lexikalische und kulturgeschichtliche Untersuchung*, Helsinki: Suomalaisen Kirjallisuuden Kirjapainon.
König, E.
1882   *Offenbarungsbegriff im Alten Testament*, II, Leipzig: J.C. Hinrichs.
Kraus, H.-J.
1961   *Psalmen*, BKAT 15/1 & 2, Neukirchen–Vluyn: Neukirchener Verlag.
1966   *Worship in Israel: A Cultic History of the Old Testament*, trans. G. Buswell, Oxford: Basil Blackwell.
1986   *Theology of the Psalms*, trans. K. Crim, Minneapolis: Augsburg.
Kreissig, H.
1984   'Eine beachtungswerte Theorie zur Organisation altvorderorientalischer Tempelgemeinden im Achämenidenreich. Zu J.P. Weinbergs "Bürger–Tempel Gemeinde" in Juda', *Klio* 66, 35-9.
Kreuzer, S.
1985   'Zur Bedeutung und Etymologie von *Histah^{a}wah/Ysthwy*', *VT* 35, 39-60.
Kropat, A.
1909   *Die Syntax des Autors der Chronik verglichen mit der seiner Quellen*, BZAW 16, Giessen: Töpelmann.
Kugel, J.L.
1980   'The Adverbial Use of *Kî Tob*', *JBL* 99, 433-39.
Kurtz, J.J.
1863   *Sacrificial Worship of the Old Testament*, trans. J. Martin, Edinburgh: T. & T. Clark.
Kutsch, E.
1958   'Erwägungen zur Geschichte der Passafest und des Massotfestes', *ZTK* 55, 1-35.
Langdon, S.
1921   'Babylonian and Hebrew Musical Terms', *JRAS* 1, 170-91.
Lawson, T.E.
1976   'Ritual as Language', *Rel* 6, 123-39.
Leach, E.R.
1976   *Culture and Communication: The Logic by which Symbols are Connected*, Cambridge: Cambridge University Press.
Leaver, R.A.
1976   'The Calov Bible from Bach's Library', *Bach* 7, 16-22.
1983   *Bachs theologische Bibliothek: Eine kritische Bibliographie*, Beiträge zur theologischen Bachforschung 1, Stuttgart: Hänssler.

1985   *J.S. Bach and Scripture: Glosses from the Calov Bible Commentary*, St Louis: Concordia.

Lemke, W.F.

1963   'Synoptic Studies in the Chronicler's History', unpublished Doctoral Dissertation, Harvard University.

1965   'The Synoptic Problem in the Chronicler's History', *HTR* 58, 349-63.

Leupold, U.S.

1969   'Worship Music in Ancient Israel. Its Meaning and Purpose', *CJT* 15, 176-86.

Levine, B.A.

1963   'The Netînîm', *JBL* 82, 207-12.

1965   'The Descriptive Tabernacle Texts of the Pentateuch', *JAOS* 85, 307-18.

1974   *In the Presence of the Lord: A Study of Cult and Some Cultic Terms in Ancient Israel*, SJLA 5, Leiden: Brill.

1987   'The Language of Holiness. Perceptions of the Sacred in the Hebrew Bible', in M.P. O'Connor and D.N. Freedman (eds.), *Backgrounds for the Bible*, Winona Lake, IN: Eisenbrauns, 241-55.

Lindblom, J.

1962   'Lot-Casting in the Old Testament', *VT* 12, 164-78.

Lo, H.C.

1986   'The Structural Relationship of the Synoptic and Non-Synoptic Passages in the Book of Chronicles', Doctoral Dissertation, Southern Baptist Seminary, Louisville.

Loader, J.A.

1976   'Redaction and Function of the Chronistic "Psalm of David" ', in W.C. van Wyk (ed.), *Studies in the Chronicler*, Ou-Testamentiese Werkgemeenskap in Suid Afrika 19, Johannesburg: University of Pretoria, 67-75.

Loretz, O.

1974   'Psalmenstudien III', *UF* 6, 175-210.

Lowery, R.H.

1991   *The Reforming Kings: Cult and Society in First Temple Judah*, JSOTSup 120, Sheffield: JSOT Press.

Lyons, J.

1977   *Semantics*, I, II, Cambridge: Cambridge University Press.

McCarter, P.K.

1980   *1 Samuel*, AB 8, Garden City, NY: Doubleday.

1984   *2 Samuel*, AB 9, Garden City, NY: Doubleday.

McCarthy, D.L.

1982   'Covenant and Law in Chronicles—Nehemiah', *CBQ* 44, 25-44.

McConville, G.

1984   'Chronicles and its Genealogies', *Ev* 2/4, 3-4.

1986   '1 Chronicles 28:9. Yahweh "Seeks out" Solomon', *JTS* 37, 105-108.

McCready, W.O.

1986   'Priests and Levites', *ISBE* 3, 965-70.

McKenna, J.H.

1976   'Ritual Activity', *Worship* 50, 347-52.

McKenzie, S.L.
1985   *The Chronicler's Use of the Deuteronomistic History*, HSM 33, Atlanta: Scholars Press.

Macy, H.R.
1975   'The Sources of the Books of Chronicles. A Reassessment', Doctoral Dissertation, Harvard University.

Madge, W.
1977   *Biblical Music and its Developments*, London: Chester House.

Maecklenburg, A.
1929   'Über die Musikinstrumente der alten Hebräer', *TSK* 101, 172-204.

Mand, F.
1958   'Die Eigenständigkeit der Danklieder als Bekenntnislieder', *ZAW* 70, 185-99.

Manson, R.
1989   'Some Chronistic Themes in the "Speeches" of Ezra and Nehemiah,' *ExpTim* 101, 72-6.
1990   *Preaching the Tradition: Homily and Hermeneutics after the Exile*, Cambridge: Cambridge University Press.

Mantel, H.D.
1973   'The Dichotomy of Judaism during the Second Temple', *HUCA* 44, 55-87.

Margulis, B.
1970   'The Canaanite Origin of Psalm 29 Reconsidered', *Bib* 51, 332-48.

Mathias, D.
1984   ' "Levitische Predigt" und Deuteronomismus', *ZAW* 96, 23-49.

Mayer, G.
1986   'ydh/tôḏâ', *TDOT*, V, 427-28, 431-43.

Mays, J.L.
1986   'The David of the Psalms', *Int* 40, 143-55.

Mazar, B.
1960   'The Cities of the Priests and the Levites', in G.W. Anderson *et al.* (eds.), *Congress Volume, Oxford 1959*, VTSup 7, Leiden: Brill, 193-205.
1963   'The Military Elite of King David', *VT* 13, 310-20.

Mead, M.
1966   'Ritual and the Expression of the Cosmic Sense', *Worship* 40, 67-72.
1973   'Ritual and Social Crisis', in J. Shaughnessy, *The Roots of Ritual*, Grand Rapids: Eerdmans, 87-101.

Mendelsohn, I.
1940[a]   'Guilds in Babylon and Assyria', *JAOS* 60, 68-72.
1940[b]   'Guilds in Ancient Palestine', *BASOR* 80, 17-21.

Mettinger, T.N.D.
1982   *The Dethronement of Sabaoth: Studies in the Shem and Kabod Theophanies*, ConBOT 18, trans. F.H. Cryer, Lund: Gleerup.
1988   *In Search of God: The Meaning and Message of the Everlasting Names*, trans. F.H. Cryer, Philadelphia: Fortress Press.

Meyers, C.
1987[a]   'David as Temple Builder', in P.D. Miller *et al.* (eds.), *Ancient Israelite Religion: Studies in Honor of Frank Moore Cross*, Philadelphia: Fortress Press, 357-76.
1987[b]   'The Israelite Empire. In Defense of King Solomon', in M.P. O'Connor and

D.N. Friedman (eds.), *Backgrounds for the Bible*, Winona Lake, IN: Eisenbrauns, 181-97.

Micheel, R.
1983   *Die Seher- und Profetenüberlieferungen in der Chronik*, BET 18, New York: Peter Lang.

Milgrom, J.
1970   *Studies in Levitical Terminology*. I. *The Encroacher and the Levite: The Term 'Avoda'*, Berkeley: University of California Press.
1976ᵃ   'Sacrifices and Offerings, OT', *IDBSup*, 763-71.
1976ᵇ   *Cult and Conscience*, SJLA 18, Leiden: Brill.
1983   *Studies in Cultic Theology and Terminology*, SJLA 36, Leiden: Brill.
1985   'Hezekiah's Sacrifices of the Dedication Services of the Purified Temple (2 Chr. 29:21-24)', in A. Kort and S. Morschauser (eds.), *Biblical and Related Studies Presented to Samuel Iwry*, Winona Lake, IN: Eisenbrauns, 159-61.
1986   'The Priestly Impurity System', in D. Assaf (ed.), *Proceedings of the Ninth World Congress of Jewish Studies 1985*, Jerusalem: Magnes, 121-25.

Milgrom, J. and L. Harper
1986   '*Mišmaeraet*', *ThWAT*, V, cols. 78-85.

Miller, M.
1970   'The Korahites in Southern Judah', *CBQ* 32, 58-68.

Miller P.D.
1973   *The Divine Warrior in Early Israel*, HSM 5, Cambridge, MA: Harvard University Press.
1985   ' "Enthroned on the Praises of Israel". The Praise of God in Old Testament Theology', *Int* 39, 5-19.
1986   *Interpreting the Psalms*, Philadelphia: Fortress Press.

Mittman, S.
1981   'Die Grabinschrift des Sängers Uriahu', *ZDPV* 95, 139-52.

Möhlenbrink, K.
1934   'Die levitischen Überlieferungen des Alten Testaments', *ZAW* 52, 184-231.

Moore, B. and N. Habel
1982   *When Religion Goes to School: Typology of Religion for the Classroom*, Adelaide: South Australian College of Advanced Education.

Morgenstern, J.
1963   *Fire upon the Altar*, Leiden: Brill.

Moriarty, F.L.
1965   'The Chronicler's Account of Hezekiah's Reform', *CBQ* 27, 399-406.

Mosis, R.
1973   *Untersuchungen zur Theologie des chronistischen Geschichtswerkes*, FTS 29, Freiburg: Herder.

Mowinckel, S.
1922   *Kultprophetie und prophetische Psalmen: Psalmenstudien 3*, Kristiania: Norske Videnskaps-Akademi.
1953   *Religion und Kultus*, Göttingen: Vandenhoeck & Ruprecht.
1967   *The Psalms in Israel's* Worship, I, II, trans. D.R. Ap-Thomas, Oxford: Basil Blackwell.
1969   'Erwägungen zum chronistischen Geschichtswerk', *TLZ* 85, 1-8.

Müller, H.-P.
1964   'Die kultische Darstellung der Theophanie', *VT* 14, 183-91.
1986   '*maśśā*', *ThWAT*, V, cols. 20-25.
Müller, K.F.
1937   *Das Assyrische Ritual*. I. *Texte zum Assyrischen Königsritual*, MVAG 41/3,
              Leipzig: J.C. Hinrichs.
Murray, J.
1954   'Instrumenta musica s. scripturae', *VD* 32, 84-89.
Myers, J.M.
1966   'The Kerygma of the Chronicler. History and Theology in the Service of
              Religion', *Int* 20, 259-73.
Nasuti, H.P.
1988   *Tradition History and the Psalms of Asaph*, SBLDS 88, Atlanta: Scholars
              Press.
Newsome, J.D.
1973   'The Chronicler's View of Prophecy', Doctoral Dissertation, Vanderbilt
              University, Nashville.
1975   'Toward a New Understanding of the Chronicler and his Purposes', *JBL* 94,
              201-17.
Nielsen, K.
1986   *Incense in Ancient Israel*, VTSup 38, Leiden: Brill.
Niles, D.P.
1974   'The Name of God in Israel's Worship. The Theological Importance of the
              Name Yahweh', Doctoral Dissertation, Princeton Theological Seminary.
North, R.
1963   'Theology of the Chronicler', *JBL* 82, 369-81.
1964   'The Cain Music (1 Chr. 2, 50)', *JBL* 83, 373-89.
1974   'Does Archaeology Prove Chronicles Sources?', in H.N. Bream *et al.* (eds.),
              A Light to my Path: Old Testament Studies in Honor of Jacob M. Myers,
              Philadelphia: Temple University Press, 375-401.
Noordtzij, A.
1940   'Les Intentions du Chroniste', *RB* 49, 161-68.
Noth, M.
1987   *The Chronicler's History*, trans. H.G.M. Williamson with an introduction,
              JSOTSup 50, Sheffield: JSOT Press.
Oesterley, W.O.E.
1937   *A Fresh Approach to the Psalms*, London: Ivor Nicholson & Watson.
Old, H.O.
1985   'The Psalms of Praise in the Worship of the New Testament Church', *Int* 39,
              20-33.
Osborne, W.L.
1979   'The Genealogies of 1 Chronicles 1–9', Doctoral Dissertation, Dropsie
              University.
Payne, D.F.
1963   'The Purpose and Methods of the Chronicler', *FT* 93, 64-73.
Peterca, V.
1985   'Die Verwendung des Verbs *BHR* für Salomo in den Büchern der Chronik',
              BZ (NF) 29, 94-96.

Petersen, D.L.
1977   *Late Israelite Prophecy: Studies in Deuteroprophetic Literature and in Chronicles*, SBLMS 23, Atlanta: Scholars Press.
Petter, G.J.
1985   'A Study of the Theology of the Books of Chronicles', Doctoral Dissertation, Vanderbilt University, Nashville.
Pfeiffer, R.H.
1941   *Introduction to the Old Testament*, New York: Harper & Brothers.
1962   'Chronicles I and II', *IDB*, I, 572-80.
Plöger, O.
1957   'Rede und Gebete im deuteronomistischen und chronistischen Geschichtswerk', in W. Schneemelcher (ed.), *Festschrift für Günther Dehn*, Neukirchen–Vluyn: Neukirchener Verlag (*Aus der Spätzeit des Alten Testaments*, Göttingen: Vandenhoeck & Ruprecht, 1971, 50-66).
Polk, T.
1979   'Levites in the Davidic–Solomonic Empire', *StBT* 9, 3-22.
Polzin, R.
1976   *Late Biblical Hebrew: Toward an Historical Typology of Biblical Hebrew Prose*, HSM 12, Atlanta: Scholars Press.
Porter, J.R.
1979   'Old Testament Historiography', in G.W. Anderson (ed.), *Tradition and Interpretation: Essays by Members of the Society for Old Testament Study*, Oxford: Clarendon Press, 125-62.
Poulssen, N.
1967   *König und Tempel im Glaubenszeugnis des Alten Testaments*, SBM 3, Stuttgart: Katholisches Bibelwerk.
Preuss, H.-D.
1980   '*hwh, hishtach^{a}vah*', *TDOT*, V, 248-56.
Quasten, J.
1941   'The Conflict of Early Christianity with the Jewish Temple Worship', *TS* 2, 481-87.
1983   *Music and Worship in Pagan and Christian Antiquity*, trans. B. Ramsey, Washington: National Association of Pastoral Musicians.
Rad, G. von
1930   *Das Geschichtsbild des chronistischen Werkes*, BWANT 54, Stuttgart: Kohlhammer.
1952   *Der heilige Krieg im alten Israel*, Göttingen: Vandenhoeck & Ruprecht.
1962   *Old Testament Theology*, I, trans. D.M.G. Stalker, London: SCM Press.
1966[a]   'The Tent and the Ark', in *The Problem of the Hexateuch and Other Essays*, trans. E.W. Trueman Dicken, Edinburgh: Oliver & Boyd, 267-80.
1966[b]   'The Levitical Sermon in I and II Chronicles', in *The Problem of the Hexateuch and Other Essays*, trans. E.W. Trueman Dicken, Edinburgh: Oliver & Boyd, 267-80.
Rainey, A.F.
1969   'The Satrapy "Beyond the River"', *AJBA* 1/2, 51-78.
1970   'The Order of Sacrifices in Old Testament Ritual Texts', *Bib* 51, 485-98.

Rehm, M.D.
    1968   'Studies in the History of the Pre-Exilic Levites', Doctoral Dissertation, Harvard University.

Reicke, B.
    1951   *Diakonie, Festfreude und Zelos in Verbindung mit der altchristlichen Agapenfeier*, UUÅ 5, Uppsala: Almqvist & Wiksell.

Rendtorff, R.
    1956   'Der Kultus im Alten Israel', *JLH* 2, 1-21.
    1967   *Studien zur Geschichte des Opfers im alten Israel*, WMANT 24, Neukirchen-Vluyn: Neukirchener Verlag.

Richardson, H.N.
    1958   'The Historical Reliability of Chronicles', *JBR* 26, 9-12.

Ringgren, H.
    1948   *The Prophetical Conception of Holiness*, UUÅ 12, Uppsala: Almquist & Wiksells, 3-30.
    1966   *Israelite Religion*, trans. D. Green, London: SPCK.
    1971   *Psalmen*, trans. U. Bracher, Stuttgart: Kohlhammer.
    1978   '*hll* I & II', *TDOT* 3, 404-10.
    1986   'ʿ*ăbōḏāh*', *ThWAT* 5, cols. 1010-1012.
    1987   'ʿ*ānaḏ*', *ThWAT* 6, cols. 194-204.

Robinson, R.
    1978   'The Levites in the Pre-Monarchic Period', *StBT* 8, 3-24.

Rogerson, J.W.
    1980   'Sacrifice in the Old Testament. Problems of Method and Approach', in Bourdillon and Fortes 1980, 45-59.

Rothkoff, A.
    1972   'Sacrifice. Second Temple Period', *EncJud* 14, 607-15.

Rowley, H.H.
    1961–62   'Hezekiah's Reform and Rebellion', *BJRL* 44, 395-431 (*Men of God: Studies in Old Testament History and Prophecy*, London: Thomas Nelson & Sons, 1963, 98-132).
    1967   *Worship in Ancient Israel: Its Forms and Meaning*, London: SPCK.

Rudolph, W.
    1949   *Ezra und Nehemia*, HAT 2O, Tübingen: Mohr (Paul Siebeck).
    1952   'Der Aufbau der Asa-Geschichte', *VT* 2, 367-71.
    1954[a]   'Zur Theologie des Chronisten', *TLZ* 79, 285-86.
    1954[b]   'Problems of the Books of Chronicles', *VT* 4, 401-409.

Saalschütz, J.L.
    1829   *Geschichte und Würdigung der Musik bei den Hebräern*, Berlin: G. Finke.

Sachs, C.
    1940   *The History of Musical Instruments*, London: J.M. Dent & Sons.
    1944   *The Rise of Ancient Music in the Ancient World East and West*, London: J.M. Dent & Sons.
    1953   *The Rise of Music in the Ancient Near East*, London: Norton.

Saebo, M.
    1980   'Messianism in Chronicles? Some Remarks to the Old Testament Background of the New Testament Christology', *HBT* 2, 85-109.
    1981   'Chronistische Theologie/Chronistisches Geschichtswerk', *TRE* 8, 74-87.

Safrai, S.
1981   *Die Wallfahrt im Zeitalter des zweiten Tempels*, Forschungen zum jüdisch-christlichen Dialog 3, Neukirchen–Vluyn: Neukirchener Verlag.
Sakenfeld, K.D.
1985   *Faithfulness in Action: Loyalty in Biblical Perspective*, OBT, Philadelphia: Fortress Press.
Sarna, N.M.
1979   'The Psalm Superscriptions and the Guilds', in S. Stein and R. Loewe (eds.), *Studies in Jewish Religious and Intellectual History*, University of Alabama: University of Alabama Press, 281-300.
Schaeffer, G.E.
1972   'The Significance of Seeking God in the Purpose of the Chronicler', Doctoral Dissertation, Southern Baptist Seminary, Louisville.
Schmitt, A.
1982   'Das prophetische Sondergut in 2 Chr. 20, 14-77', in L. Rupprecht *et al.* (eds.), *Künder des Wortes: Beiträge zur Theologie der Propheten: Joseph Schreiner zum 60. Geburtstag*, Würzburg: Echter Verlag, 273-85.
Schottroff, W.
1978   '*zkr* gedenken', *THAT*, I, cols. 507-18.
Schreiner, J.
1983   'Gebet in der Gemeinde des Zweiten Tempels', in *idem*, *Freude am Gottesdienst: Aspekte ursprünglicher Liturgie: Festschrift für J.G. Plöger*, Stuttgart: Katholisches Bibelwerk, 55-66.
Schürer, E.
1979   *The History of the Jewish People in the Age of Jesus Christ*, II, revised by G. Vermes, F. Millar and M. Black, Edinburgh: T. & T. Clark.
Seeligmann, I.L.
1978   'Die Auffassung von der Prophetie in der deuteronomistischen und chronistischen Geschichtsschreibung (mit einem Exkurs über das Buch Jeremia)', in J.A. Emerton *et al.* (eds.), *Congress Volume, Göttingen 1977*, VTSup 29, Leiden: Brill, 254-84.
Segal, H.
1963   *The Hebrew Passover from the Earliest Times to AD 70*, London Oriental Series 12, London: Oxford University Press.
Segal, R.A.
1983   'Victor Turner's Theory of Ritual', *Zygon* 18, 327-35.
Seidel, H.
1956–57 'Horn und Trompete im alten Israel unter Berücksichtigung der Kriegsroll von Qumran', *Wissenschaftliche Zeitschrift der Karl-Marx-Universität Leipzig* 6, 589-99.
1980   *Auf den Spuren der Beter: Einführung in die Psalmen*, Berlin: Evangelische Verlagsanstalt.
1981   'Psalm 150 und die Gottesdienstmusik in Altisrael', *NTT* 35, 89-100.
1983   'Untersuchung zur Aufführungspraxis der Psalmen im altisraelitischen Gottesdienst', *VT* 33, 503-509.
1989   *Musik in Altisrael: Untersuchungen zur Musikgeschichte und Musikpraxis Altisraels anhand Biblischer und Ausserbiblischer Texte*, BEATAJ 12, New York: Peter Lang.

Sellers, O.R.
  1941   'Musical Instruments of Israel', *BA* 4, 33-47.
Sendrey, A.
  1969   *Music in Ancient Israel*, London: Vision Press.
  1974   *Music in the Social and Religious Life of Antiquity*, New York: Farleigh
              Dickenson University Press.
Seybold, K.
  1973   *Das Gebet des Kranken im Alten Testament: Untersuchungen zur
              Bestimmung und Zuordnung der Krankheits- und Heilungspsalmen*,
              BWANT 99, Stuttgart: Kohlhammer.
  1984   '*nebael*', *ThWAT*, V, cols. 185-88.
Shaver, J.
  1984   'Torah and the Chronicler's History Work. An Inquiry into the Chronicler's
              References to Laws, Festivals, and Cultic Institutions in Relation to
              Pentateuchal Legislation', Doctoral Dissertation, University of Notre Dame.
Shiner, L.E.
  1972   'Sacred Space, Profane Space, Human Space', *JAAR* 40, 425-36.
Smend, R.
  1970   *Yahweh War and Tribal Confederation*, trans. M.G. Rogers, Nashville:
              Abingdon.
Smith, J.Z.
  1980   'The Bare Fact of Ritual', *HR* 20, 112-27.
  1987   *To Take Place: Toward Theory in Ritual*, Chicago: University of Chicago
              Press.
Smith, M.S.
  1991   'The Levitical Compilation of the Psalter', *ZAW* 103, 258-63.
Smith, W. Robertson
  1914   *Lectures on the Religion of the Semites: The Fundamental Institutions*,
              revised edn, London: A. & C. Black.
Snaith, N.H.
  1934   'The Psalter of the Chronicler', *The London Quarterly and Holburn Review*
              149, 39-46.
Solomon, A.M.
  1989   'The Structure of the Chronicler's History. A Key to the Organisation of the
              Pentateuch', *Semeia* 46, 51-64.
Sperling, S.D.
  1989   'Rethinking Covenant in Late Biblical Books', *Bib* 70, 50-73.
Spieckermann, H.
  1989   *Heilsgegenwart: Eine Theologie der Psalmen*, FRLANT 148, Göttingen:
              Vandenhoeck & Ruprecht.
Stainer, J.
  1879   *The Musik of the Bible*, London; revised edn by F.W. Galpin, London:
              Carsell, Petter, Galpin & Co., 1914.
Stauder, W.
  1961   *Die Harfen und Leiern Vorderasiens in babylonischer und assyrischer Zeit*,
              Frankfurt: n.p.

Stevenson, W.B.
1950 'Hebrew *Olah* and *Zebach* Sacrifices', in W. Baumgartner *et al.* (eds.), *Festschrift A. Bertholet zum 80. Geburtstag*, Tübingen: Mohr, 488-97.

Stinespring, W.F.
1961 'Eschatology in Chronicles', *JBL* 80, 209-16.

Stoebe, H.J.
1971 'ḥāesaed Güte', *THAT*, I, cols. 600-21.

Stolz, F.
1972 *Jahwes und Israels Kriege: Kriegstheorien und Kriegserfahrungen im Glauben des alten Israels*, ATANT 60, Zürich: Theologischer Verlag.

Sugimoto, T.
1989 'Chronicles as Historiography. An Investigation in Scripture's Use of Scripture', Doctoral Dissertation, University of Sheffield.

Szörinyi, A.
1961 *Psalmen und Kult im Alten Testament: Zur Formgeschichte der Psalmen*, Budapest: Sankt Stefans Gesellschaft.

Talshir, D.
1988 'A Reinvestigation of the Linguistic Relationship between Chronicles and Ezra–Nehemiah', *VT* 38, 165-93.

Terrien, R.
1978 *The Elusive Presence: Toward a New Biblical Theology*, New York: Harper & Row.

Thackeray, H.S.J. (ed.)
1934 *Josephus: Jewish Antiquities*, Books 5–8, LCL, London: Heinemann.

Thiel, W.
1981 'Gottesdienst und Psalmengesang in Israel. Zu Anton Arens, *Die Psalmen im Gottesdienst des Alten Bundes*', *JLH* 25, 55-69.

Thirtle, J.W.
1904 *The Titles of the Psalms: Their Nature and Meaning Explained*, London: Henry Frowde.

Throntveit, M.A.
1982 'Linguistic Analysis and the Question of Authorship in Chronicles, Ezra and Nehemiah', *VT* 32, 201-16.
1987 *When Kings Speak: Royal Speech and Royal Prayer in Chronicles*, SBLDS 93, Atlanta: Scholars Press.
1988 'Hezekiah in the Books of Chronicles', *SBLSP* 27, ed. D.J. Lull, Atlanta: Scholars Press.

Torczyner, H.
1949 'A Psalm by the Sons of Heman', *JBL* 68, 247-49.

Torrey, C.C.
1954 *The Chronicler's History of Israel: Chronicles–Ezra–Nehemiah Restored to its Original Form*, New Haven: Yale University Press.

Tournay, R.J.
1991 *Seeing and Hearing God with the Psalms: The Prophetic Liturgy of the Second Temple in Jerusalem*, trans. J.E. Crowley, JSOTSup 118, Sheffield: JSOT Press.

Townsend, J.L.
1987 'The Purpose of 1 and 2 Chronicles', *BSac* 144, 277-92.

Trautmann, C.
    1969   ' "Calvoii Schriften. 3 Bände" aus Johann Sebastian Bachs Nachlass und ihre Bedeutung für das Bild des lutherischen Kantors Bach', *Musik und Kirche* 39, 145-60 (*J.S. Bach: New Light on his Faith*, trans. H. Oswald, CTM 42, 1971, 88-99).
    1972   'Bach's Bible', *American Choral Review* 14, 3-11.

Turner, V.W.
    1957   *Schism and Continuity in an African Society: A Study of Ndembu Village Life*, Manchester: Manchester University Press.
    1967   *The Forest of Symbols*, Ithaca, NY: Cornell University Press.
    1968   *The Drums of Affliction: A Study of Religious Processes Among Ndembu of Zambia*, Oxford: Clarendon Press.
    1969[a]   *The Ritual Process: Structuralism and Anti-Structuralism*, Ithaca, NY: Cornell University Press.
    1969[b]   'Forms of Symbolic Action. Introduction', *Proceedings of the 1969 Annual Spring Meeting of the American Ethnological Society*, ed. R.F. Spencer, Seattle, 3-25.
    1974   *Dramas, Fields, and Metaphors: Symbolic Action in Human Society*, Ithaca, NY: Cornell University Press.
    1977   'Sacrifice as Quintessential Process. Prophylaxis or Abandonment?', *HR* 16, 189-215.
    1983   'Body, Brain, and Culture', *Zygon* 8, 221-45.

Ulrich, E.
    1978   *The Qumran Text of Samuel and Josephus*, HSM 19, Atlanta: Scholars Press.

Vaux, R. de
    1961   *Ancient Israel: Its Life and Institutions*, trans. J. McHugh, London: Longman & Todd.

Vogt, E.
    1960   'Der Aufbau von Ps 29', *Bib* 41, 17-24.

Vos, H.F.
    1949   'The Music of Israel', *BSac* 106, 446-57.
    1950   'The Music of Israel', *BSac* 107, 64-70.

Vries, S.J. de
    1986   'The Forms of Prophetic Address in Chronicles', *HAR* 10, 15-36.
    1988   'Moses and David as Cult Founders in Chronicles', *JBL* 107, 619-39.
    1989   *1 and 2 Chronicles*, FOTL 11, Grand Rapids: Eerdmans.

Wacholder, B.Z.
    1988   'David's Eschatological Psalter 11 Q Psalms', *HUCA* 59, 23-72.

Warmuth, G.
    1978   '*hādhār*', *TDOT*, III, 335-41.

Wauchope Stewart, G.
    1917   'Musik (Hebrew)', *ERE*, IX, 39-43.

Wegner, M.
    1950   *Die Musikinstrumente des Alten Orients*, OrAnt 2, Münster: Aschendorff.

Wehmeier, G. and D. Vetter
    1971   '*hadar* Pracht', *THAT*, I, cols. 469-72.

Weinberg, J.P.

1972 'Demographische Notizen zur Geschichte der nachexilischen Gemeinde in Juda', *Klio* 54, 45-59.

1973 'Das *Beit Abot* Im 6.–4. Jh. v.u.z.', *VT* 23, 400-14.

1974ᵃ 'Der *'am ha'ares* der 6.–4. Jhr v.u.z.', *Klio* 56, 325-35.

1974ᵇ 'Die Agrarverhältnisse in der Bürger-Tempel-Gemeinde der Achämenidenzeit', *AASH* 22, 473-86.

1975 '*Nᵉtînîm* und "Söhne der Sklaven Salomos" in 6.–4. Jh. v.u.z.', *ZAW* 87, 355-71.

1976 'Bemerkungen zum Problem der Vorhellenismus im vorderen Orient', *Klio* 58, 5-20.

1977 'Zentral- und Partikulargewalt im achämenidischen Reich', *Klio* 59, 25-43.

1978 'Die "Ausserkanonischen Prophezeiungen" in den Chronikbüchern', *AASH* 24, 387-404.

1979 'Das Eigengut in den Chronikbüchern', *OLP* 10, 161-81.

1981ᵃ 'Die Natur im Weltbild des Chronisten', *VT* 31, 324-45.

1981ᵇ 'Das Wesen und die funktionelle Bestimmung der Listen in 1 Chr 1–9', *ZAW* 93, 91-114.

1982 'Der Mensch im Weltbild des Chronisten: Sein Korper. Die allgemeinen Begriffe', *OLP* 13, 71-93.

1983 'Der Mensch im Weltbild des Chronisten: Seine Psyche', *VT* 33, 298-316.

1984 ' "Wir" und "Sie" im Weltbild des Chronisten', *Klio* 66, 19-35.

1985 'Krieg und Frieden im Weltbild des Chronisten', *OLP* 16, 111-29.

1986 'Die soziale Gruppe im Weltbild des Chronisten', *ZAW* 98, 72-95.

1987 'Königtum und Königreich im Weltbild des Chronisten', *Klio* 69, 28-45.

1988 'Gott im Weltbild des Chronisten. Die vom Chronisten verschwiegenen Gottesnamen', in O. Kaiser (ed.), *Lebendige Forschung im Alten Testament*, BZAW 100, Berlin: de Gruyter, 170-89.

1989 'Der König im Weltbild des Chronisten', *VT* 39, 415-37.

Weintraub, D.

1985 'Music and Prophecy', *Dor le Dor* 14, 94-100.

Weippert, H.

1980 ' "Der Ort, den Jahwe erwählen wird, um dort seinen Namen wohnen zu lassen". Die Geschichte einer alttestamentlichen Formel', *BZ* (NF) 24, 76-94.

Weippert, M.

1972 ' "Heiliger Krieg" in Israel und Assyrien. Kritische Anmerkungen zu Gerhard von Rads Konzept des "Heiligen Krieges" im alten Israel', *ZAW* 84, 460-93.

Weisberg, D.B.

1967 *Guild Structure and Political Allegiance in Early Achaemenid Mesopotamia*, YNER 1, New Haven: Yale University Press.

Weiser, A.

1950 'Zur Frage nach den Beziehungen der Psalmen zum Kult. Die Darstellung der Theophanie in den Psalmen und im Festkult', in W. Baumgartner *et al.* (eds.), *Festschrift Alfred Bertholet zum 80. Geburtstag*, Tübingen: Mohr, 513-31.

1962 *The Psalms: A Commentary*, trans. H. Hartwell, London: SCM Press.

Weiss, J.
1895   *Die musikalischen Instrumente in den heiligen Schriften des Alten
            Testaments*, Graz: Leuschner & Lubensky.

Welch, A.C.
1935   *Postexilic Judaism*, The Baird Lecture, 1934, Edinburgh: William
            Blackwood & Sons.
1939   *The Work of the Chronicler: Its Purpose and Date*, The Schweich Lectures,
            1939, London: Oxford University Press.

Wellhausen, J.
1885   *Prolegomena to the History of Israel*, trans. J.S. Black and A. Menzies from
            the 2nd German edn. of 1883, Edinburgh: T. & T. Clark.
1898   'Music of the Ancient Hebrews', *The Book of Psalms: A New English
            Translation*, trans. J.A. Paterson, London: James Clarke, 217-37.

Welten, P.
1973   *Geschichte und Geschichtsdarstellung in den Chronikbüchern*, WMANT 42,
            Neukirchen–Vluyn: Neukirchener Verlag.
1979   'Lade–Tempel–Jerusalem. Zur Theologie der Chronikbücher', in
            A.H.J. Gunneweg and O. Kaiser (eds.), *Textgemäss: Aufsätze und Beiträge
            zur Hermeneutik des Alten Testaments: Festschrift für Ernst Würthwein zum
            70. Geburtstag*, Göttingen: Vandenhoeck & Ruprecht, 196-83.

Wenham, G.J.
1979   *The Book of Leviticus*, NICOT, London: Hodder & Stoughton.
1981   *Numbers*, TOLC, Leicester: Inter-Varsity Press.

Werner, E.
1957   'Musical Aspects of the Dead-Sea-Scrolls', *MQ* 43, 21-37.
1962   'Music', 'Musical Instruments', *IDB*, III, 457-76.

Westerholm, S.
1988   'Temple', *ISBE*, IV, 759-76.

Westermann, C.
1960   'Musik III. Instrumentale Musik, Gesang und Dichtung in Israel', RGG, IV,
            cols. 1201-1205.
1966   *The Praise of God in the Psalms*, trans. K.R. Crim, London: John Knox.
1978[a]   '*hll* pi. loben', *THAT*, I, cols. 493-502.
1978[b]   '*jdh* hi. preisen', *THAT*, I, cols. 674-82.

Wheelock, W.T.
1982   'The Problem of Ritual Language. From Information to Situation', *JAAR* 50,
            49-71.

Wilda, G.
1959   *Das Königsbild des chronistischen Geschichtswerkes*, Bonn: Rheinische
            Friedrich-Wilhelms-Universität.

Willi, T.
1972   *Die Chronik als Auslegung: Untersuchungen zur literarischen Gestaltung der
            historischen Überlieferung Israels*, FRLANT 106, Göttingen: Vandenhoeck
            & Ruprecht.
1980   '*Thora* in den Biblischen Chronikbüchern', *Jud* 36, 102-105, 148-151.

Williamson, H.G.M.
1973   'A Note on 1 Chronicles VII 12', *VT* 23, 375-79.
1976   'The Accession of Solomon in the Books of Chronicles', *VT* 26, 351-61.

1977[a]   *Israel in the Books of Chronicles*, Cambridge: Cambridge University Press.
1977[b]   'Eschatology in Chronicles', *TynBul* 28, 115-54.
1978   'The Sure Mercies of David: Subjective or Objective Genitive?', *JSS* 23, 31-49.
1979[a]   'The Origins of the Twenty-Four Priestly Courses. A Study of 1 Chronicles XXIII–XXVII', in J.A. Emerton (ed.), *Studies in the Historical Books of the Old Testament*, VTSup 30, Leiden: Brill, 251-68.
1979[b]   'Sources and Redaction in the Chronicler's Geneaology of Judah', *JBL* 98, 351-59.
1981   ' "We are yours, O David": the Setting and Purpose of 1 Chronicles XII: 1-23,' in van der Woude 1981, 164-76.
1982   'The Death of Josiah and the Development of the Deuteronomic History', *VT* 32, 242-48.
1983[a]   'The Dynastic Oracle in the Books of Chronicles', in A. Rofi and Y. Zakovitch (eds.), *Isaac Leo Seeligmann Volume: Essays on the Bible and the Ancient World*, III, Jerusalem: Rubenstein, 305-18.
1983[b]   'The Composition of Ezra I–VI', *JTS* 34, 1-30.
1985   *Ezra, Nehemiah*, WBC, Waco, TX: Word Books.
1988   'History', in D.A. Carson and H.G.M. Williamson (eds.), *It is Written: Scripture Citing Scripture: Essays in Honour of Barnabas Lindars*, Cambridge: Cambridge University Press, 25-38.
1989   'The Concept of Israel in Transition', in R.E. Clements (ed.), *The World of Ancient Israel: Sociological, Anthropological and Political Perspectives: Essays by Members of the Society for Old Testament Study*, Cambridge: Cambridge University Press, 141-61.

Wilms, F.-W.
1981   *Freude vor Gott: Kult und Fest in Israel*, Regensburg: Friedrich Pustet.
Wilson, R.R.
1975   'The Old Testament Genealogies in Recent Research', *JBL* 94, 169-89.
1977   *Genealogy and History in the Biblical World*, New Haven: Yale University Press.
1979   'Between "Azel" and "Azel": Interpreting Biblical Genealogies', *BA* 42, 11-22.
1980   *Prophecy and Society in Ancient Israel*, Philadelphia: Fortress Press.
Winter, P.
1956   'Twenty-Six Priestly Courses', *VT* 6, 215-17.
Wohlenberg, D.
1967   'Kultmusik in Israel. Eine forschungsgeschichtliche Untersuchung', Doctoral Dissertation, Hamburg.
Woude, A.S. van der
1976   '*šēm*', *THAT*, II, cols. 935-63.
Woude, A.S. van der (ed.)
1981   *Remembering All the Way*, OTS 21, Leiden: Brill.
Wright, D.P.
1987   *The Disposal of Impurity: Elimination Rites in the Bible and in Hittite and Mesopotamian Literature*, SBLDS 101, Atlanta: Scholars Press.

Wright, J.W.
1989   'The Origin and Function of 1 Chronicles 23–27', Doctoral Dissertation,
            University of Notre Dame.
1990   'Guarding the Gates. 1 Chronicles 26.1-19 and the Roles of Gatekeepers in
            Chronicles', *JSOT* 48, 69-81.
1991   'The Legacy of David in Chronicles. The Narrative Function of 1 Chronicles
            23–27', *JBL* 110, 229-42.

Wypych, S.
1987   'Das Werk des Chronisten', in E. Sitarz (ed.), *Höre, Israel! Jahwe ist
            einzig*', Biblische Basis Bücher 5, Stuttgart: Katholisches Bibelwerk, 121-
            41.

Yadin, Y.
1962   *The Scroll of the War of the Sons of Light against the Sons of Darkness*,
            trans. B. and C. Rabin, Oxford: Oxford University Press.

Yeivin, S.
1953   'Social, Religious and Cultural Trends in Jerusalem under the Davidic
            Dynasty', *VT* 3, 149-66.

Yerkes, R.K.
1953   *Sacrifice in Greek and Roman Religions and Early Judaism*, London:
            A. & C. Black.

Zalewski, S.
1968   'Cultic Officials in the Book of Chronicles', Doctoral Dissertation, University
            of Melbourne.
1989   'The Purpose of the Story of the Death of Saul in Chronicles', *VT* 39, 449-
            67.

Zeitlin, S.
1960–61   'The Temple and Worship. A Study in the Development of Judaism. A
            Chapter in the History of the Second Jewish Commonwealth', *JQR* 51, 209-
            41.

Zeron, A.
1974   'Tag für Tag kam man zu David, um ihm zu helfen, 1 Chr. 12, 1-22', *TZ* 30,
            257-61.
1977   'Die Anmassung des Königs Usia im Lichte von Jesajas Berufung', *TZ* 33,
            65-68.

Zobel, H.-J.
1986   '*ḥeseḏ*', *TDO I*, V, 44-64.

Zimmerli, W.
1969   *Ezechiel*, BKAT 13/2, Neukirchen–Vluyn: Neukirchener Verlag.

Zirker, H.
1964   *Die kultische Vergegenwärtigung der Vergangenheit in den Psalmen*, BBB
            20, Bonn: Peter Hanstein.

Zuesse, E.
1974   'Taboo and the Divine Order', *JAAR* 42, 482-504.
1975   'Meditation on Ritual', *JAAR* 43, 517-30.
1987   'Ritual', *Encyclopedia of Religion*, XII, 405-22.

Zunz, L.
1832   *Die gottesdienstlichen Vorträge der Juden historisch entwickelt*, Berlin; repr.
            edn Hildesheim: Georg Olms, 1966.

INDEXES

INDEX OF REFERENCES

OLD TESTAMENT

29.20-35	101, 108	29.31	19, 68, 103,	31.16-17	42
29.20-30	21		125, 128	31.16	53
29.20-24	102	29.32	125	31.17	40, 170
29.20	170	29.33-35	103	31.18	94
29.21-30	102, 112	29.34	94	31.21	30, 31
29.21-29	111	29.35	101	32.8	171
29.21-24	102, 112	30	75	32.12	105
29.21	68, 103, 107	30.2	170	32.21	88
29.22-24	101	30.3	94	32.24-26	127
29.22	103	30.5	29	32.24	127
29.24	68, 102,	30.6-9	111	32.25-26	127
	111, 112,	30.6	29, 170	32.25	127
	117	30.8	106	32.31	127
29.25	16, 29, 32,	30.12	29, 170	32.32	128
	40, 68, 73,	30.15	94	33.4	65
	78, 82-84,	30.16	29, 30, 40,	33.7	65
	89, 91, 149		70	33.8	31
29.25-30	14, 17, 23,	30.17	89	33.12-13	127
	102, 110,	30.18	29	33.13	129
	116	30.19	30, 94	33.16	125, 127,
29.25-29	61, 68, 113	30.20	67		128
29.25-26	102	30.21-26	169	34.12-13	14, 23
29.26-28	36, 62	30.21-22	14, 21, 23,	34.12	16, 46
29.26-27	93		76, 91, 110,	34.13	46
29.26	40, 78		124, 126,	34.24-26	127
29.27-30	120-22		129	34.25	105
29.27-29	103, 120	30.21	16, 65, 76,	34.31	40, 70
29.27-28	80, 109, 121		78, 88, 121,	34.32	121
29.27	43, 66, 68,		156	34.33	121
	78, 80, 86,	30.22	74, 88, 89,	35.1-19	75
	102, 107,		92, 125, 126	35.2	40, 42
	117	30.23	76, 88	35.3	29, 47, 94
29.28-29	81	30.24	94	35.4	29, 40, 170
29.28	82, 95, 117,	30.25	76, 88	35.5-6	94
	120, 121,	30.26	76, 88	35.5	40, 70, 94
	176	30.27	34, 111	35.6	29, 89
29.29	107, 120,	31.1	121	35.7	121
	121, 122	31.2	14, 16, 21,	35.10	29, 40, 70,
29.30	16, 37, 45,		23, 34, 40,		170
	61, 65, 66,		61, 70, 71,	35.12	29
	68, 91, 120,		91, 117,	35.13	29, 30
	121, 149,		126, 170	35.14	107, 117
	155, 169,	31.3	29, 30, 55,	35.15	14, 16, 21,
	170		74, 75, 108		40, 61, 70,
29.31-35	102, 103		170, 179		86, 89, 149,
29.31-34	123	31.8	46, 78, 115		151
29.31-33	125	31.12	170	35.16	29, 107
		31.15-16	170	35.17	121
		31.15	40, 58, 73		

NEW TESTAMENT

INDEX OF AUTHORS

JOURNAL FOR THE STUDY OF THE OLD TESTAMENT

Supplement Series